POSTCARD HISTORY SERIES

Along Wyoming's Historic Highway 20

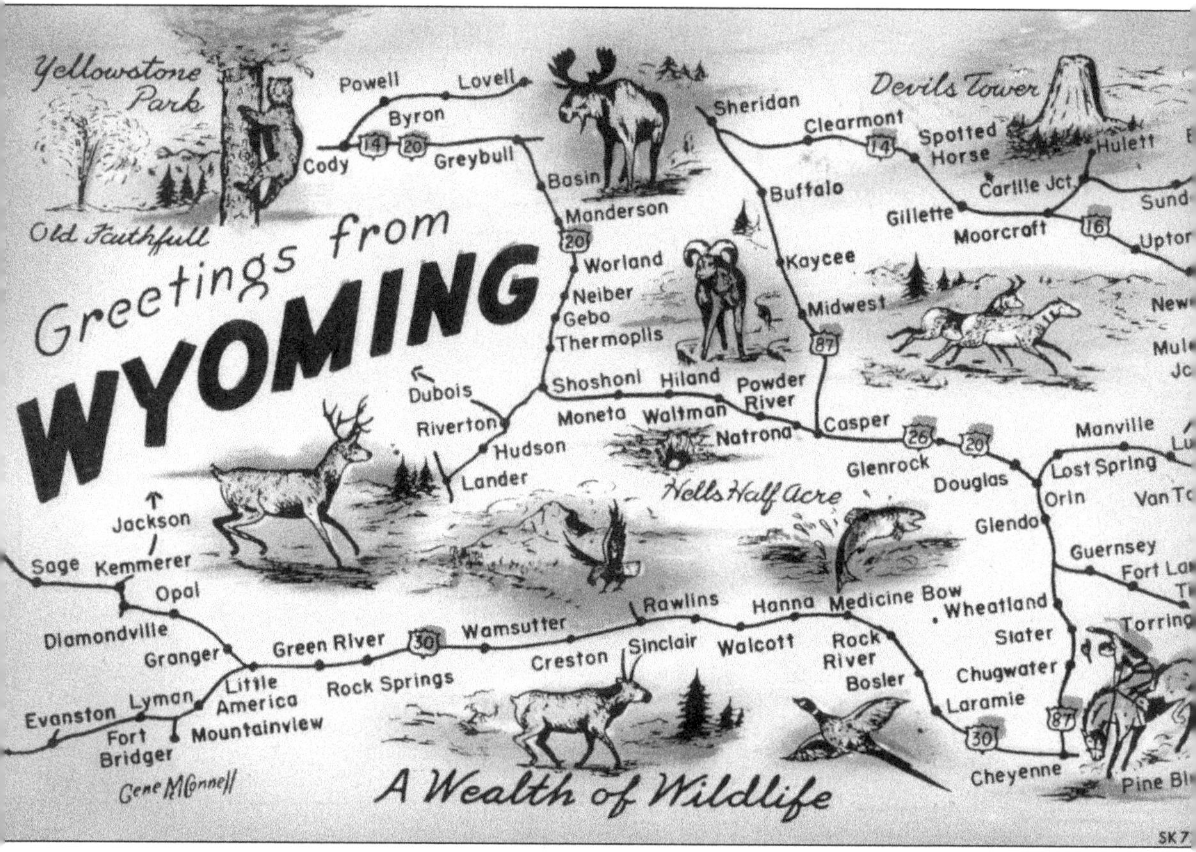

Historic Highway 20 across Wyoming. For almost a century, historic Highway 20 has been the road followed by travelers across northern Wyoming, connecting towns and villages with the state's abundant natural wonders. It still remains the favorite road of those seeking closeness to nature, beauty, and a slower pace of life. (Author's collection.)

On the Front Cover: US Highway 20 is the only cross-country road that goes directly through Yellowstone National Park. For early travelers the opportunity for close-up views of wild animals was a hard-to-beat experience. This scene could not be repeated today, as feeding animals from cars is now strictly prohibited. (Author's collection.)

On the Back Cover: Pres. Theodore Roosevelt called the journey between Cody, Wyoming, and Yellowstone National Park the "50 most scenic miles in America." The road treats travelers to awe-inspiring scenery and is testament to the skill of the engineers who planned and built the road through rugged mountain terrain. (Author's collection.)

POSTCARD HISTORY SERIES

Along Wyoming's Historic Highway 20

Michael J. Till

ARCADIA PUBLISHING

ISBN 978-1-4671-1598-8

Published by Arcadia Publishing
Charleston, South Carolina

Library of Congress Control Number:

For all general information contact Arcadia Publishing at:
Telephone 843-853-2070
Fax 843-853-0044
E-mail sales@arcadiapublishing.com
For customer service and orders:
Toll-Free 1-888-313-2665

Visit us on the Internet at www.arcadiapublishing.com

To all who remember the crowding and heat in the backseat of the family sedan before the days of air-conditioning, iPods, and smartphones

Contents

ACKNOWLEDGMENTS

Thanks are due to the long-ago civic leaders and business owners who had the foresight to recognize the value of picture postcards in promoting their communities. These visual and historic records provide invaluable insights into "the way it was" in the days when two-lane highways and mom-and-pop tourist courts reigned supreme. Thanks also to the vendors of vintage postcards without whose help this book would have been more difficult if not impossible. Many searched for Highway 20 cards for me, which was greatly appreciated. The same is true for persons responsible for modern web pages describing towns and historical sites on Highway 20. I have borrowed freely from their descriptions and wish to acknowledge their contributions.

Librarians and staffs of county historical societies and museums along Highway 20 were helpful in directing me to interesting information about the road. Many shared personal memories of the postcard sites, and if someone did not know the answer to a question, a telephone call to a longtime resident of the community usually produced the information; thus, many grandparents, uncles, aunts and community elders contributed indirectly to this book.

Last, but certainly not least, I wish to thank my wife, Christine, for her help. A librarian herself, she knows sources of information and how to access them. She was also an excellent collaborator as we drove historic Highway 20 researching specific sites. Many of her observations have been incorporated into the captions in the book.

All images in this book appear courtesy of the author's personal collection.

INTRODUCTION

The Federal Aid Highway Act of 1921 was enacted to answer the demand for better roads as motorized travel gained in popularity during the early 20th century. The act provided funding for development and maintenance of seven percent of each state's road system provided the roads were "interstate in character," meaning that the designated roads in one state must connect with similarly designated roads in adjacent states. Thus, the original federal highways were existing roads that provided a contiguous roadway system throughout the country that would be convenient for motorists to follow and would assure funding for their ongoing maintenance. The roads to be included were identified in 1923, and in 1926 the first Federal Highway System came into existence. The numbering system was adopted, which is still in use today. Major east–west routes were assigned a number ending in "0" and the numbering sequence was from north to south. Major north–south roads ended in "5" with the sequence going from west to east. To avoid the unique number "0," the number "2" was assigned to the highway that extended from Maine through New York and then was separated by the Great Lakes before continuing its western section from Michigan. The remaining roads were designated 10, 20, 30, etc. to 90. Highway 10 extended only from the Midwest to the West Coast, whereas the others were all cross-country.

From 1926 to 1940, historic Highway 20 extended from Boston to the east entrance of Yellowstone National Park. In 1940, the western section was completed to Newport, Oregon. The roads within the park were connecting links between the eastern and western sections, making Highway 20 the northernmost of the true cross-country highways and, at 3,365 miles, the longest. Federal highway designations are not used in national parks, causing some observers to suggest that Highway 20 is not a cross-country highway. That argument carries very little weight, as the road continues uninterrupted through the park with the only change being the signage. For decades, travelers on Highway 20 have happily passed through Yellowstone National Park without questioning the road's continuity and have enjoyed the views shown on the cards in this book.

Wyoming officials chose wisely in selecting the route of historic Highway 20. They ensured efficient travel from place to place and recognition of the importance of good roads for the state's economic progress. Highway 20 was located near many of Wyoming's most productive oil fields, which benefitted greatly from convenient access to highway transportation. In the middle of the state, the road was routed past Boysen Lake, the beautiful Wind River Canyon, and the Hot Springs in Thermopolis, all important locations for tourists and vacationers. In northern Wyoming, the road leads directly to Yellowstone National Park. Planners knew that automobiles would become the preferred mode of transportation in the future, and they were determined that Wyoming would provide a highway system capable of meeting that trend. Although not as famous as its cousins Highway 30 (much of which coincided with the original Lincoln Highway) or Route 66 (which is not cross-country), Highway 20 nonetheless has served with equal importance in introducing automobile and truck traffic to America.

Early motorists got a close-up view of the towns and cities along the path of their journey, and they took advantage of the stores, restaurants, service stations, and tourist accommodations. City officials and entrepreneurial merchants quickly recognized the value of advertising their wares to the traveling public. Inexpensive or even free picture postcards were a popular vehicle for showing off their cities. Professionally produced picture postcards provided a convenient record of the trip, and typically they were less expensive and of higher quality than travelers could produce with their own cameras. Many picture postcards found their way into personal scrapbooks. These postcards provide the basis for this book.

The advent of the Interstate Highway System in the 1950s was a boon for motorized travel, but it also had a downside; frequently, the course of the new superhighways was directly over the former local roads. The latter were simply bulldozed away, thus completely obliterating their existence together with the memories they evoked. Fortunately, Highway 20 has escaped this fate. The original road has survived almost entirely intact and to this day epitomizes the charm and beauty of Wyoming throughout its length. Modern interstate highways parallel original Highway 20 rather than being superimposed directly on top. "Original" Highway 20 still exists, and one can follow historic Highway 20 across Wyoming much as our ancestors did decades ago. *Along Wyoming's Historic Highway 20* is not a book of roadside curiosities; rather, the purpose was to re-create a journey across Wyoming as close to its original route as possible using vintage picture postcards as illustrations. It is intended to give a glimpse of where early travelers might have stopped for gas, to eat, or to spend the night—and especially what they would have seen along the way. The route was determined by following road maps and travel guides from the 1920s to the 1940s and extrapolating information to current streets and roads. Whenever possible, local knowledge of the route was included. The postcards show main streets, service stations, diners, tourist homes, cabin courts, and early motels. Notable scenic and historical locations along the route also are included. Many of the scenes were located directly on historic Highway 20 or could be viewed by a person traveling by automobile on the highway. Many of the sites still exist, although not necessarily serving their original purpose. The overall objective was to provide a guide as well as a nostalgic record for anyone wishing to replicate the experience of driving across Wyoming on Highway 20 in the pre-interstate era.

The final chapter of this book is about West Yellowstone, Montana, located at the western extremity of Yellowstone National Park and the beginning of Historic Highway 20's western route to the Pacific Ocean. Failure to include it would be a disservice to historic Highway 20 as West Yellowstone is an integral part of Highway 20 in northern Wyoming.

One

Niobrara and Converse Counties

Niobrara County is the easternmost county through which historic Highway 20 passes in Wyoming. It holds the distinction of being the least populous of any of Wyoming's 23 counties. The county, named for the Niobrara River, was created in 1911, having been separated from Converse County immediately to the west. The county has only three communities, and all are located along Historic Highway 20: Van Tassell is near the Nebraska border; Lusk, the county seat, is the largest; and Manville is located farther west. The population of the county has declined steadily since its peak in 1920, when the arrival of the railroad and discovery of oil brought many new residents to the area. The county's 1920 population was 6,321, and by 2012 the number had fallen to 2,456; nonetheless, the county has continued to be attractive to residents and visitors alike.

Converse County also is notable for its small population. Its two major communities, Douglas and Glenrock, lie directly on historic Highway 20. In contrast to many other eastern Wyoming communities, Douglas's population grew during the first half of the 20th century from under 1,000 to its present size of approximately 6,000 citizens. Glenrock's growth was more modest, expanding from under 1,000 in 1910 to it present size of approximately 3,600. Much of the region's growth can be attributed to the arrival of the railroad and discovery of oil. The Big Muddy oil field especially drew residents to the area, many of whom established homes and families there where their descendants remain today.

Eastern Wyoming was graced with several colorful Western characters during its formative years. Tops among them were Mother Featherlegs, a frontier madam known for her ruffled pantalettes; George Lathrop, a famous driver the Deadwood stage; and George Pike, an alleged rustler and outlaw who despite an unsavory reputation was known for his loyalty to friends. All are part of the early fabric of the area and have been memorialized by the placement of monuments in their honor.

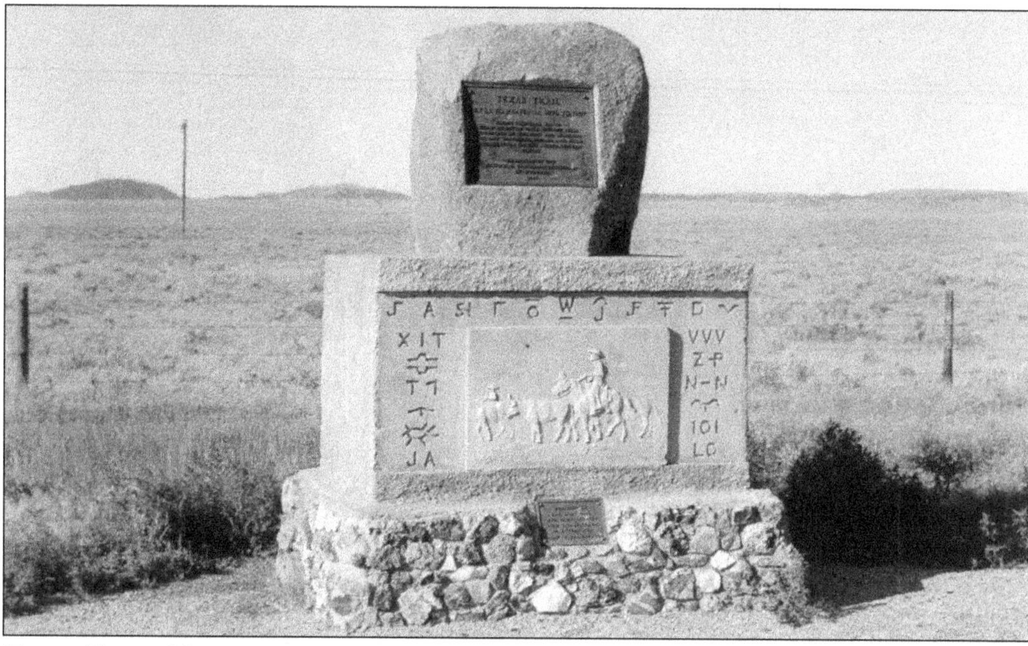

Texas Trail Monument, Three Miles East on Highway 20, Lusk. With the exception of the tiny village of Van Tassell, Lusk is the most eastern town in Wyoming on the trail that became historic Highway 20. During the final quarter of the 19th century, many herds of cattle coming from distant Texas were driven north along this trail to replace the fast vanishing buffalo herds in Wyoming and Montana.

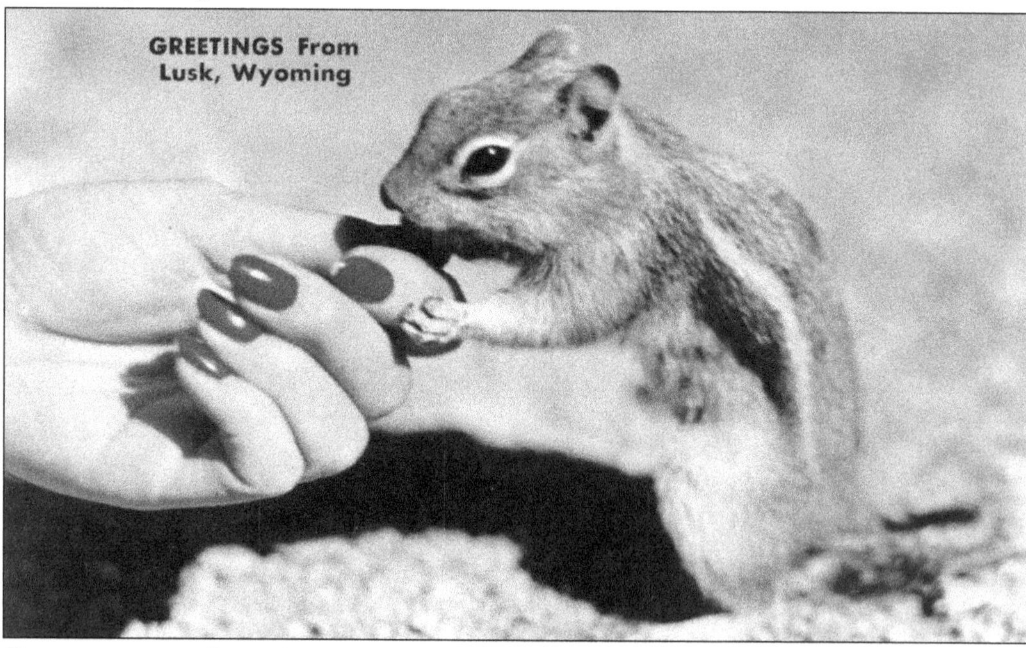

Greetings from Lusk. Many communities extended greetings to visitors via generic postcards showing a variety of scenes typical of the region. Chipmunks were among the most abundant animals in eastern Wyoming, often near towns and parks where peanuts and snacks were sold. The chipmunk shown on this card is especially friendly and daring.

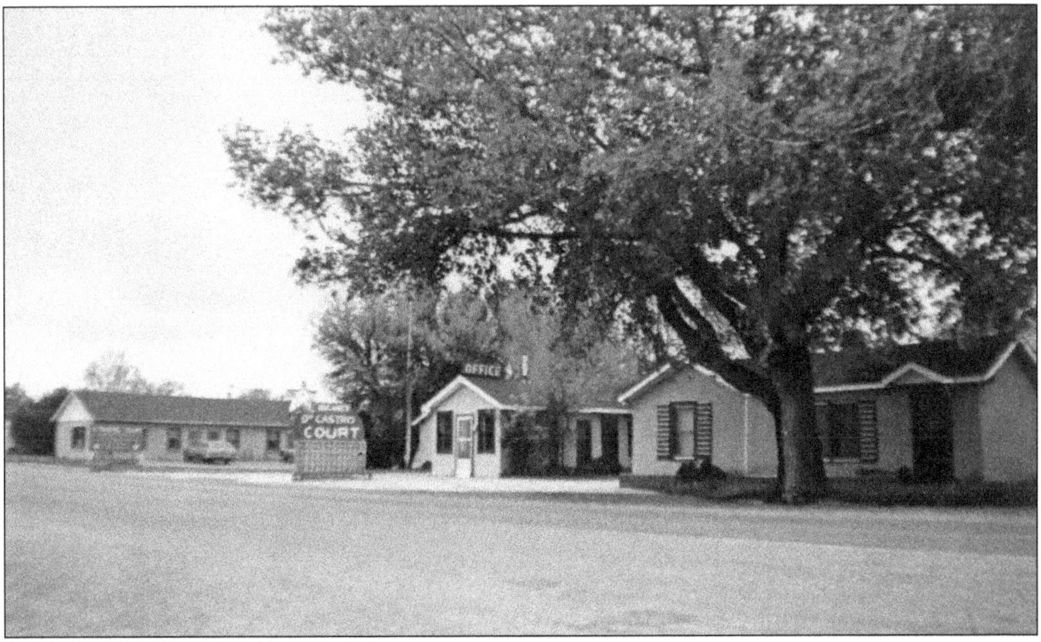

De Castro Court, East on Highway 20, Lusk. This motel near Lusk's eastern city limit was one of the first tourist accommodations for westbound travelers on Highway 20 after entering Wyoming. Given that many tourists used state boundaries as an objective for their day's drive, saying, "We'll stop at the first nice place we see after we cross the border," this motel probably did good business.

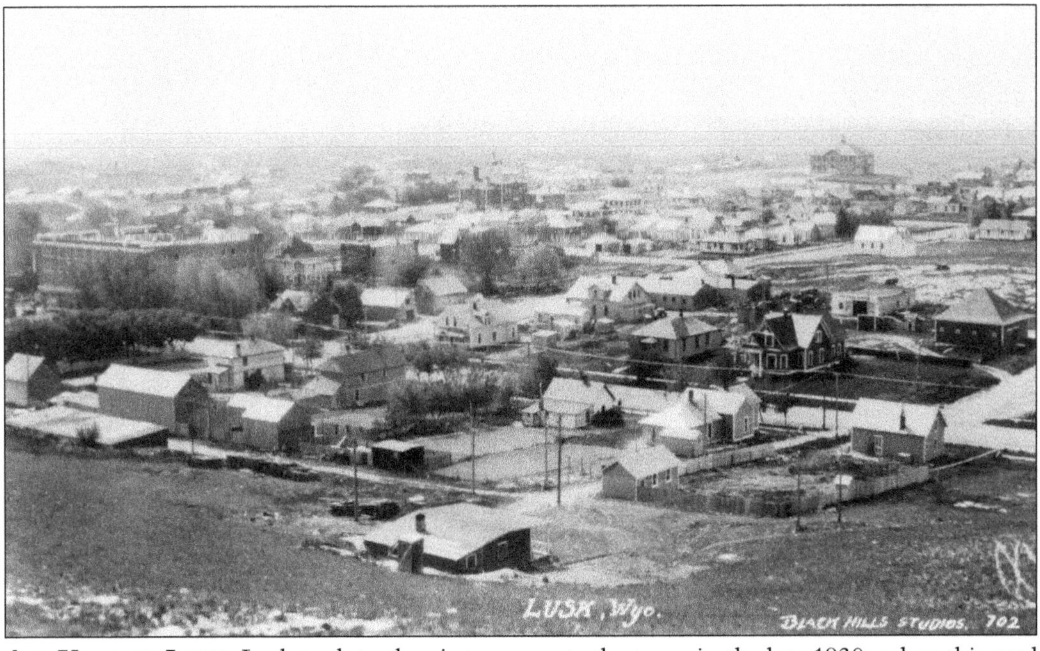

Air View of Lusk. Lusk took to the air to promote the town in the late 1930s when this card was mailed. Highway 20 is shown running horizontally in the center of the photograph. The writer was driving east and expected to be in Chicago in a few days. She reported having a flat tire, but on the bright side she had a steak dinner at a local restaurant for 50¢.

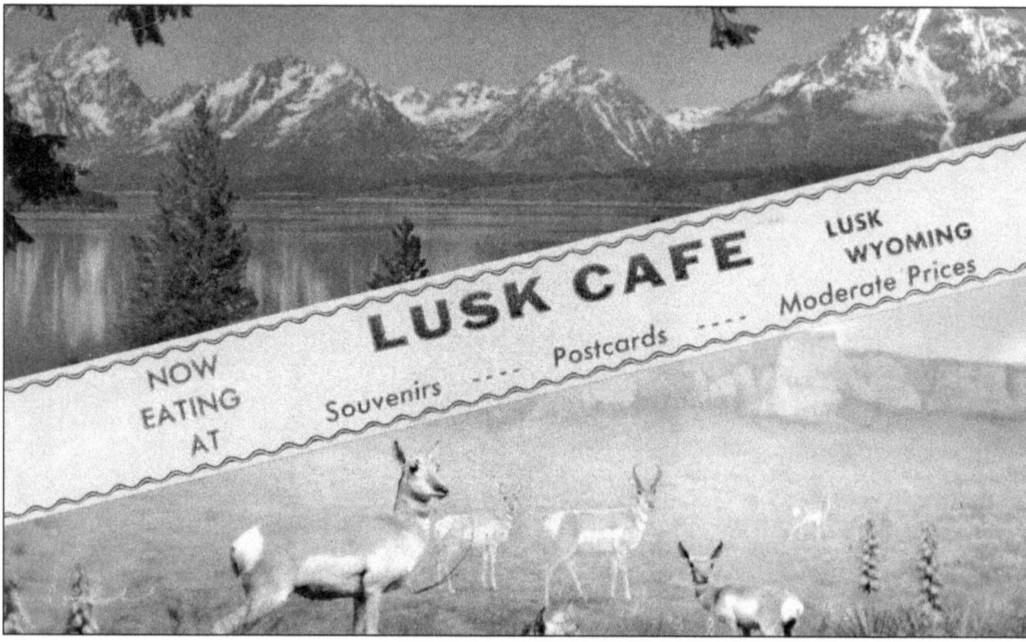

Lusk Cafe, Main Street, Lusk. Advertising cards that displayed the beauty of the surrounding countryside were popular during the early decades of Highway 20. This writer was in Lusk to visit his grandfather's former ranch but was unimpressed. He described the ranch as a desolate, godforsaken place. He had taken pictures of grandpa's log cabin but was more interested in seeing the oil fields in the area.

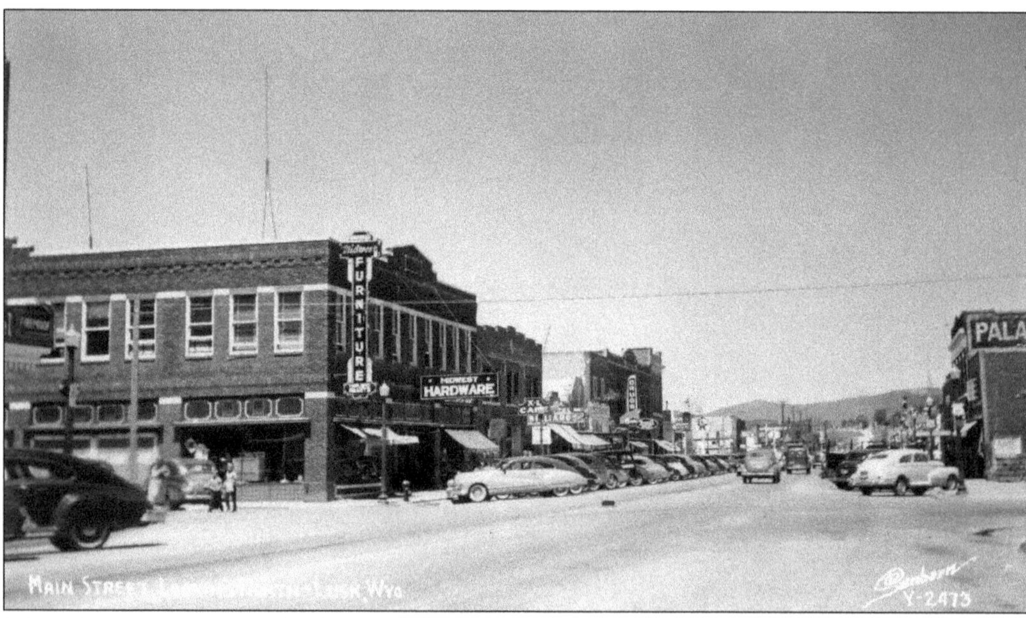

Main Street, Lusk. The thoroughfare was busy when this photograph was taken in the late 1940s. Diagonal parking was common, and establishments such as cafes, furniture, and hardware stores occupied both sides of Main Street. A drugstore and billiards parlor also can be identified. The writer told her dad that she had petted "a real live deer" near Mount Rushmore, and she had seen burros, mountain goats, and buffalo herds.

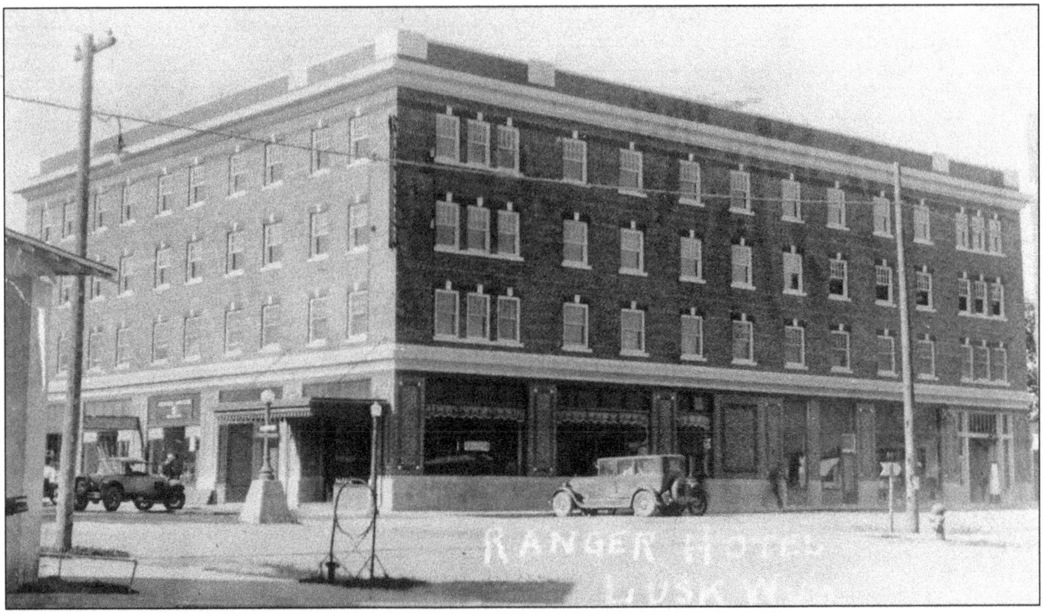

Ranger Hotel, 302 South Main Street, Lusk. Construction of the hotel began in 1919 during Wyoming's boom period following the arrival of the railroad and discovery of oil in the area. It was completed in 1928. The exterior was typical of most small-town hotels: a three-story brick building on a prominent corner of Main Street. The hotel's Oasis Bar was popular with travelers and locals alike.

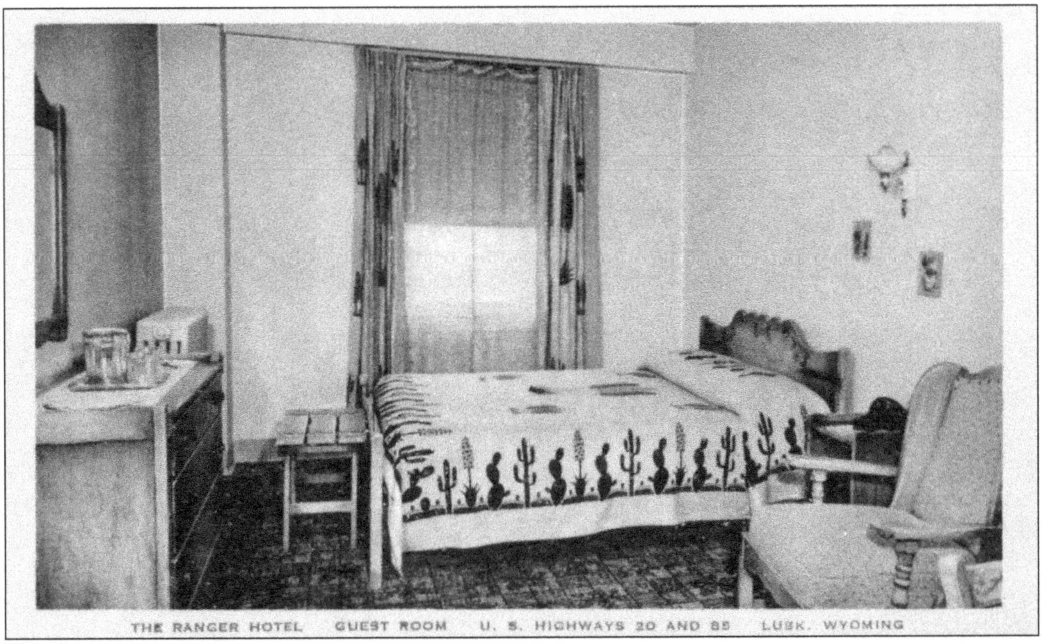

Guest Room, Ranger Hotel, Lusk. During its heyday, the Ranger was recognized as one of the finest hotels in eastern Wyoming. Guests were accommodated in rooms that were small and sparsely furnished, but comfortable. The room shown here had a bed, chair, dresser, and a pitcher for water. The hot-water radiator in the corner provided heat. Separate bathrooms were located on each floor.

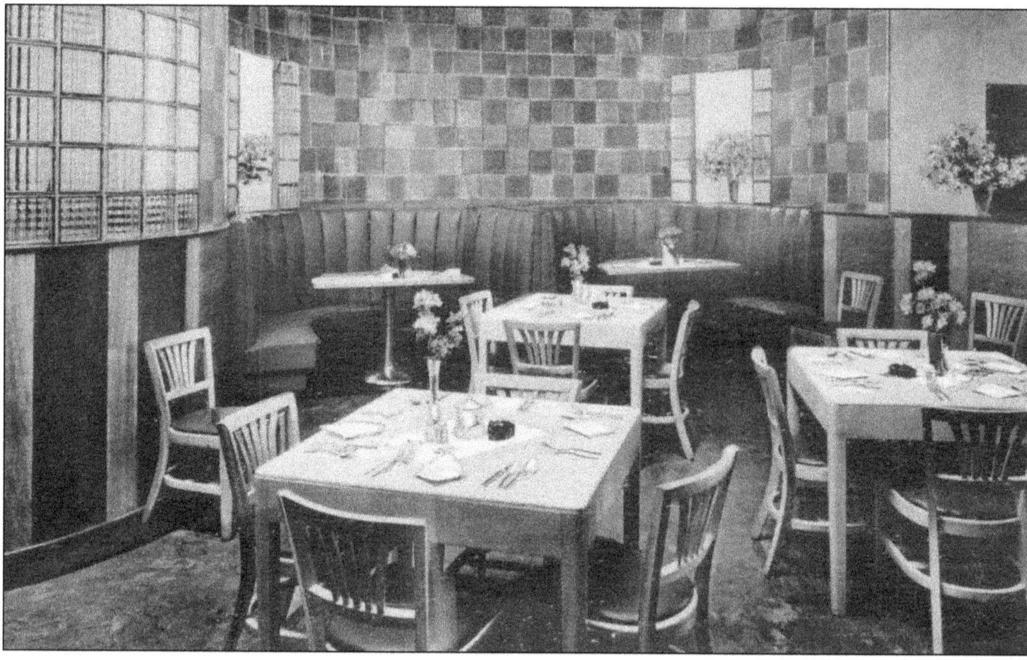

RANGER HOTEL COFFEE SHOP, LUSK. The decor of this dining room clearly shows that the management of the Ranger Hotel was keeping up with the interior design tastes of the day. Glass brick and tile walls, built in banquettes, and the stylish tables and chairs all are characteristic of the Art Deco style of the era.

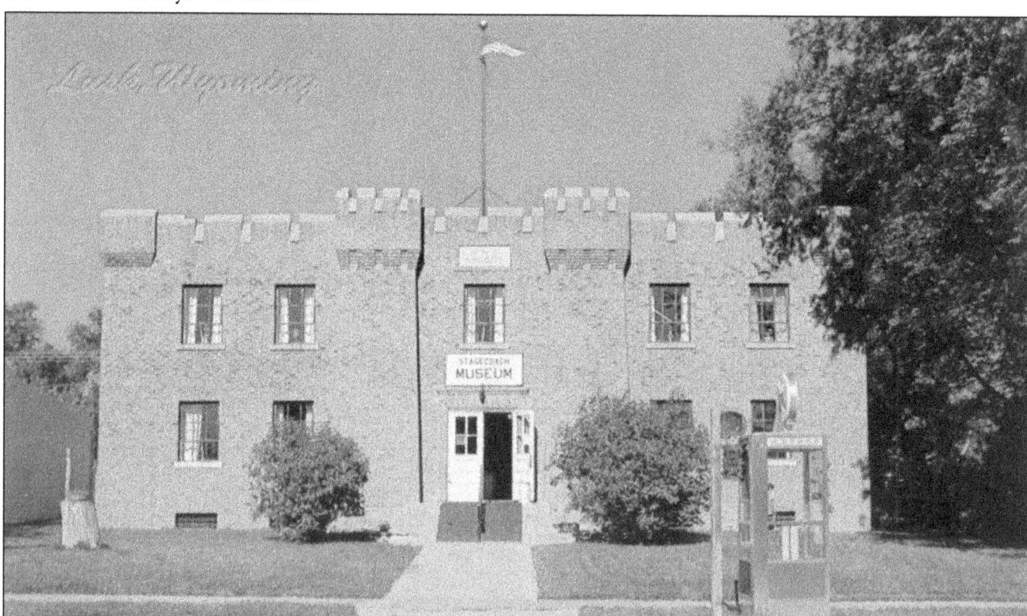

STAGECOACH MUSEUM, 322 SOUTH MAIN STREET, LUSK. The National Guard Armory, built in 1927, provided an ideal space for the expanded Stagecoach Museum when the building was no longer needed for military use. Exhibits include a stagecoach used on the famed Cheyenne and Black Hills Stage Line, plus several buggies, early farm implements, and a general store. A one-room schoolhouse and newspaper building also are located on the site.

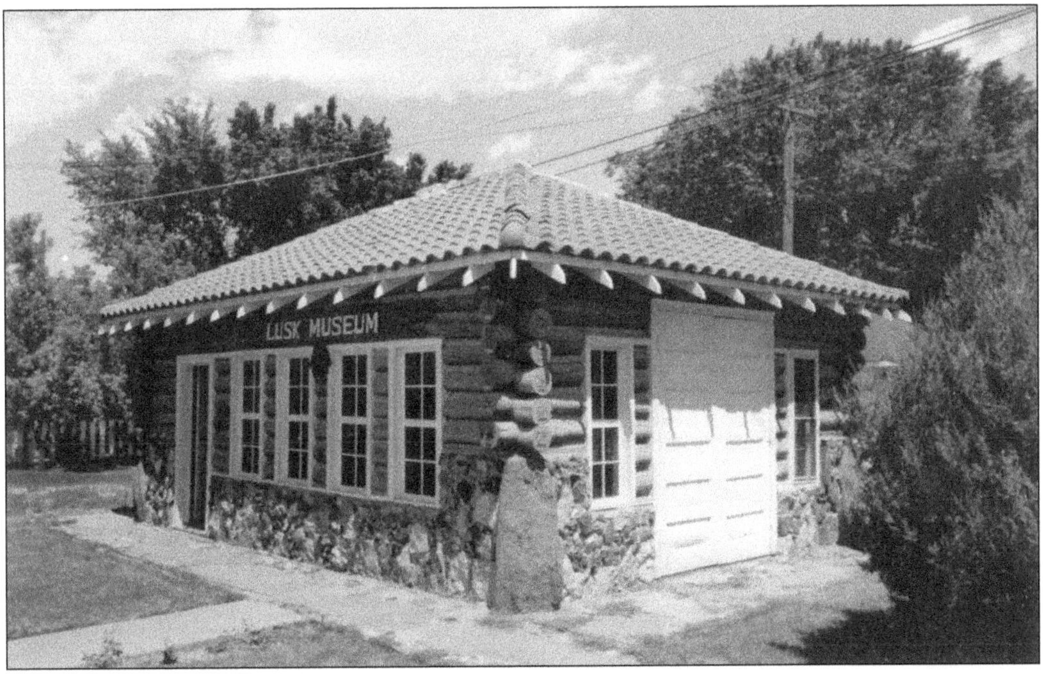

ORIGINAL LUSK MUSEUM AND FRONTIER STAGE COACH, LUSK. The original Lusk Museum shown in the image above was constructed as a WPA project intended only to house the stagecoach used on the Cheyenne and Black Hills Line, seen below. It was donated by Russell Thorp Jr., a leading citizen of Lusk, and is the centerpiece of the museum now located in the former National Guard Armory shown on the previous page. Coincidentally, Thorp also was instrumental in establishing a granite monument at the gravesite of Charlotte Shepard, better known as Mother Featherlegs, a famous frontier madam and brothel operator near Lusk.

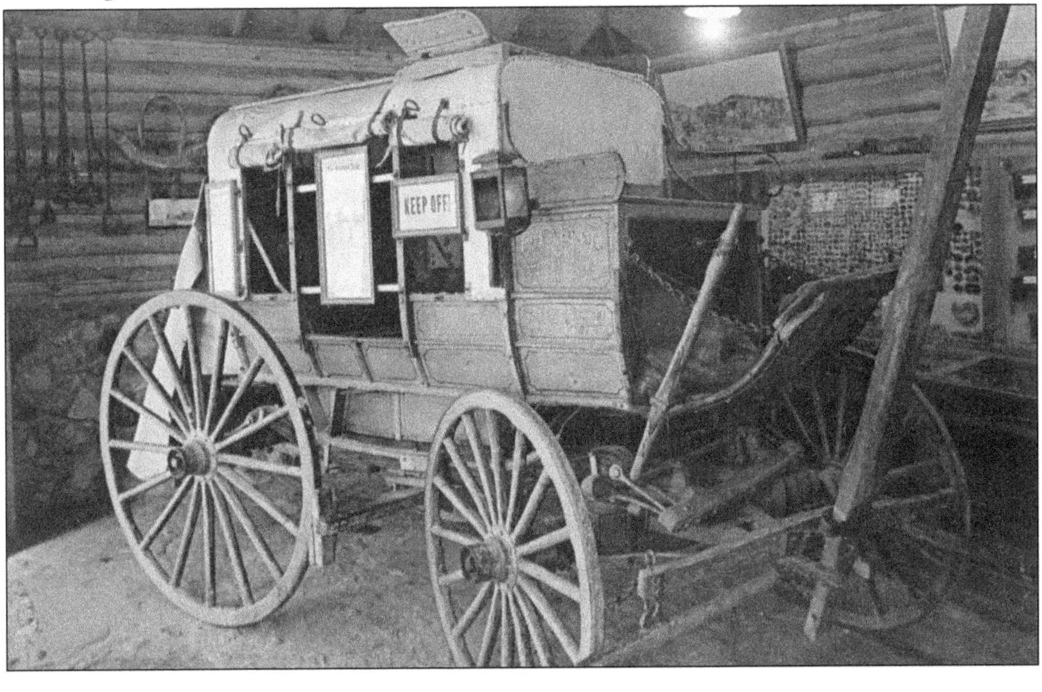

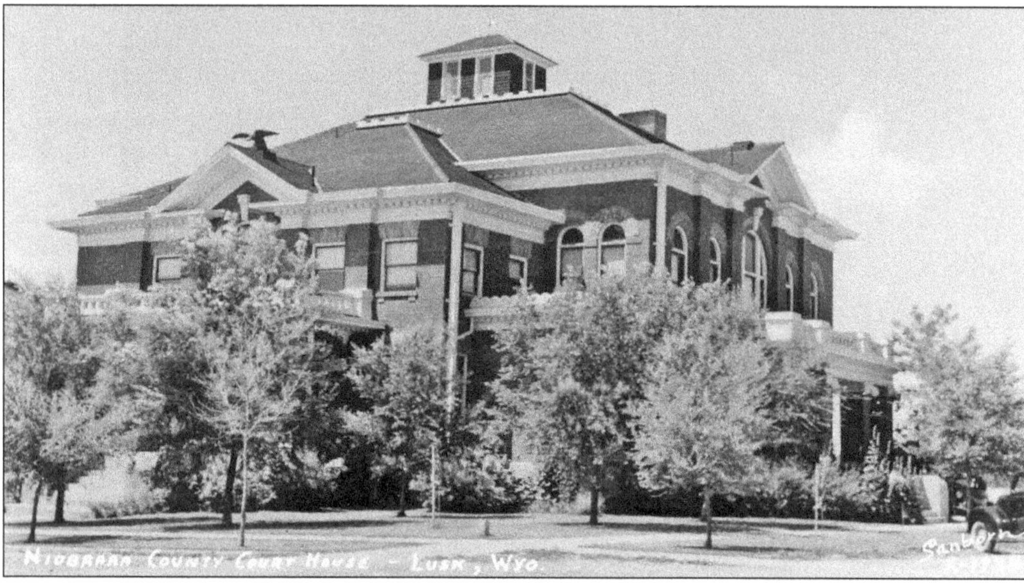

Niobrara County Courthouse, 424 South Elm Street, Lusk. Originally, Lusk and the surrounding communities were included in Converse County with Douglas as the county seat. As the population and commercial importance of Lusk expanded, and following a long and sometimes bitter campaign, Niobrara County was created in 1911. County commissioners were not sworn in until January 1, 1913.

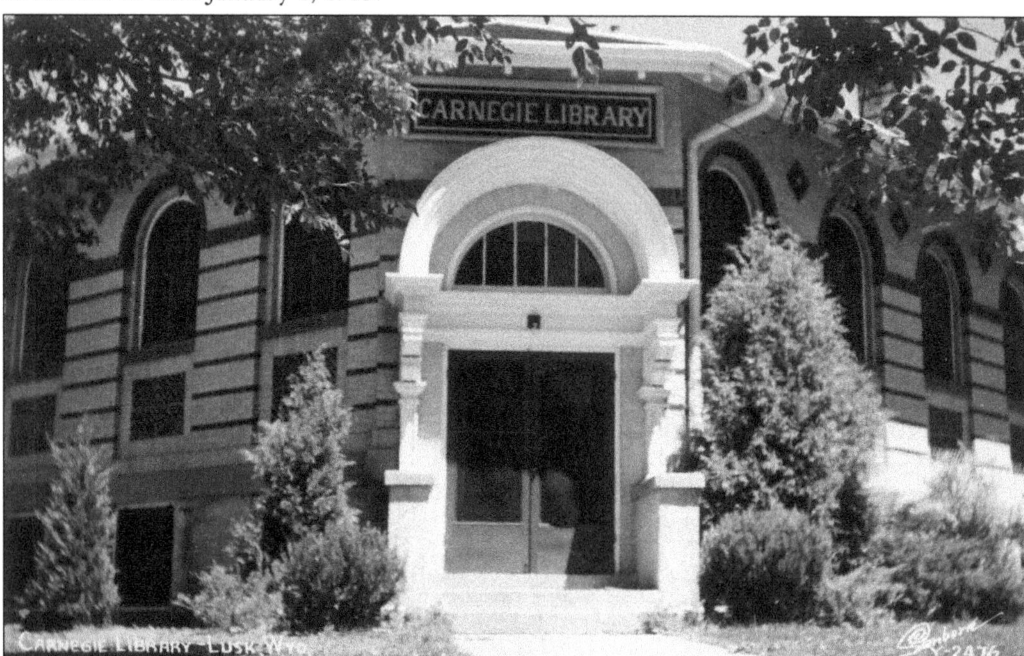

Carnegie Library, 425 South Main Street, Lusk. Early Lusk citizens recognized the importance of a library in their new town and they began a campaign to obtain a grant from the Carnegie Foundation to construct a suitable building. An award of $11,000 was made in 1911, and the classic building was completed in 1914. It continues to serve its original purpose to this day.

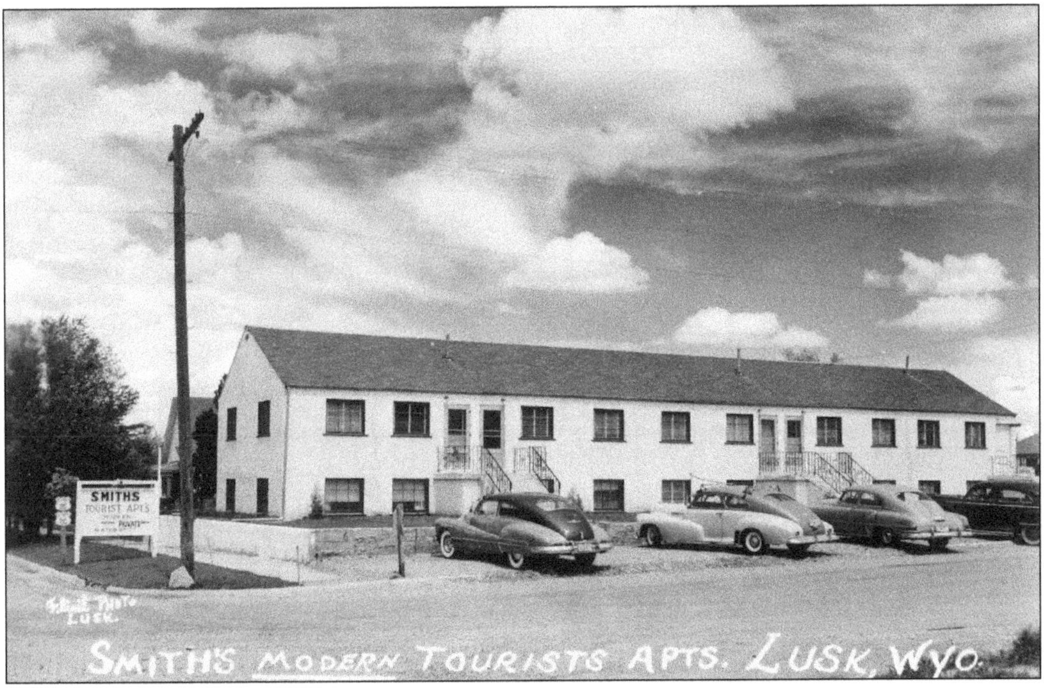

Smith's Modern Tourist Apartments, Highway 85 and 20, Lusk. This 1940s tourist court, located south of the business district in Lusk, boasted two levels of accommodations. It appears that most of the tenants preferred slant-back General Motors cars or maybe a local dealer loaned them for the photograph. A Highway 20 shield can be seen immediately to the left of the motel sign.

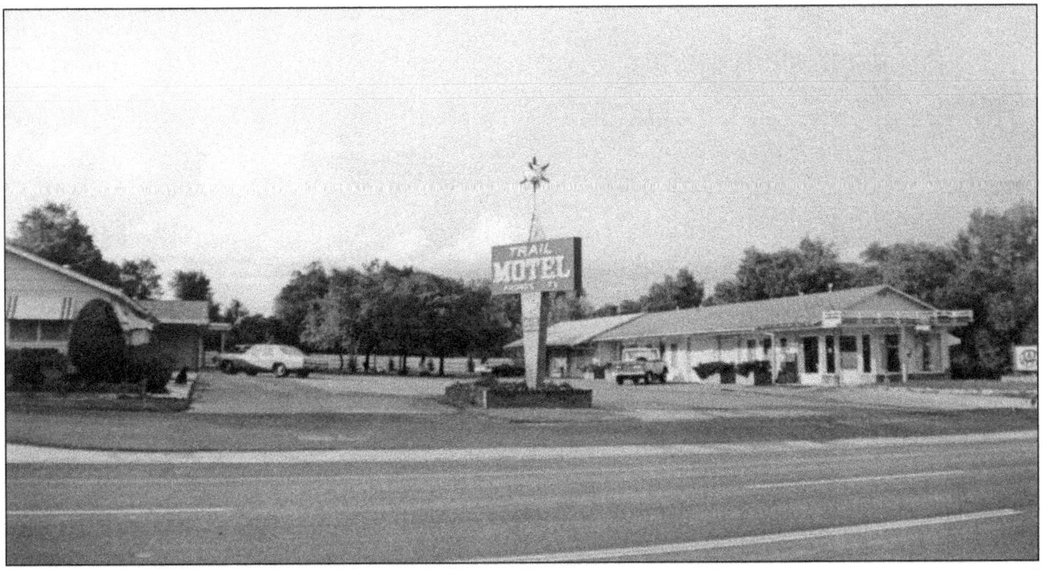

Trail Motel, Highways 20 and 85, Lusk. All 16 units of the Trail Motel were equipped with combination tub and showers and thermostatically controlled heat. The motel proudly displayed its AAA approval rating on a large sign at the entrance. Its location, just one block from the junction of Highways 20 and 85 south of Lusk's business district, made it a convenient stop for travelers on both highways.

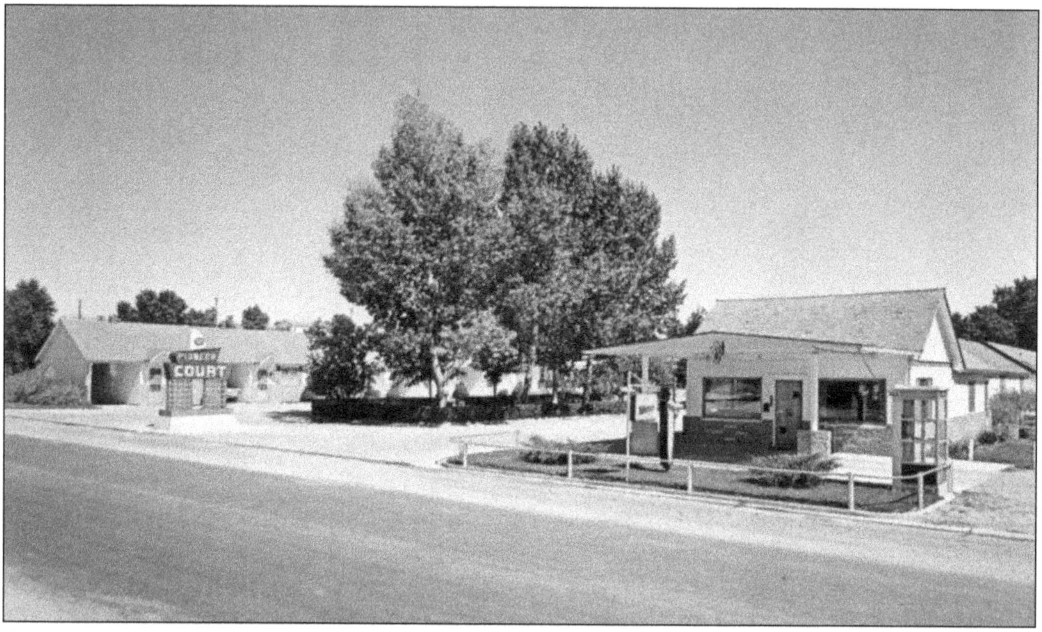

PIONEER COURT, SOUTH JUNCTION OF HIGHWAYS 85 AND 20, LUSK. The 3-3-9 telephone number of this motel gives an indication of the era this card was produced. Garages were available, but they were a rapidly passing feature of early motels as most operators preferred to convert the space into rentable rooms. Another passing feature was the telephone booth on the premises, which was common before in-room telephones were installed.

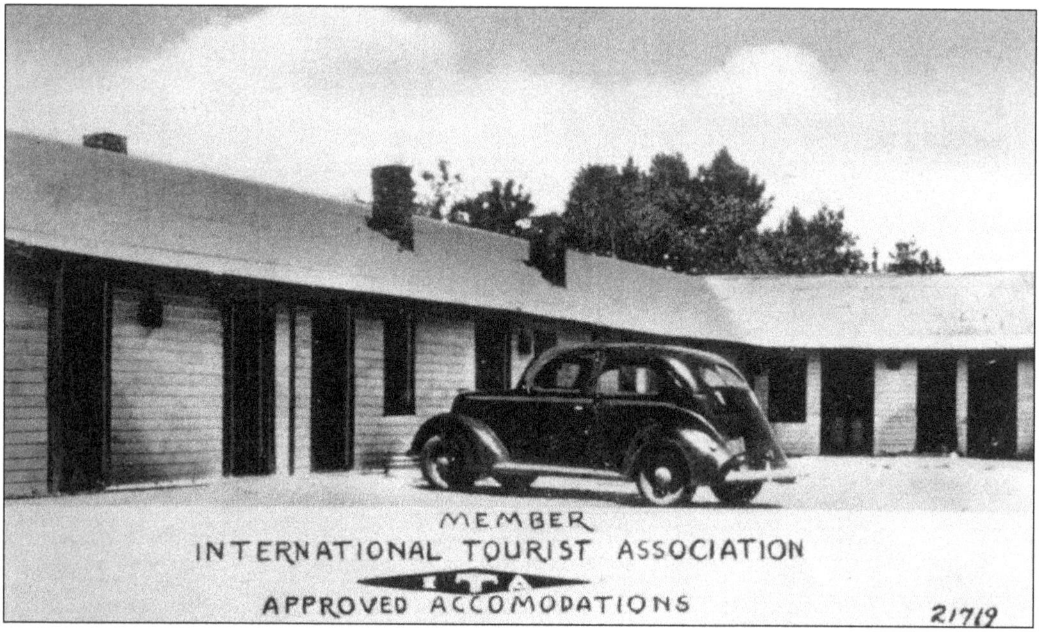

WYOMING CAMP, LUSK. The owners of this early motel were proud that the International Tourist Association approved their business. Certain units had chimneys, indicating that they were heated by in-room stoves whereas other units must have used other heating systems. The back contains the message, "You are cordially invited to stay with us." Someone driving a shiny 1937 Ford sedan had accepted that kind invitation.

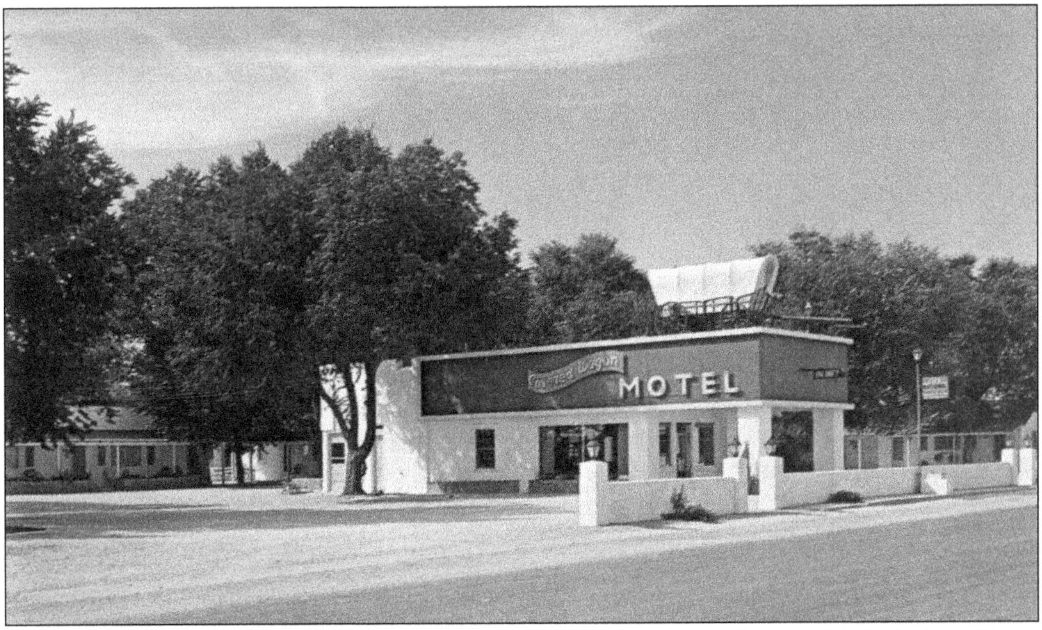

COVERED WAGON MOTEL, HIGHWAYS 18, 20, AND 85, LUSK. The motel definitely had kept up with the times. It boasted modern conveniences, including wall-to-wall carpets, ceramic tile bathrooms, and thermostatically controlled heat. In-room television was still in the future, but a TV lounge near the office was available for guests. The Covered Wagon Motel was open only from April to November.

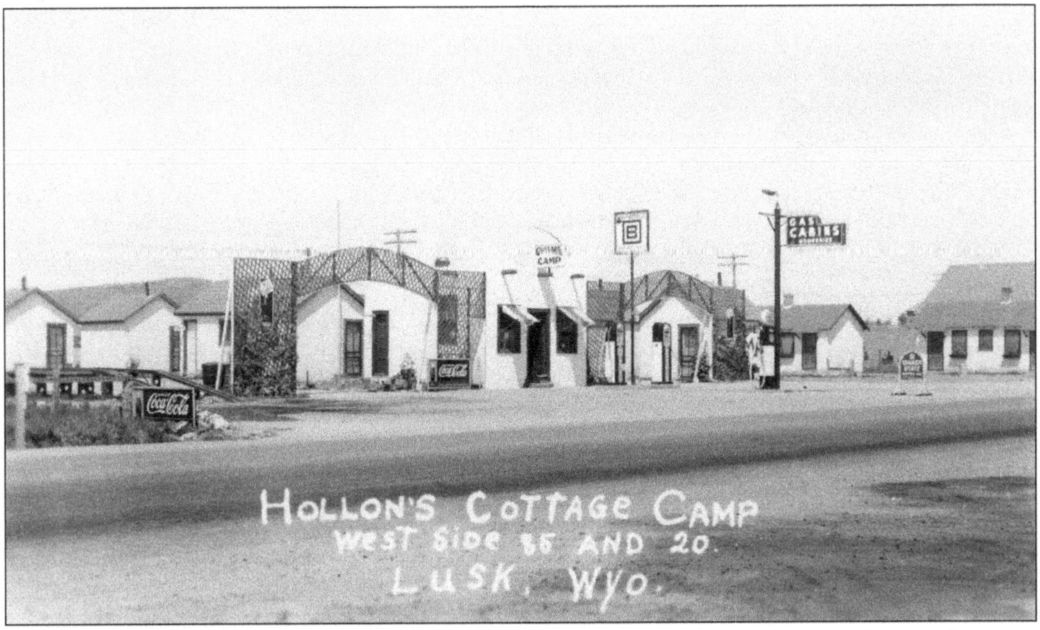

HOLLON'S COTTAGE CAMP, HIGHWAYS 85 AND 20, LUSK. Gas, cabins, and groceries were available at Hollon's, located adjacent to the Covered Wagon Motel. The service station had two gas pumps, and Quaker State oil products were featured. The outdoor, elevated rack on the left probably was used for oil changes and minor auto repair. Hollon's Cottage Camp eventually was incorporated into the Covered Wagon Motel.

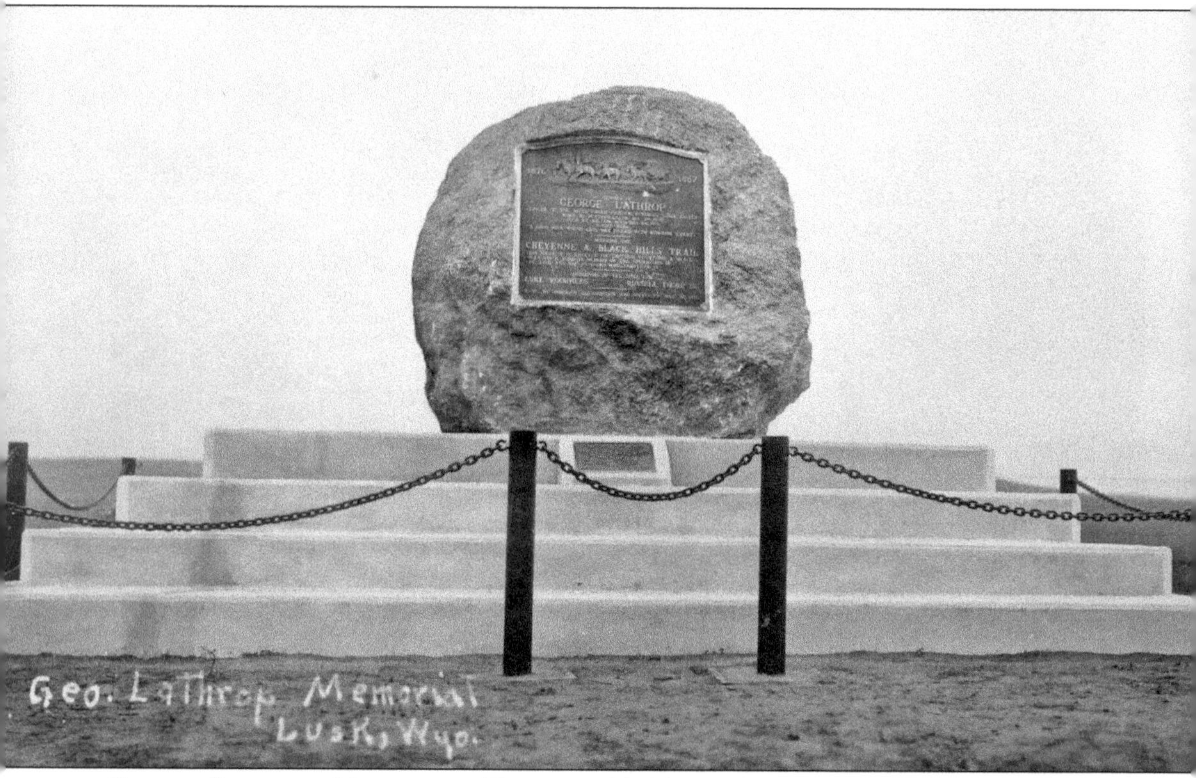

George Lathrop Memorial, Highway 20, Three Miles West of Lusk. This stone monument marks the grave and pays tribute to George Lathrop, a prominent character in early Wyoming history. During his lifetime, he was described as a bullwhacker, muleskinner, and stage driver. It is the latter activity for which he was honored by the City of Lusk. As a longtime driver of the "Deadwood Stage" (properly known as the Cheyenne and Black Hills Stage and Express Line), he faithfully delivered his passengers and cargo to their destinations despite several Indian and outlaw attacks. He was the driver on the final run of this famous stage line on February 19, 1887. Engraved on the stone marker is a simple epitaph: "In memory of George Lathrop, 1820–1915, a good man whose life was filled with stirring events."

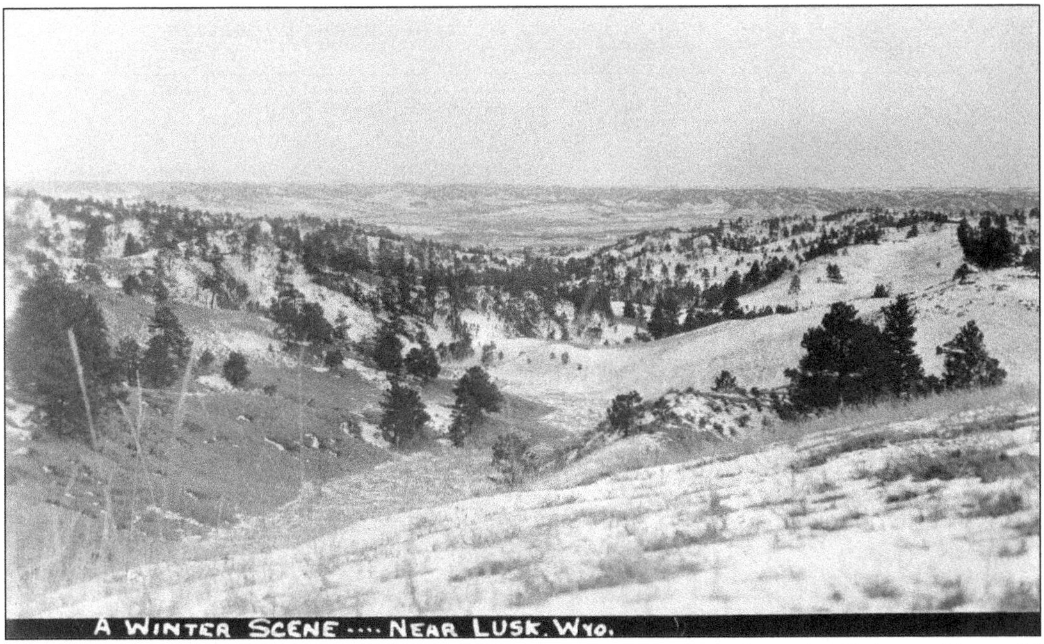

TWO WINTER SCENES NEAR LUSK. A motorist traveling west on historic Highway 20 would have noticed the change from the flat Midwestern plains to more rugged countryside that characterized eastern Wyoming. Mountains and canyons that provided an introduction to the higher mountains farther west surrounded Lusk, located in the foothills of the Rocky Mountains. The scenery throughout the region remains much the same as in earlier years when settlers arrived in covered wagons. Both of these images were taken in winter and show the land covered in a blanket of snow. The changing seasons, a positive feature of Wyoming, provided scenic beauty throughout the year.

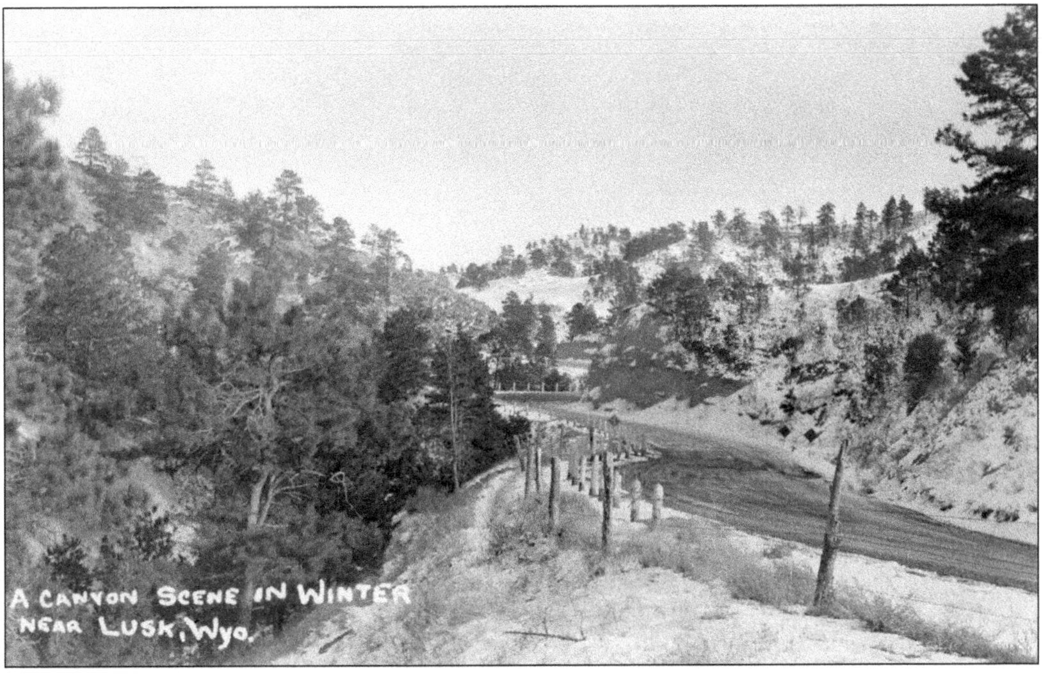

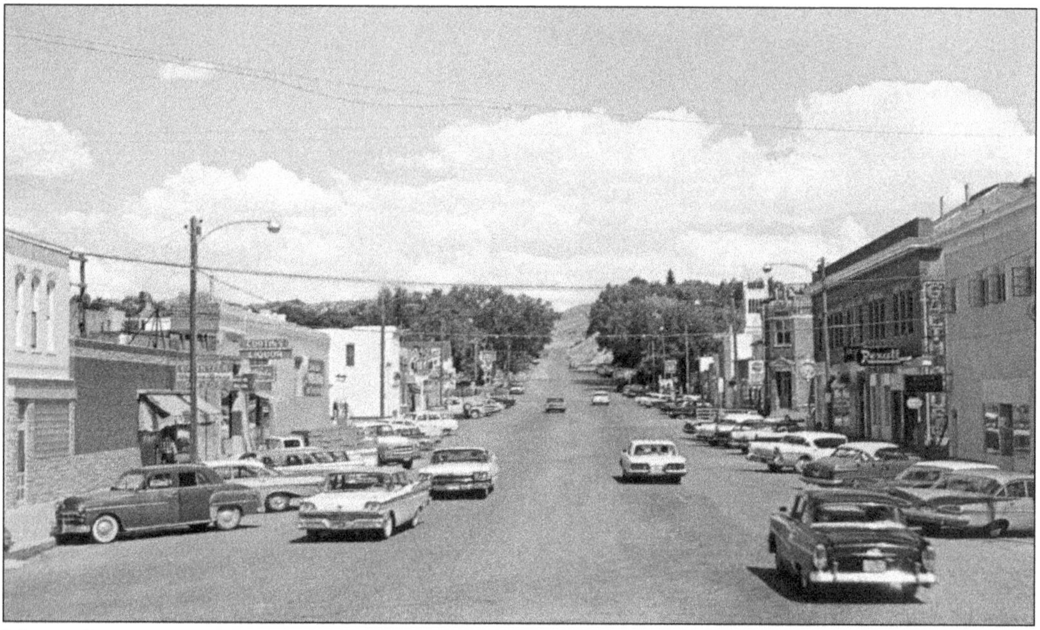

MAIN STREET, DOUGLAS, WYOMING. Douglas, the seat of Converse County, had a busy business district in the 1950s. A liquor store and three service stations can be identified. The Rexall drugstore, a fixture in almost every small town, is located on the right side of the street, and a tavern featuring Schlitz beer is located on the left at the far end of the street.

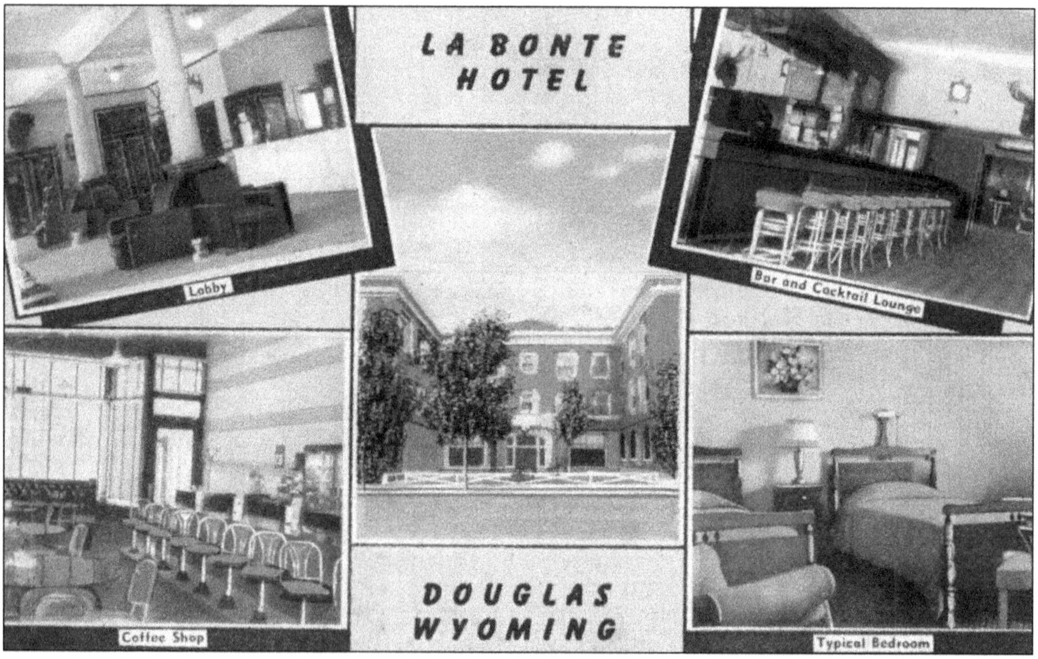

LABONTE HOTEL, 206 WALNUT STREET, DOUGLAS. The hotel was built in 1913, and its grand opening was held on January 26, 1914. Several foresightful businessmen recognized the need for a first-class hotel and financed the project. The hotel had 54 guest rooms, a bar and billiards room, and meeting rooms. For the first half of the 20th century, the LaBonte was the center of business and social activities in Douglas.

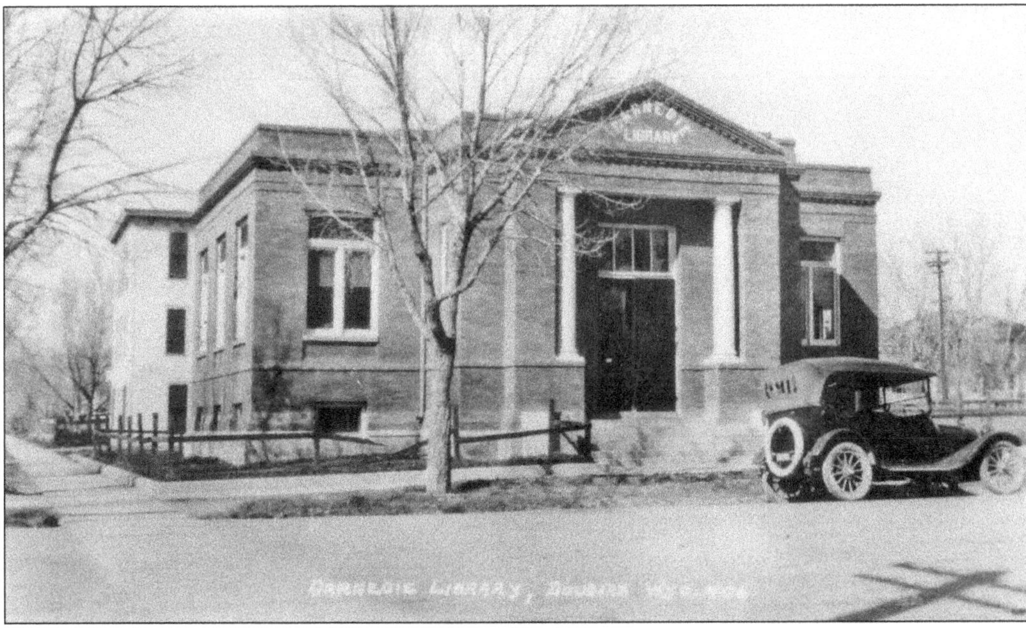

Carnegie Library, 300 Walnut Street, Douglas. This beautiful library building was completed in 1911 following a $10,000 award from the Carnegie Foundation. It replaced the town's earlier library located in the courthouse. A pillar on either side of the front door distinguished the stately building. The library served Douglas until 1966, when it was torn down to make room for a more modern library building.

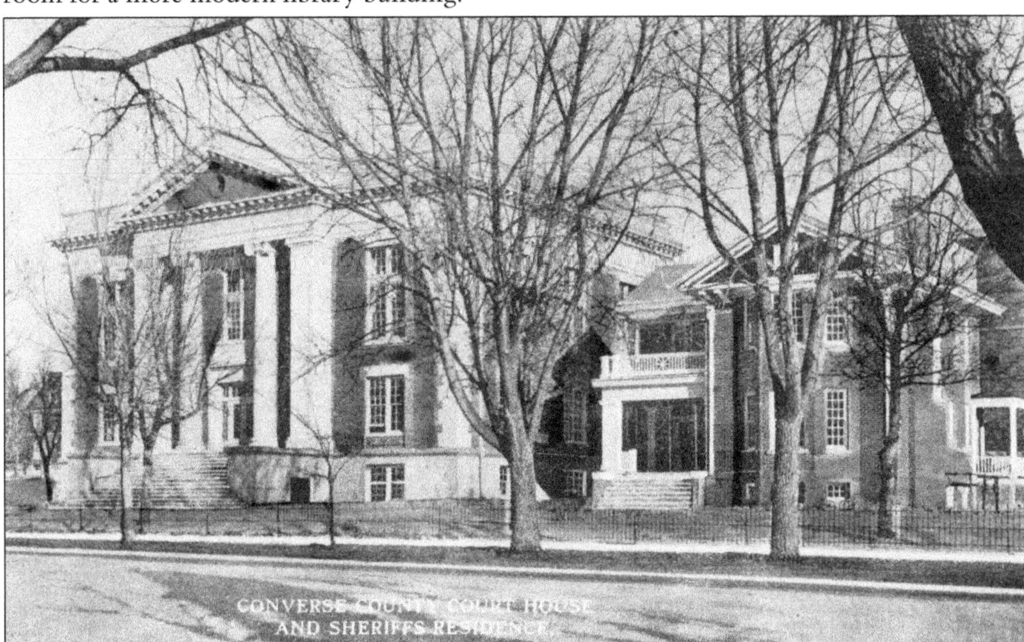

Converse County Courthouse and Sheriff's Residence, Douglas. In many early communities, the sheriff's office and home were in close proximity to the courthouse and more importantly to the local jail; often they were in the same building. Douglas differed slightly from this practice by providing an office within the courthouse and a large brick home next door.

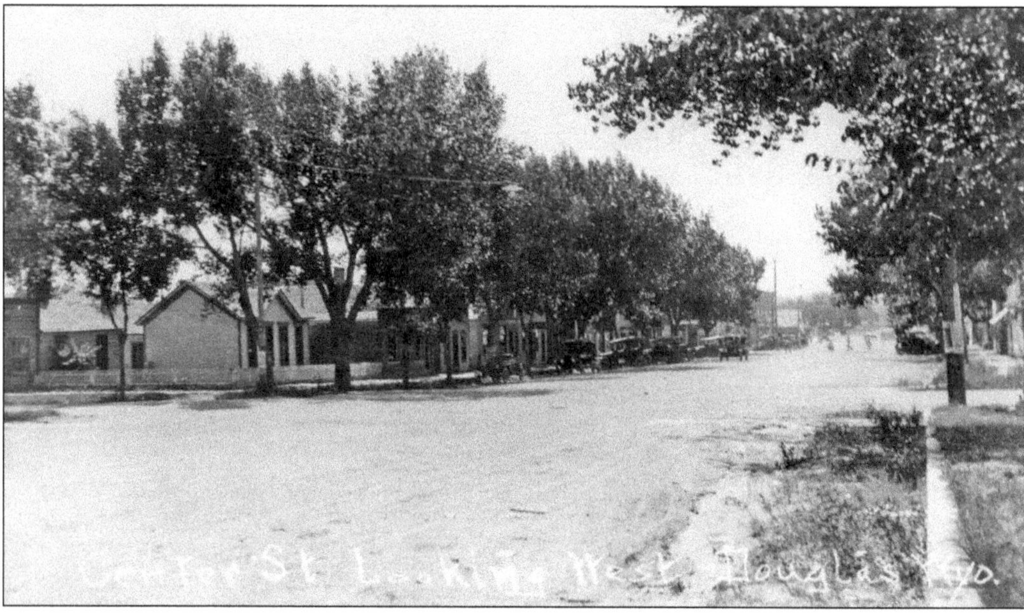

Center Street Looking West, Douglas. Historic Highway 20 followed Center Street through Douglas, giving motorists an opportunity to view both the business and residential districts. This image shows the road heading west toward downtown. The street surface was still gravel when this photograph was taken, and sidewalks were yet to be installed. Several cars from the mid-1920s can be seen in the distance.

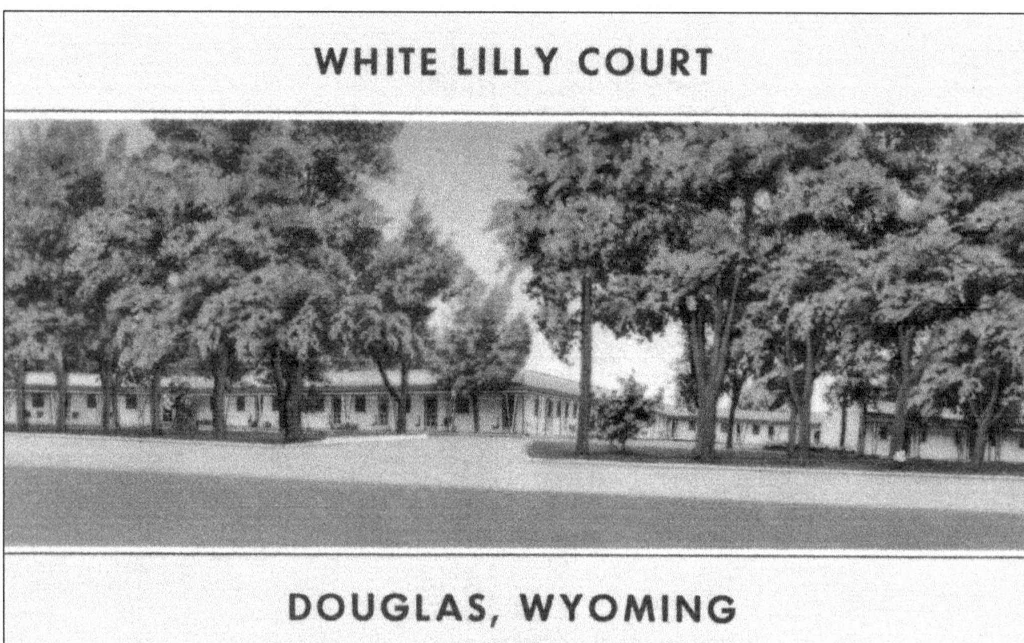

White Lilly Court, West Douglas Highway (Highways 20, 26, and 87), Douglas. A selling point for this early motel was that its units could accommodate up to six persons and were "air-cooled," possibly by opening the windows! Most likely, the court catered to families on their way to Yellowstone National Park and hunters and fishermen who frequented the area.

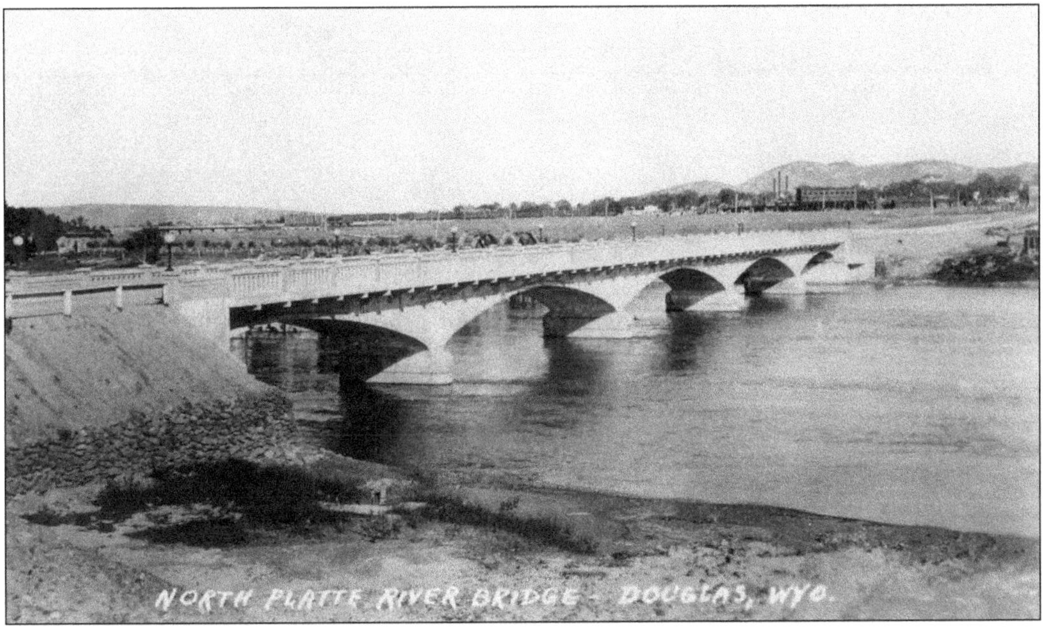

North Platte River and Bridge, Douglas. The concrete-arch bridge shown in the photograph above carried historic Highway 20 traffic across the North Platte River just west of Douglas. The graceful design of the six-span bridge was a visual complement to the surrounding countryside. The North Platte River, shown in both images, was noted for its good fishing. Access points were well marked, and fishing took place both from the riverbanks and from boats farther out on the water. The river produced several species of trout, including brown, rainbow, and cutthroat, as well as walleye and catfish.

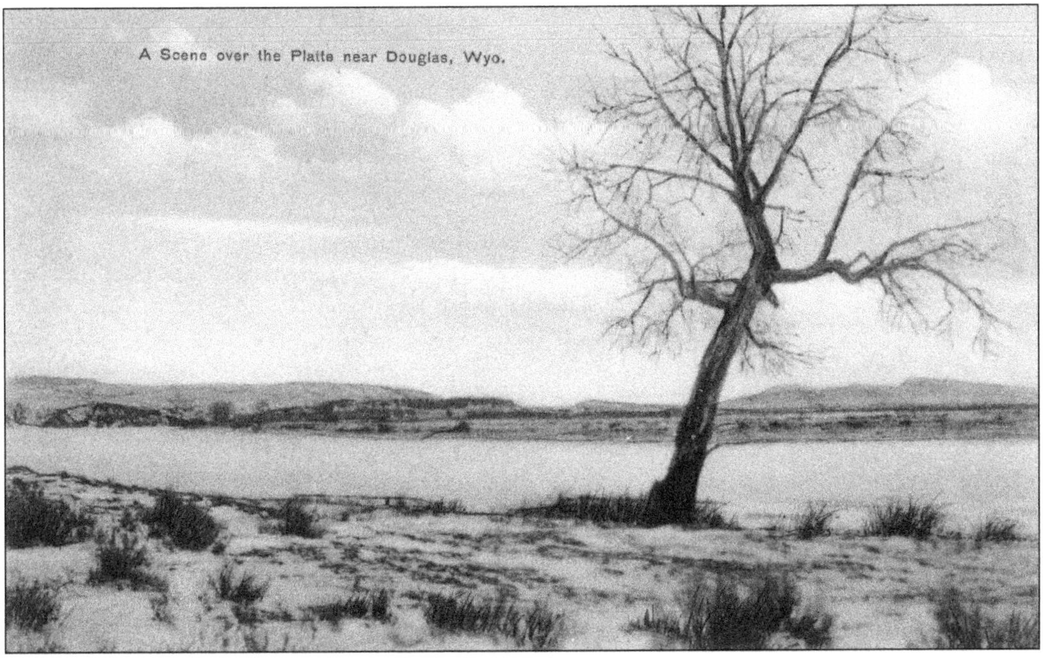

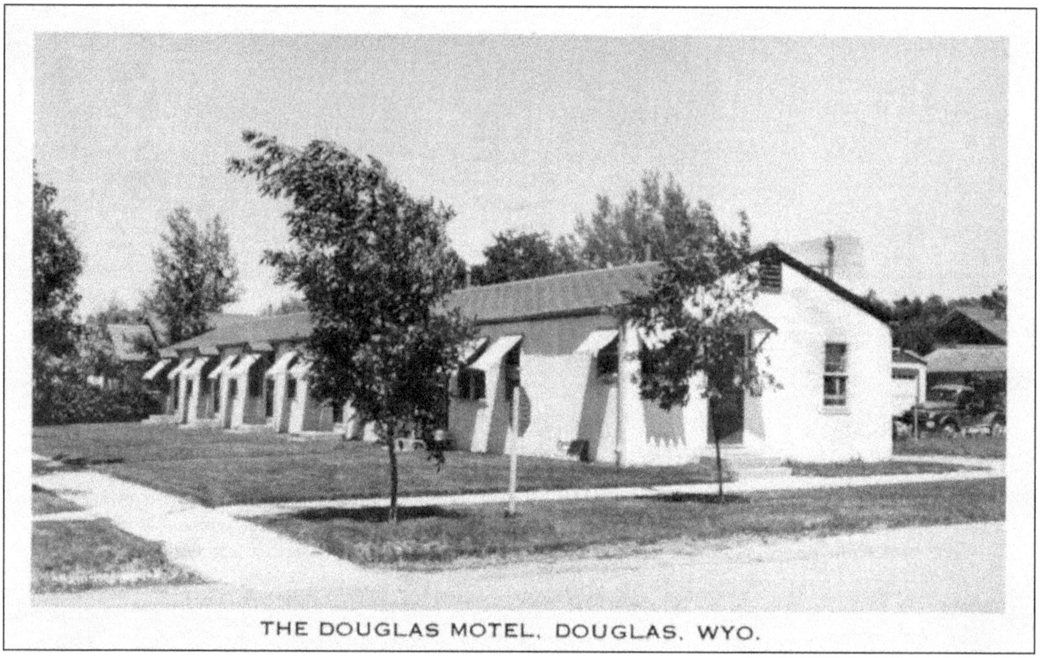

DOUGLAS MOTEL, HIGHWAYS 20, 26, AND 87, DOUGLAS. Although Yellowstone National Park was more than 300 miles northwest of Douglas, the message on the back of this card promoted this motel's location on the main highway (US 20) to and from the park. Its rooms were described as nicely furnished, with some kitchenette equipped, and moderately priced.

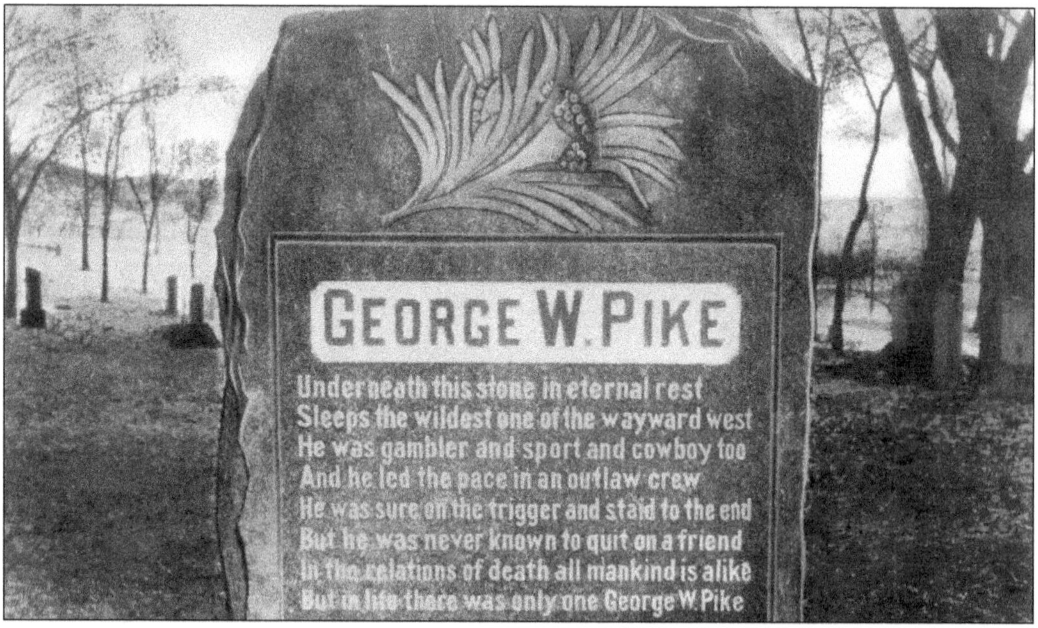

GEORGE W. PIKE MEMORIAL, DOUGLAS. This grave marker in Douglas Park Cemetery memorializes George Pike, a notorious cowboy in Douglas in the late 1800s who was alleged to be a gambler and rustler and leader of an outlaw gang. In spite of his unsavory reputation, he was never convicted of any crimes. His loyalty to friends was legendary, as shown by his epitaph carved in stone over his grave.

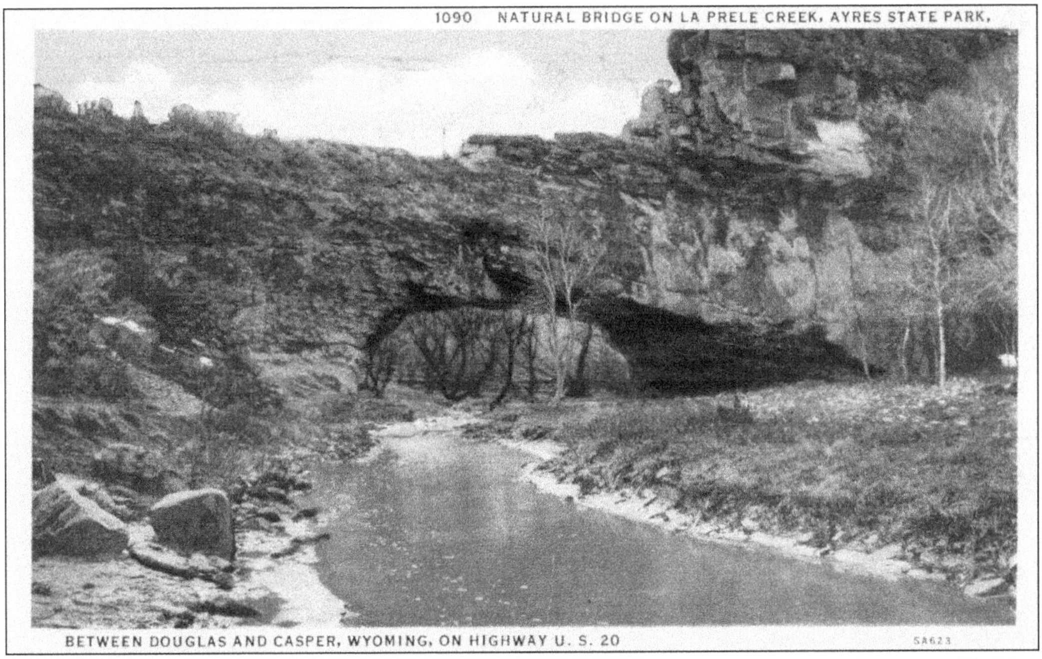

NATURAL BRIDGE ON LA PRELE CREEK, AYRES STATE PARK, DOUGLAS. This natural bridge is located in Ayres State Park just a short distance from historic Highway 20. The arch lies in a secluded, picturesque glen spanning La Prele Creek. The park is a popular location, and most visitors photograph the unique geologic structure. This card was mailed in 1938.

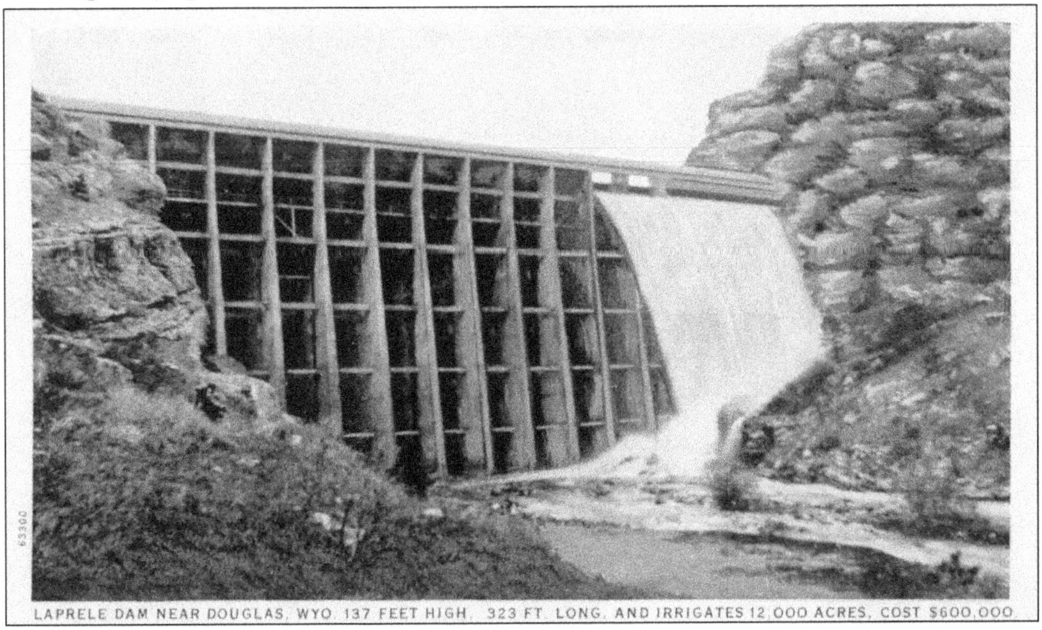

LA PRELE DAM, NEAR DOUGLAS. Since its completion in 1909, visitors and experts have been drawn to the unique design of the La Prele Dam. The "concrete slab and buttress" design required only slightly more than half the concrete used in traditional dams. The designer, Norwegian engineer Nils Amberson, went on to build more than 100 similar dams throughout the country during the early decades of the 20th century.

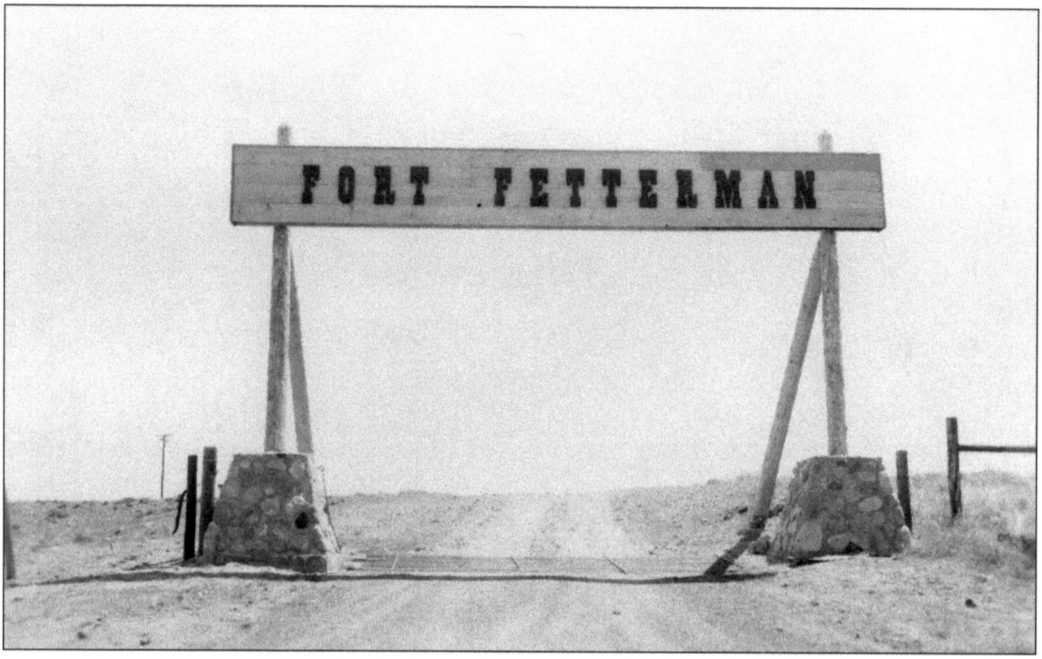

Fort Fetterman, near Douglas. Fort Fetterman was established in 1867 on a plateau overlooking the convergence of La Prele Creek and the North Platte River. It was a short-lived military post intended to help tame the Western frontier and serve as a haven for westbound settlers. The fort was abandoned in 1882. It now is a state historic site containing two original buildings and the ruins of several other structures.

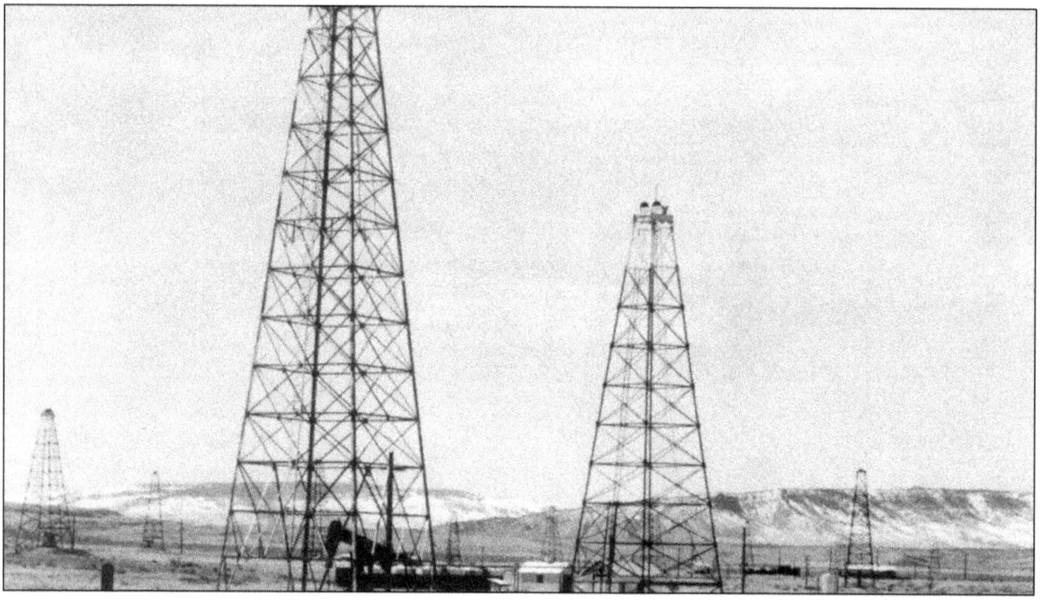

Big Muddy Oil Field, Glenrock. A historical marker on US 20 and 26, about five miles west of Glenrock, notes: "Big Muddy is a typical Wyoming oil producing structure. It was discovered in 1916 and throughout its history more than 50 million barrels have been produced." In 1919, nearly 10,000 barrels of oil per day were produced, making Big Muddy the second-most prolific oil field in the state of Wyoming.

Two

Natrona and Fremont Counties

In the 20-year period from 1910 to 1930, Natrona County grew from a population of 4,776 to 24,272 before it leveled off during the Great Depression. Casper continues to be the dominant city in this area of Wyoming. It owes much of its population growth to Wyoming's oil boom. Both the discovery of oil, and subsequently the refining of crude oil, brought many new residents to the county. This in turn spurred the building of homes and businesses. In the 1930s and 1940s, Casper boasted many hotels offering basic to luxurious accommodations that were needed to house newly arrived workers and businessmen who were involved in the oil industry.

Geologic phenomenon Hell's Half Acre is located approximately 45 miles west of Casper. The name does not give full credit to the site, which actually consists of 320 acres of multicolored canyon walls and depressions. Its depth and unique rock formations in what is flatland for miles in every direction have caused certain observers to attach the name "Baby Grand Canyon." The origin of Hell's Half Acre has been argued for decades. Some geologists attribute it to wind and water erosion from the nearby Power River, whereas others consider it to be of volcanic origin. Irrespective of its name and formation, the site has attracted tourists since the inception of historic Highway 20.

Shoshoni, about 50 miles west of Hell's Half Acre, is the only town through which historic Highway 20 passes in Fremont County. The town and region are famous for the Boysen Reservoir, an artificial lake created by the Boysen Dam that lies a few miles north of Shoshoni. Historic Highway 20 provides excellent views of the lake and easy access to its fishing and other recreational facilities. This area is also the beginning of one of the country's most scenic drives. A few miles north of Boysen Lake, Highway 20 enters the Wind River Canyon Scenic Byway, where motorists are treated to miles of precipitous cliffs, rushing river water, and colorful vegetation and wildlife.

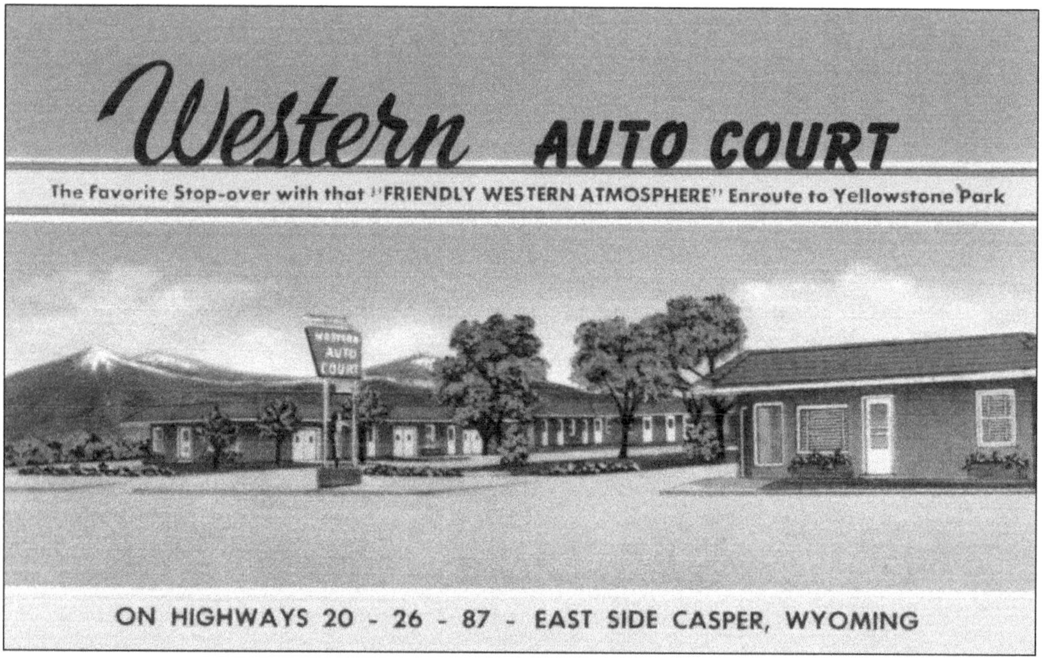

WESTERN AUTO COURT, 2325 EAST YELLOWSTONE HIGHWAY, CASPER. This is one of many early motels that catered to travelers en route to Yellowstone National Park. Located five minutes east of the city center in Casper, the motel featured luxurious, modern rooms. Family and kitchenette units were also available. Guests were assured, "You will like our accommodations."

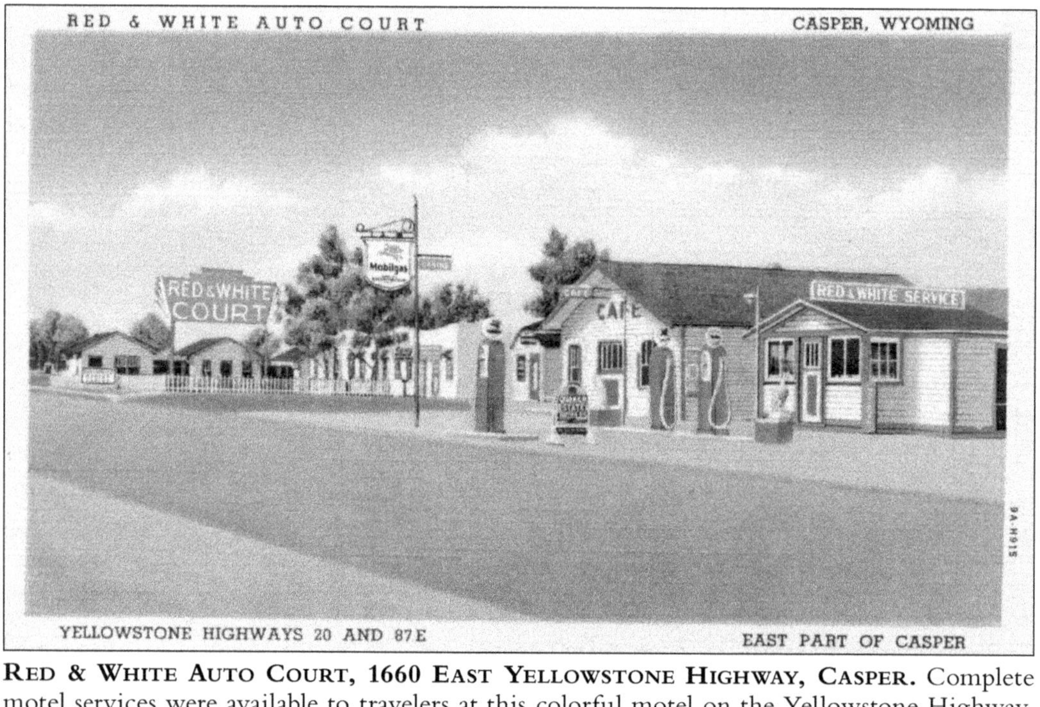

RED & WHITE AUTO COURT, 1660 EAST YELLOWSTONE HIGHWAY, CASPER. Complete motel services were available to travelers at this colorful motel on the Yellowstone Highway, including laundry, showers, and trailer space for a price of $1 and up. A combined cafe and store selling groceries and meats was part of the Mobilgas service station component.

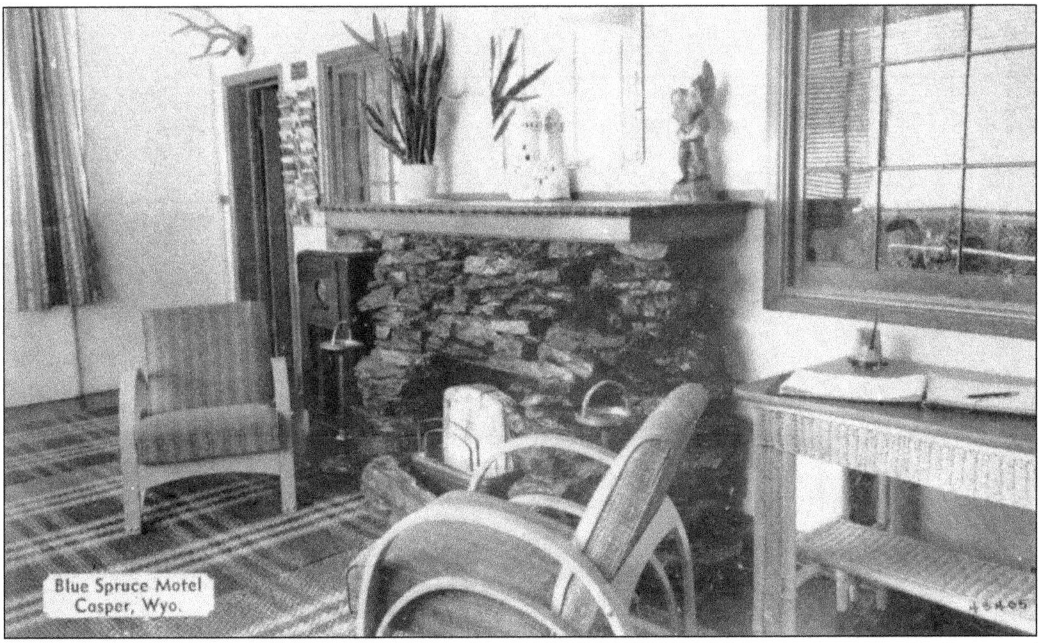

Blue Spruce Motel, East on Highways 20 and 87, Casper. The slogan of this motel was "where real hospitality is a matter of personal pride." Although a gas heater had replaced the wood-burning hearth in the reception lounge, the rough-hewn stone fireplace and the antlers on the wall were testimony to the authenticity of this Western motel.

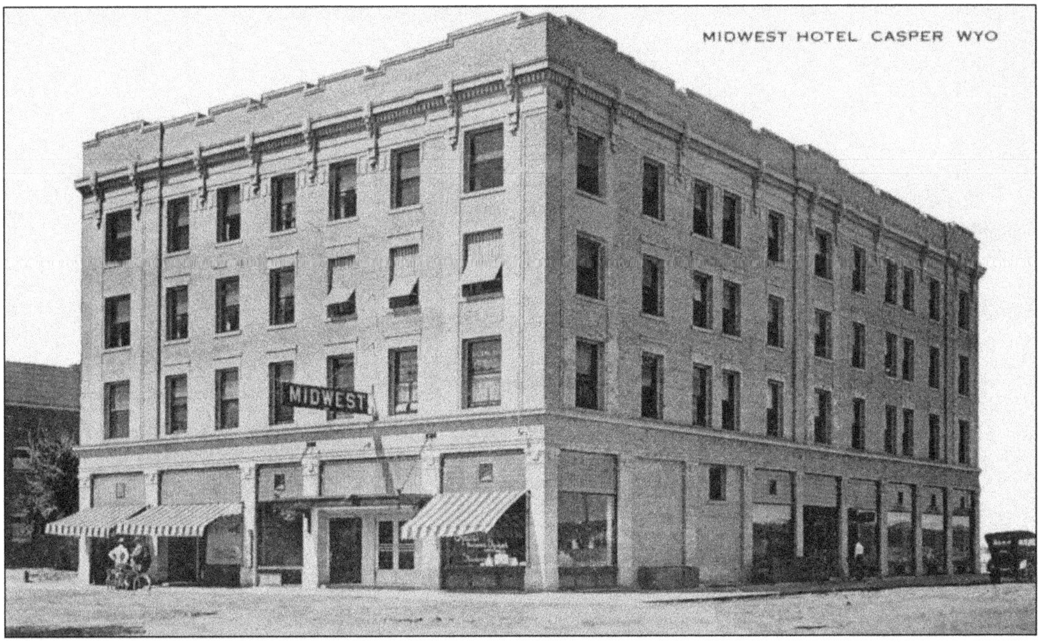

The Midwest Hotel, Casper. This hotel opened in 1914 and almost immediately plans were made to expand, with the addition to be named the Midwest Annex. Unfortunately, serious financial difficulties intervened, and in 1915 the property was sold to a group headed by businessman Welker Henning. Henning bought out his partners, completed the construction of the annex, and renamed the enlarged facility the Hotel Henning, shown on the following page.

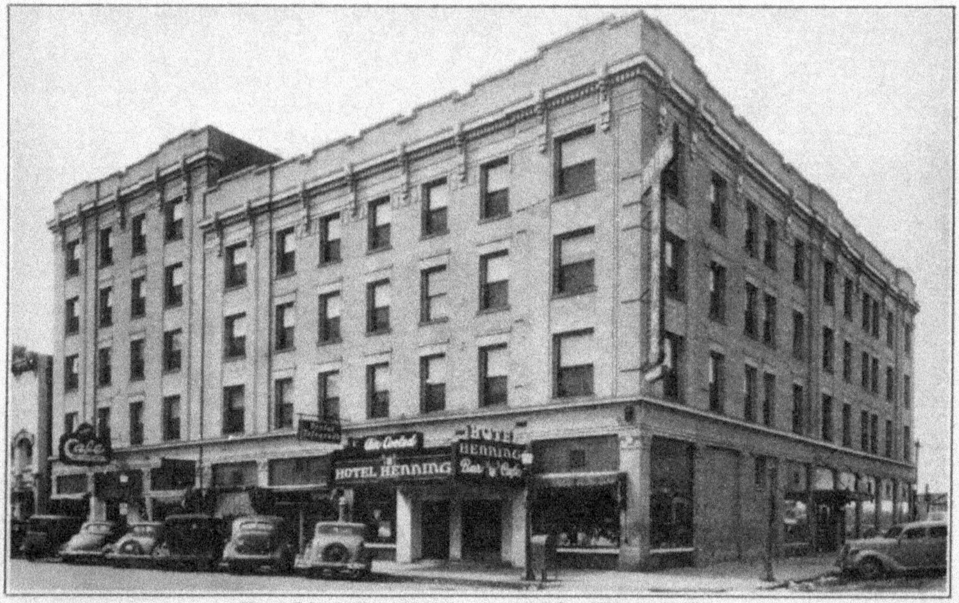

HOTEL HENNING, CASPER, WYOMING

HOTEL HENNING, SOUTHWEST CORNER OF FIRST AND CENTER STREETS, CASPER. The facade of the original Midwest Hotel is clearly visible in the 1930s view of the Hotel Henning. With the development of the Salt Creek, Midwest, and Big Muddy oil fields, Casper became the center of Wyoming's oil boom. The classic 150-room Hotel Henning was a popular gathering spot for oil field workers, owners, and tradesmen who supplied the equipment. Below is the imposing lobby of the hotel, which was formal and first class in all respects. Welker Henning, reputed to be Casper's first millionaire, took great care to please hotel guests, including the provision of transportation for business and social engagements in a 1920s version of a stretch limousine. The building was torn down in the mid-1960s. The site is now a parking lot.

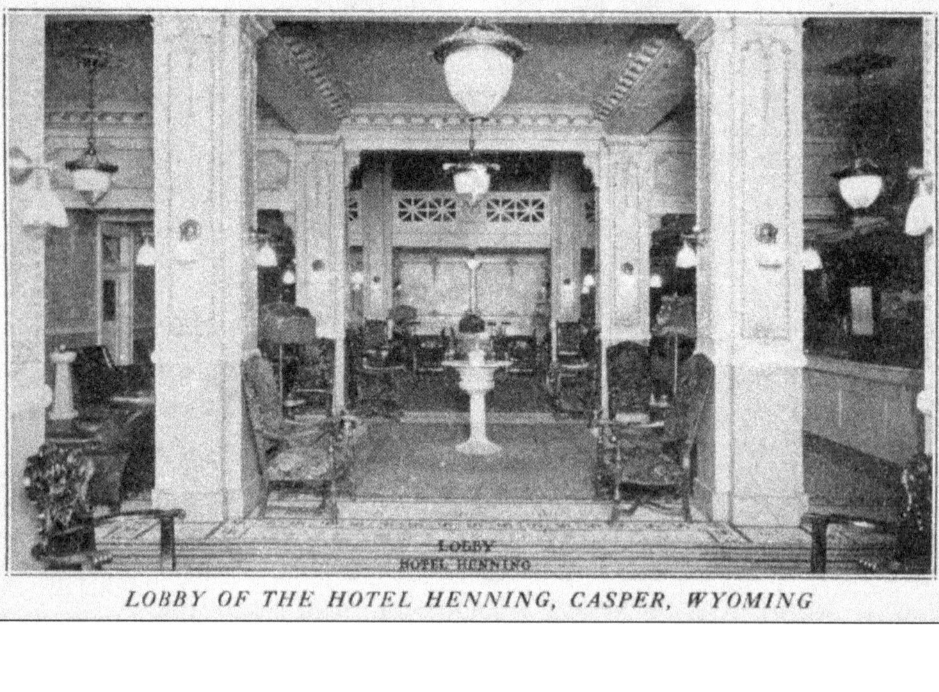

LOBBY OF THE HOTEL HENNING, CASPER, WYOMING

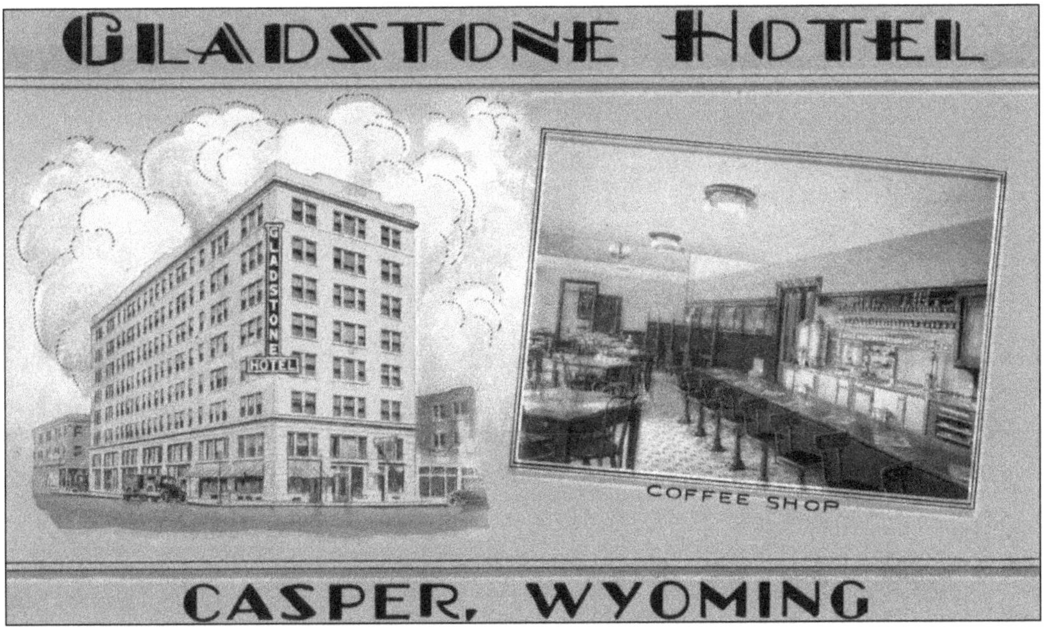

GLADSTONE HOTEL, CENTER STREET, CASPER. The Gladstone opened in 1923 and boasted 160 exterior, fireproof rooms, all with baths. The hotel featured a coffee shop and dining room and was the home of the Crystal Room, a favorite spot for dancing and receptions. Following the end of Prohibition, a bar and lounge were added. Guests could "sleep in safety and comfort, without extravagance." Rates were $1.50 and up.

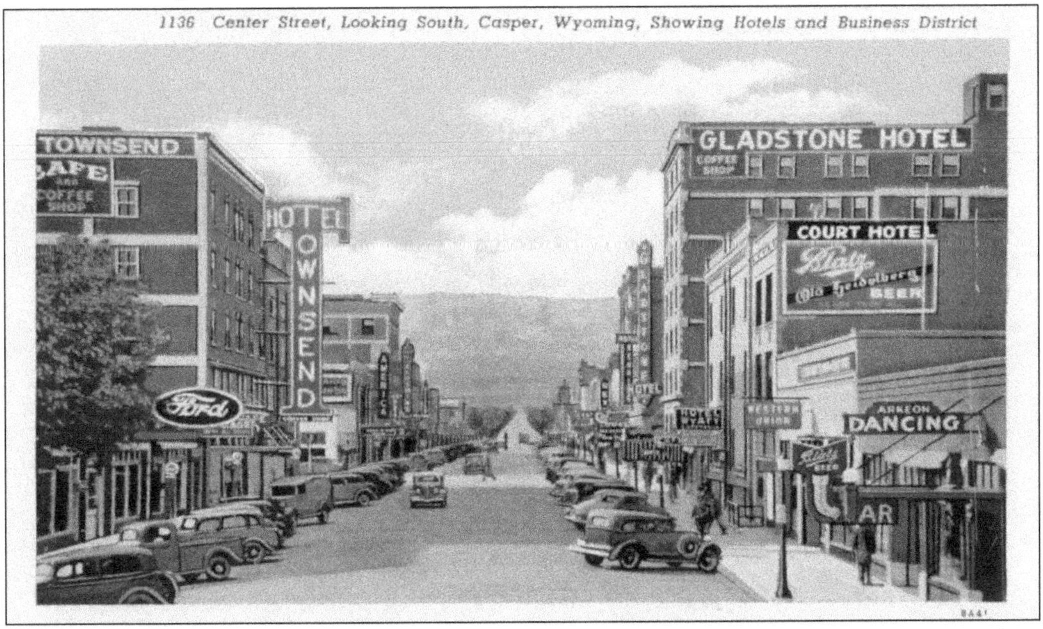

CENTER STREET, CASPER. Casper was a booming community in the 1930s. Tourists on their way to Yellowstone National Park, as well as newcomers attracted by the nearby oil fields, spurred the local economy. At least five hotels can be identified in this view of Center Street, which ran north–south through the downtown business district, intersecting with Yellowstone Highway (Highway 20).

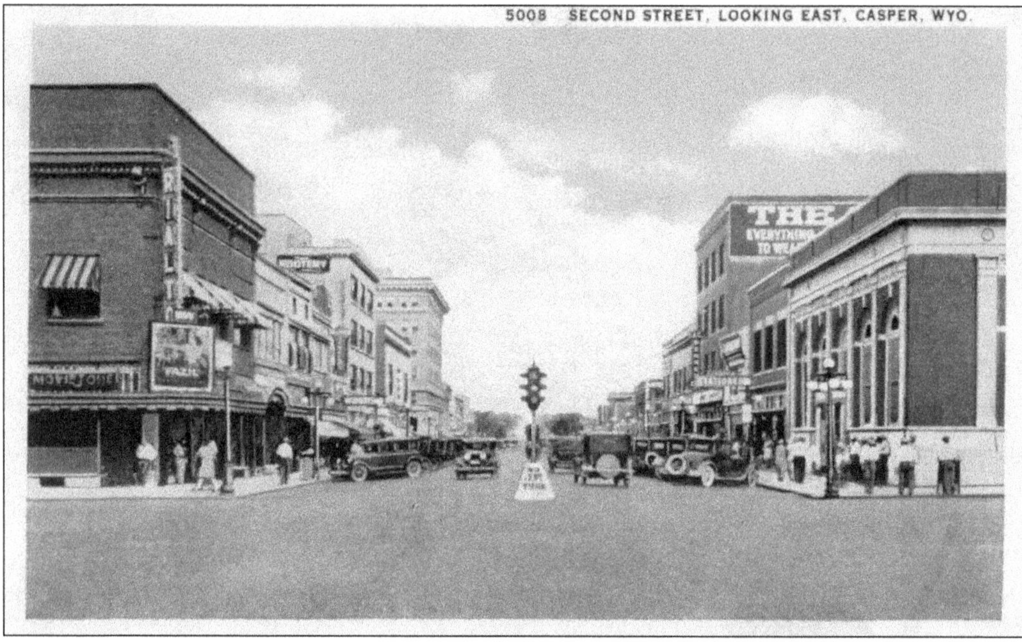

Second Street, Looking East (above) and West (below), Casper. Second Street was the main east–west thoroughfare through Casper's downtown business district in the 1920s and 1930s when these photographs were taken. Both views show a thriving business community spurred by rapid growth in the population due to the burgeoning oil industry. Traffic signals in the middle of the intersections were common at the time, but as automobile traffic increased they became an impediment and were moved to the corners or suspended from overhead wires. Diagonal parking also was replaced by parallel parking as traffic increased. Both images include many classic retail establishments of the day. Montgomery Ward, J.C. Penney, Western Auto, and Gamble stores all are located prominently along the street.

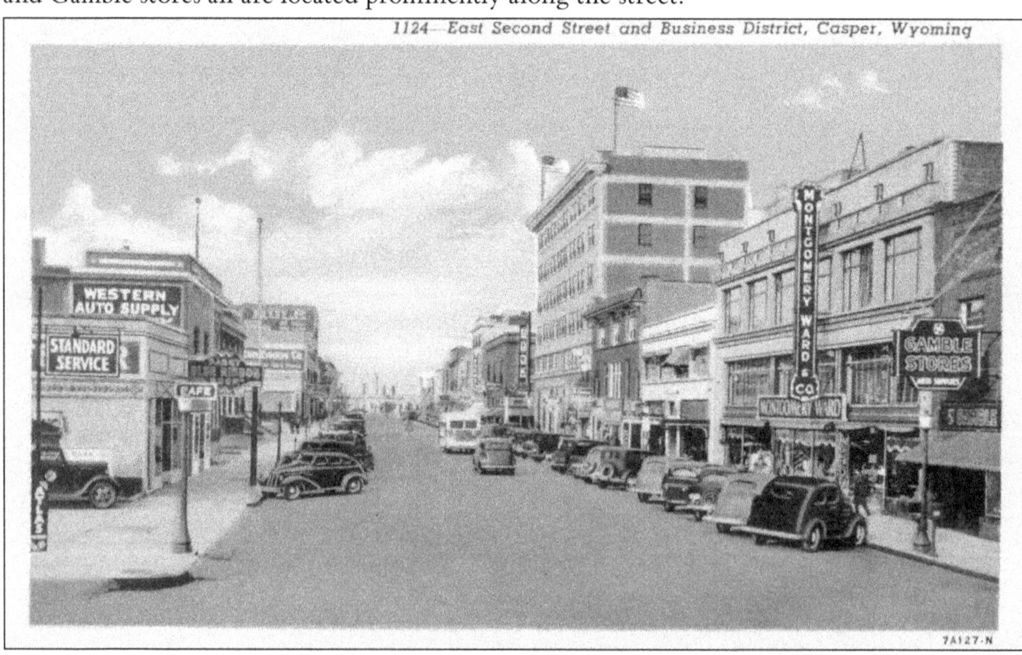

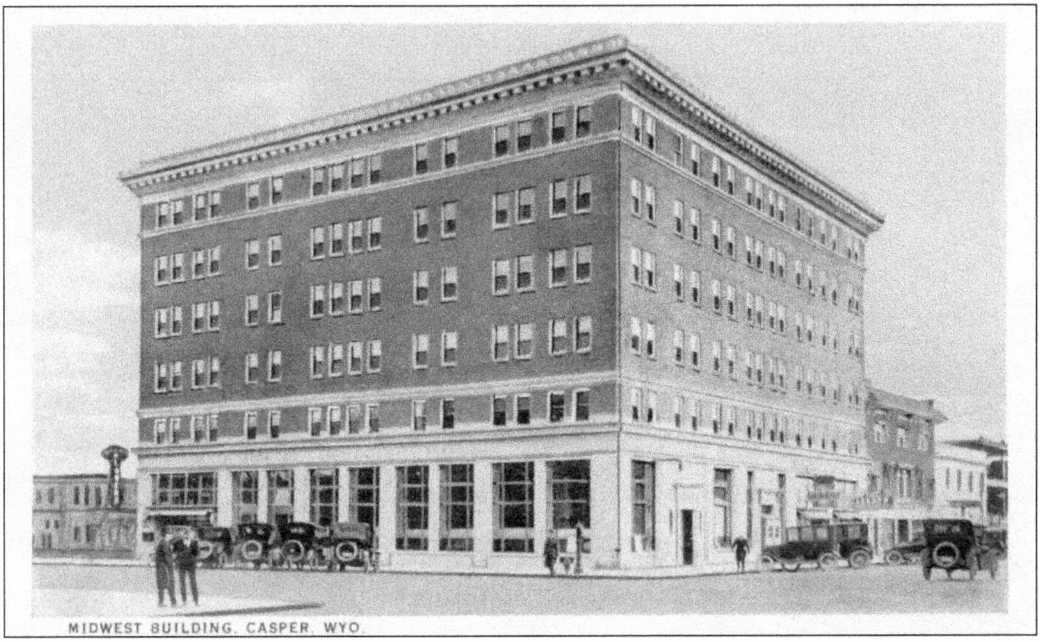

Midwest Building, 202 East Second Street, Casper. The automobiles in this view indicate that the photograph was taken only a short time after the Midwest Building was completed in 1920. It was downtown Casper's first large office building and subsequently became known as the Wyoming Building. It was converted to apartments in 2007 and is now the Wyoming National Apartments.

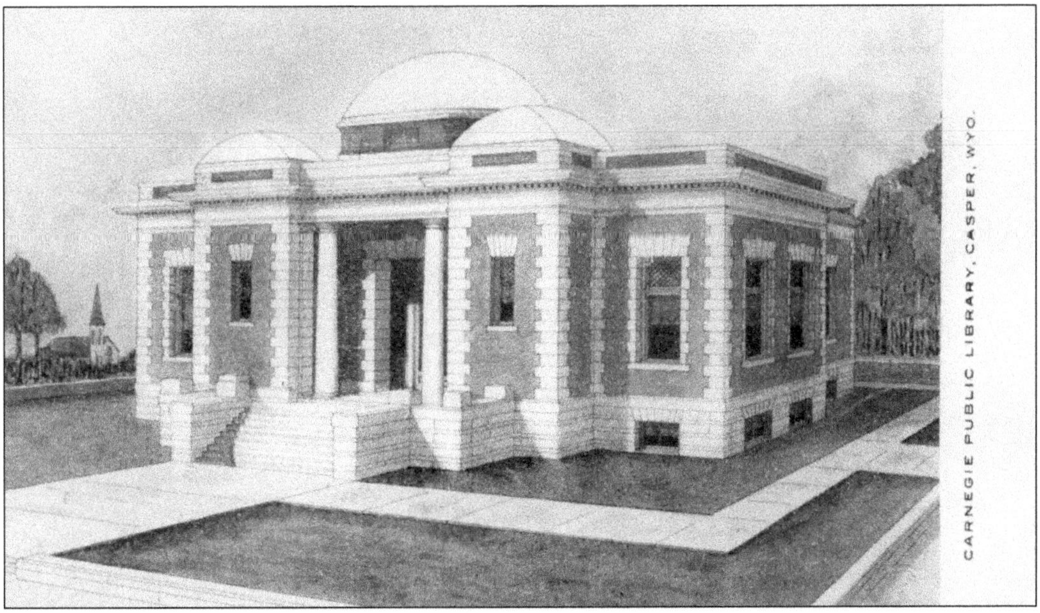

Carnegie Public Library, Second and Durban Streets, Casper. Casper received a $10,000 grant from the Carnegie Foundation in 1906 to construct a public library. The classical-style brick building was completed in 1910 and opened with a collection of 850 books. It was distinguished by domes, pillars, and contrasting colored stone on every corner and surrounding the windows. The building served Casper citizens until it was demolished in 1970.

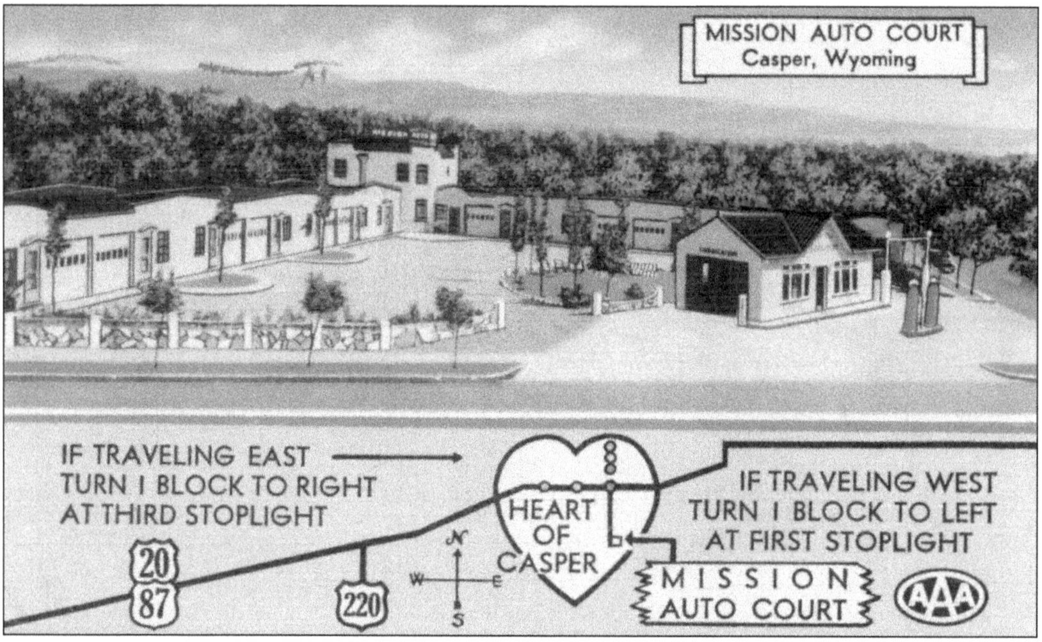

MISSION AUTO COURT, ONE BLOCK SOUTH OF HIGHWAYS 20 AND 87, CASPER. Traveling from either east or west, the map on this card clearly directs motorists to the Mission Auto Court near the center of Casper. The name obviously was derived from the architectural style of the motel, which resembled an early Spanish mission. The attractive, walled-in courtyard led to rooms equipped with garages. A full-service gas station was also available.

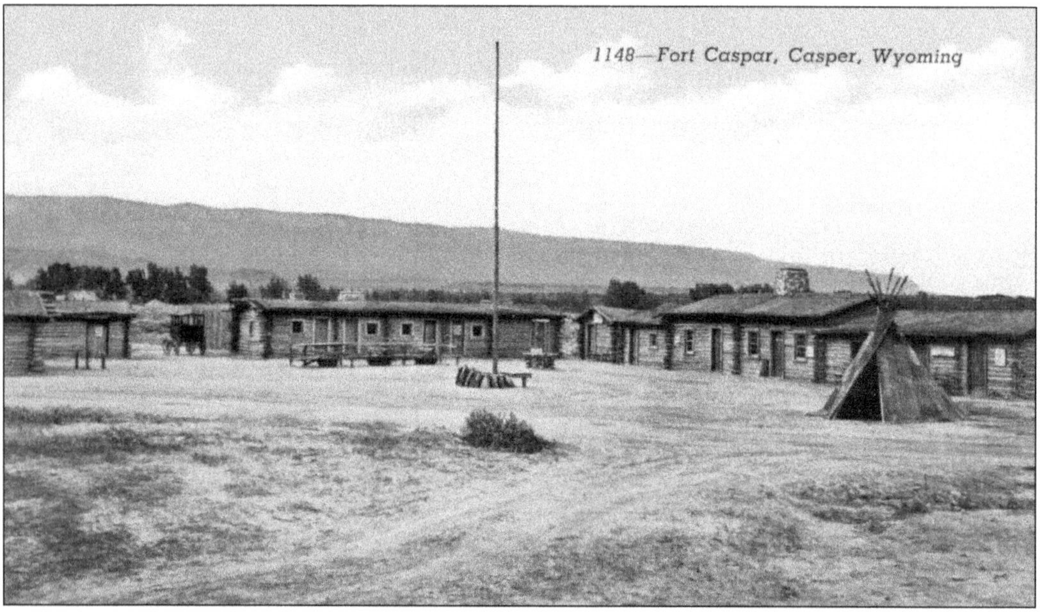

OLD FORT CASPAR, CASPER. This fort memorialized Lt. Caspar Collins, who was killed in the Battle of Platte Bridge in 1865. The structure dates to 1849, when Louis Guinard established a trading post here. The fort was taken over by the US Army in the 1860s to protect immigrant settlers and the newly installed telegraph line but was abandoned shortly thereafter in favor of Fort Fetterman in nearby Douglas.

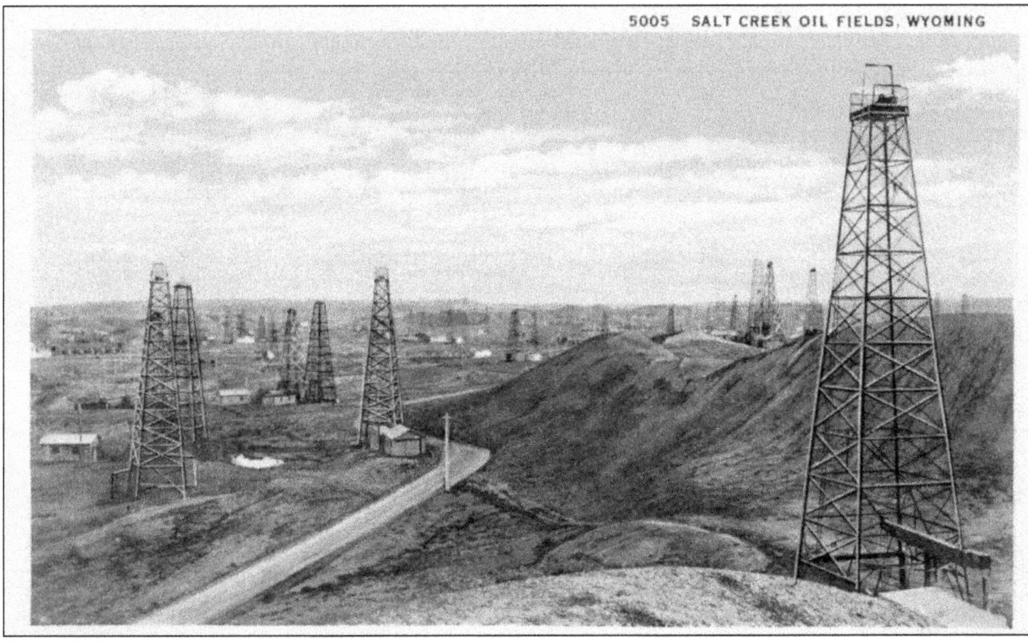

OIL FIELDS, CASPER. Oil was discovered in Wyoming in the 1880s, and by the second decade of the 20th century the economic boon was realized. The Salt Creek, Midwest, and Big Muddy Oil Fields extended east from Casper and included Glenrock, Douglas, Manville and Lusk. Casper became the center of oil-related activities. The production of oil (above) and its refinement (below) are illustrated on this page. Both led to major investments by local, national, and international companies. The Salt Creek oil field was the largest oil producer in Wyoming, accounting for 10,000 barrels per day. This in turn required the development of refineries to process the crude oil into usable commodities. Hundreds of employees were required to supply the needs of the oil industry, which resulted in a rapid influx of new families into the area.

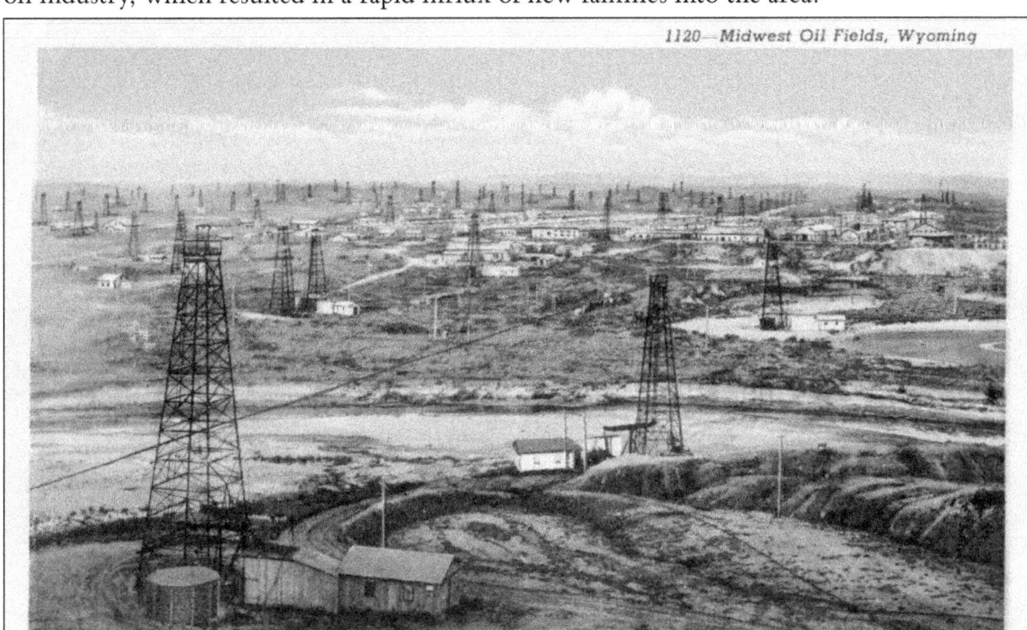

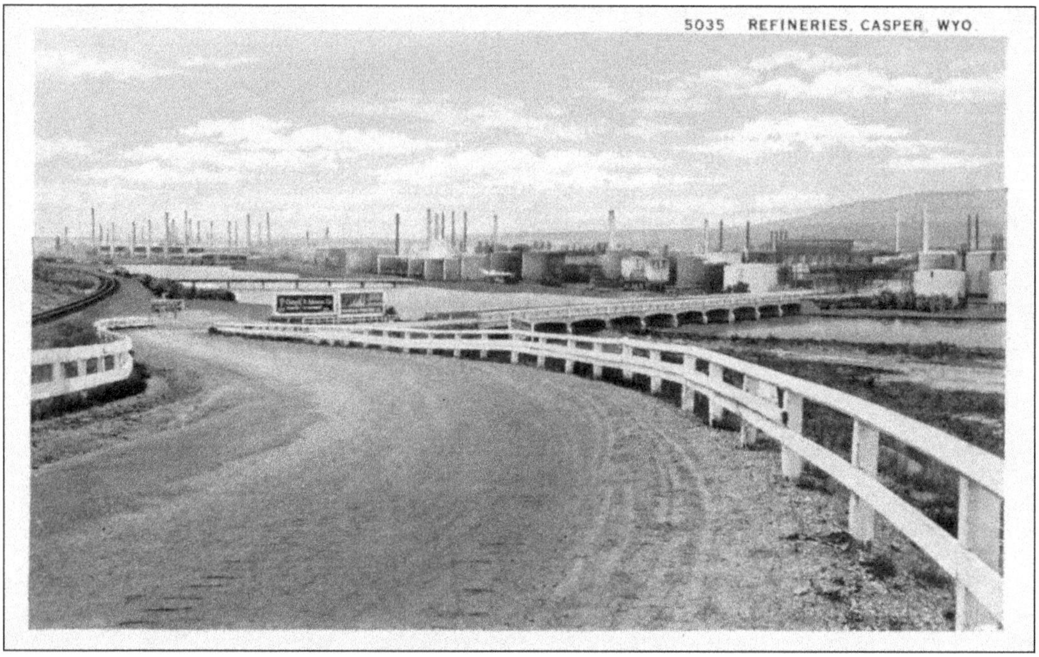

Oil Refinery, Casper. The magnitude of the oil industry near Casper is clearly evident in this image. This refinery, which serviced the major oil fields in eastern Wyoming, stretched for miles and contributed to Casper's becoming known as "Oil City." Ownership of this refinery is not cited on the card, but it possibly was the property of the Midwest Oil Company, which later was acquired by Standard Oil of Indiana.

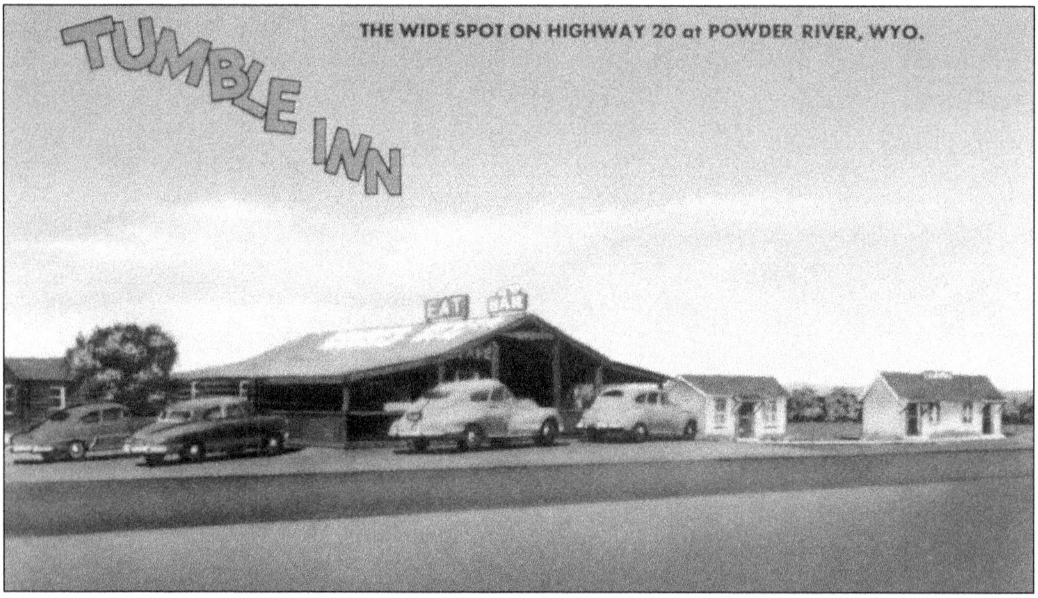

Tumble Inn, West Highway 20, Powder River. The Powder River was described on this 1940s card as "a mile wide and an inch deep." In its heyday, the Tumble Inn was a popular restaurant and bar along a lonely stretch of Highway 20. The log cabin structure, with its overweight cowboy sign, beckoned travelers from the highway. Unfortunately, the Tumble Inn fell on hard times and closed in 2005.

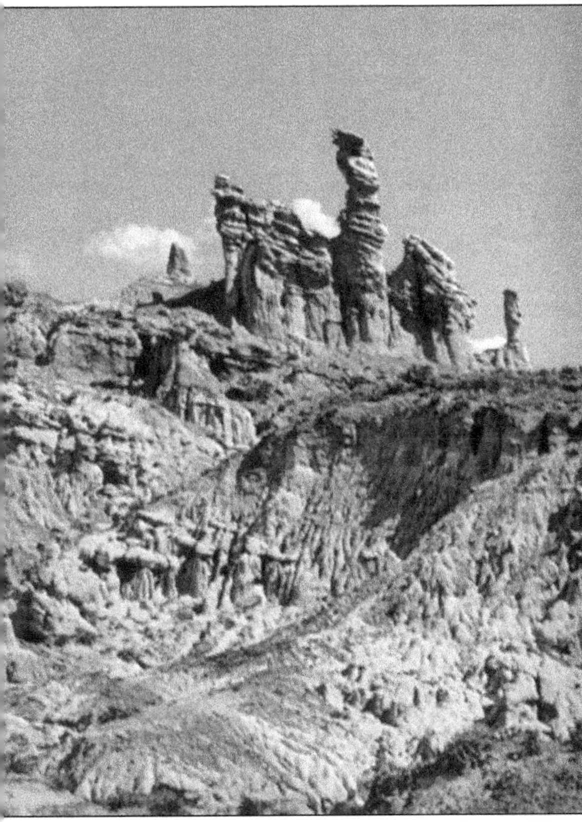

Hell's Half Acre

A depression on the vast plains of Central Wyoming, approximately 44 miles west of Casper, on Highways 20 and 26, consists of several hundred acres and is approximately 500 feet in depth. The depression is highly colored with fantastic and grotesque figures and is considered by many as one of the highlights of nature - and is often called the "baby grand canyon". In the early days when the Indians were roaming the plains of Wyoming it was used by them as a buffalo trap, where game was slaughtered and even today Indian artifacts are found in and around Hell's Half Acre. Indian legend gave it the name 'Burning Mountain' as they claimed there were flames and gaseous fumes emitting from it and this information was given to Capt. Bonneville, apparently the first white man to visit the location in the early 1800's. What caused it is debatable as scientists are not agreed on it, some saying it is erosion from the wind and water while others say it is volcanic and that the caprock is lava proving their point. Regardless of which is right nature has done a marvelous job in revealing her handiwork to man in its formation.

HELL'S HALF ACRE, DESCRIPTIVE CARD, POWDER RIVER. Hell's Half Acre is a rare geologic phenomenon adjacent to historic Highway 20 near Powder River, Wyoming. It was first reported in 1833. For years, the massive depression, which reaches a depth of more than 500 feet, has been a favorite stopping point for travelers. "Half Acre" is a misnomer, as the depression actually exceeds more than 300 acres. Hell's Half Acre and approximately 1,000 additional acres surrounding it were granted to Natrona County by Pres. Calvin Coolidge in 1924. A fuller description of the unique site is provided on the postcard above.

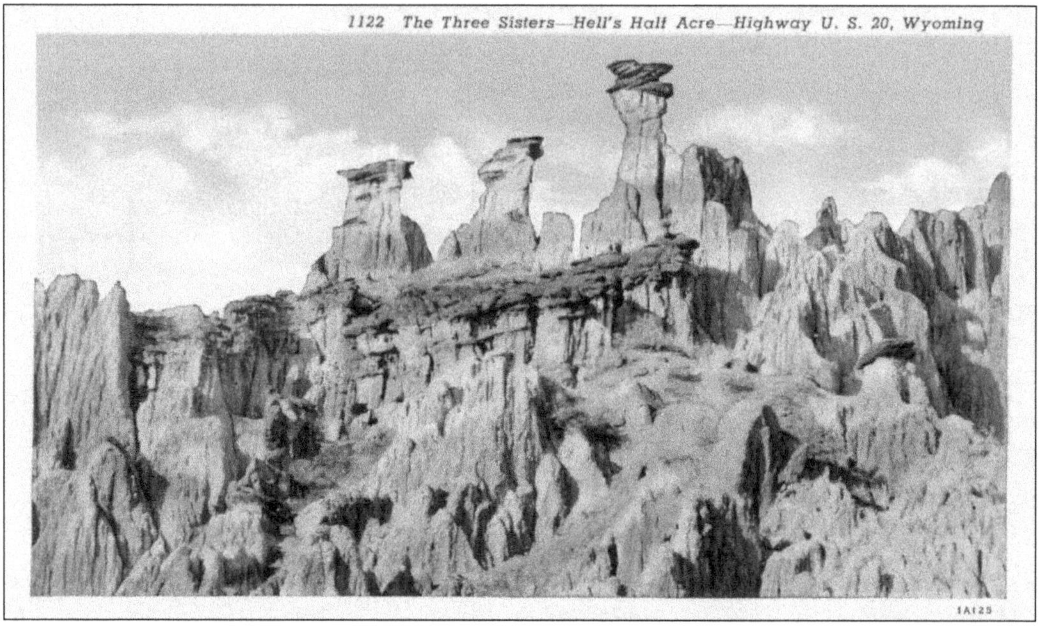

The Three Sisters, Hell's Half Acre, Powder River. Native Americans and early explorers called this depression "Burning Mountain" from the appearance of the multicolored rocks that appeared to have been the result of a fire. Some reports even said that the mountain was actually burning due to it emitting sulfurous fumes and gasses. The three towers shown on this card are among the canyon's most recognizable formations.

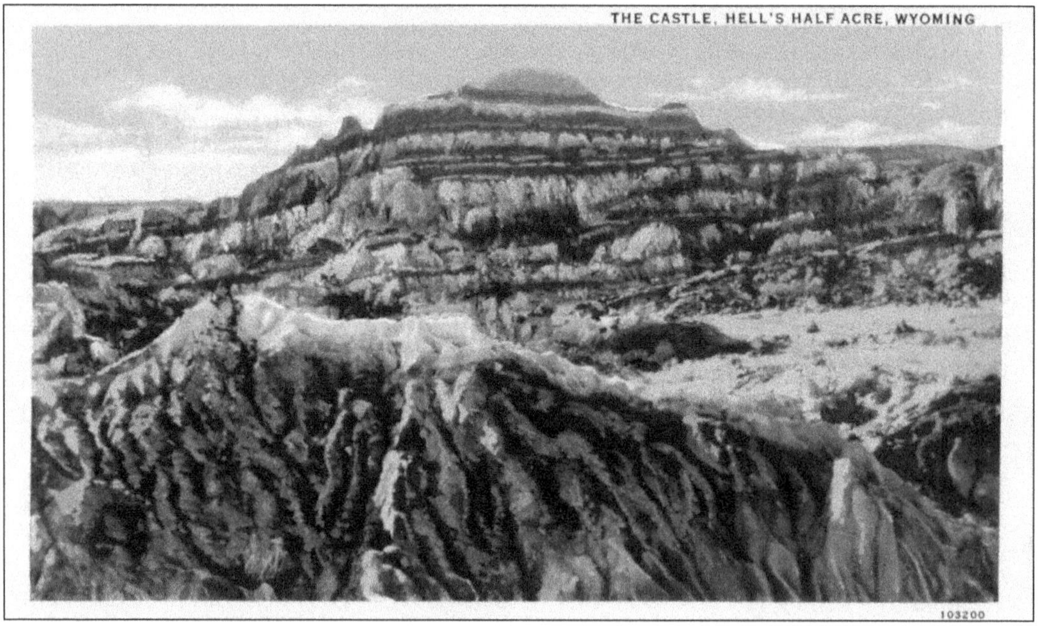

The Castle, Hell's Half Acre, Powder River. The legend on this card describes the appearance of the canyon as a burned-out coal bed. Many scientists feel that it is an ancient volcano crater, and the dome on this card supports the theory that it was formed by a mass of molten lava. Also in the depression are myriads of pinnacles and rock forms rising from 5 to 150 feet high.

TOADSTOOL, HELL'S HALF ACRE, POWDER RIVER. The name of this formation is obvious. It is one of several similar rocks throughout Hell's Half Acre, some of which are only inches in height whereas others are many feet high. Toadstool rocks are among the many fascinating and sometimes grotesque rocks that can be spotted within the canyon.

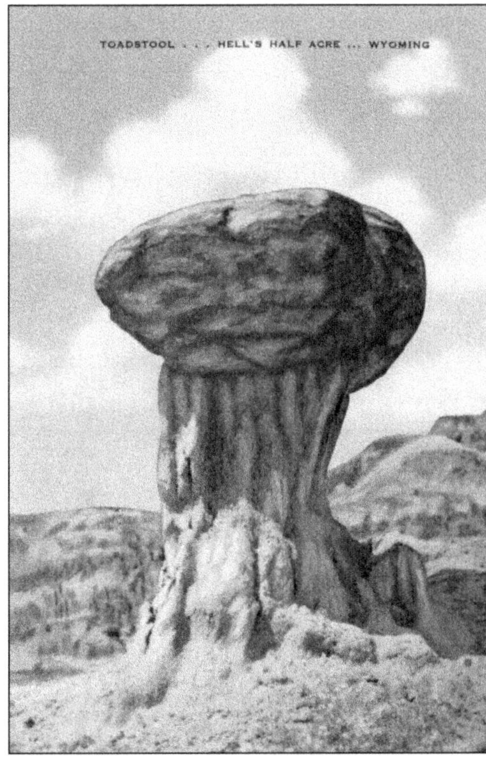

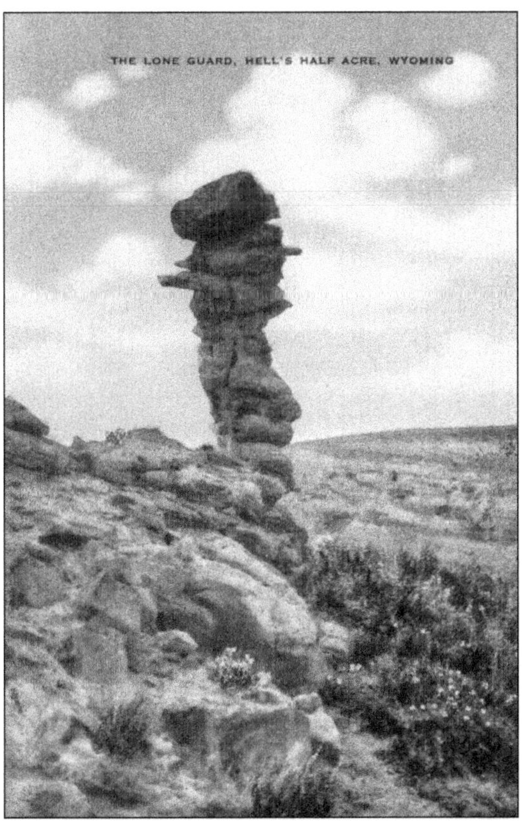

THE LONE GUARD, HELL'S HALF ACRE, POWDER RIVER. Spread throughout Hell's Half Acre are balanced rocks perched precariously among the cliffs and outcroppings of the canyon. The creator of this card describes the status poetically rather than geologically, stating that these structures implied "come hither and admire nature's beauty in Hell's Half Acre."

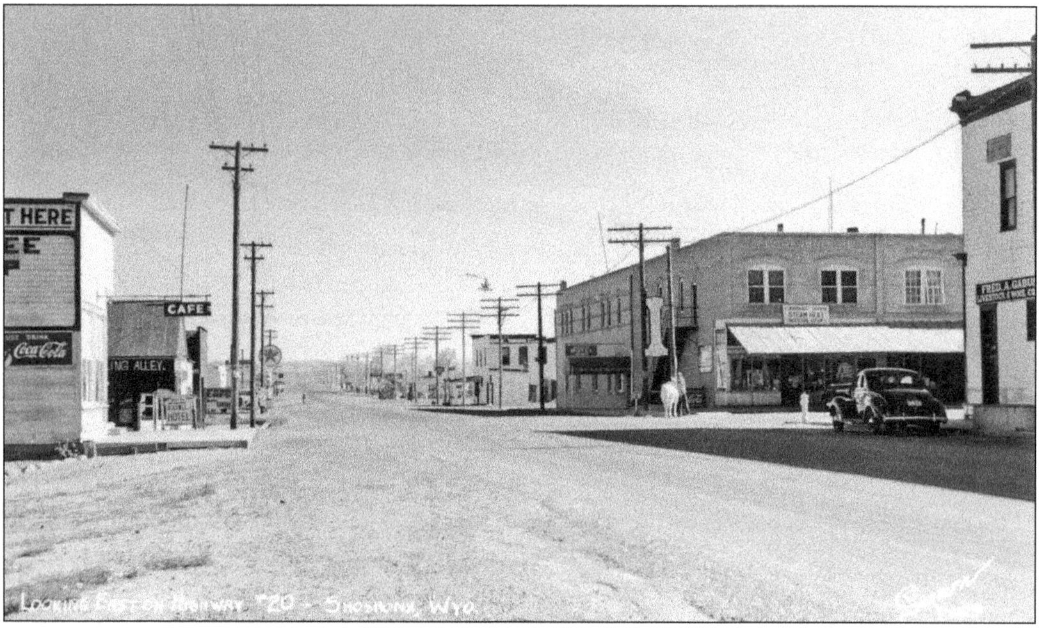

LOOKING EAST ON HIGHWAY 20, SHOSHONI. A mid-1930s car was parked at the right curb on Shoshoni's main street when this card was published. Typical of small Western towns, its stores could supply most of the residents' basic needs. The street was still gravel at the time, and in keeping with its Western location, a horse is tied to a lamppost by the hotel.

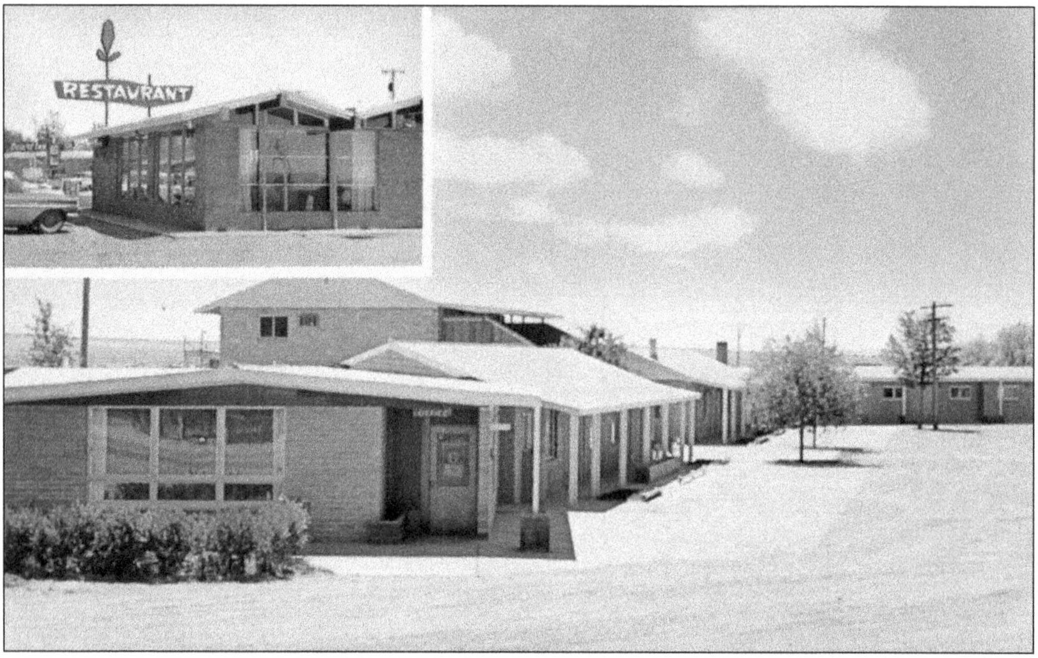

DESERT INN, JUNCTION OF HIGHWAYS 20 AND 26, SHOSHONI. All units of this 1950s motel had modern amenities, including in-room telephones. A restaurant was located on the property, and TV was available in the reception lounge. The Desert Inn advertised that it was four hours from both the east and south entrances to Yellowstone Park, making for an easy drive irrespective of the direction one was traveling.

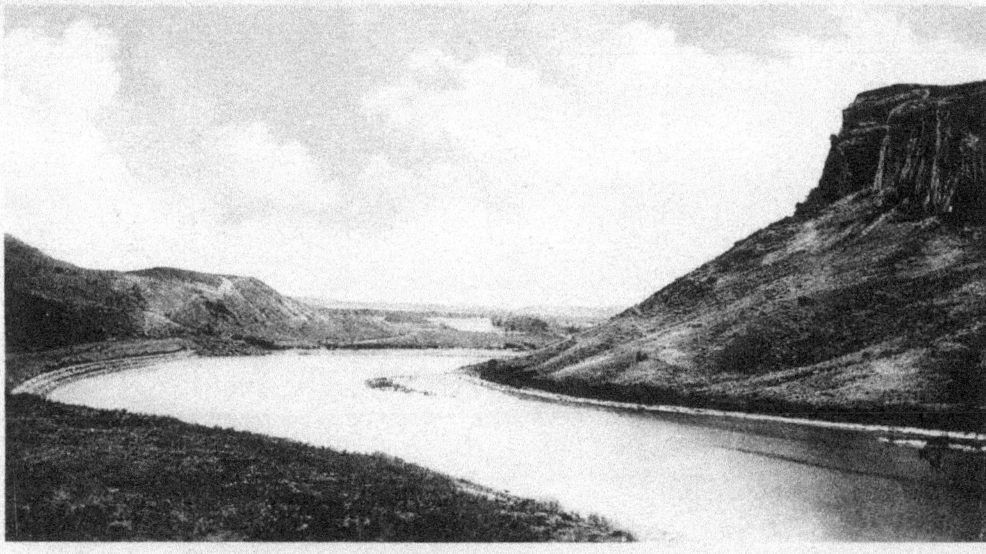

BOYSEN LAKE, YELLOWSTONE HIWAY, NEAR SHOSHONI, WYO.

BOYSEN LAKE AND DAM, US 20, NORTH OF SHOSHONI. The Wind River flows south to north in this section of Wyoming, thus Boysen Lake (above) lies south of the Boysen Dam (below). In 1900, Asmus Boysen recognized the potential of the Wind River for generating electrical power and irrigation of the surrounding farmland. He built the original dam in 1908. Unfortunately, the lake regularly flooded the Burlington Northern Railroad, so the dam was modified in 1925. The dam remained in use until 1948, when it was replaced. The present artificial lake, still carrying the name Boysen, has a surface area of 19,000 acres and a 77-mile shoreline. It is a popular fishing and recreational area. Historic Highway 20 is close to the eastern shore of the reservoir through much of its length.

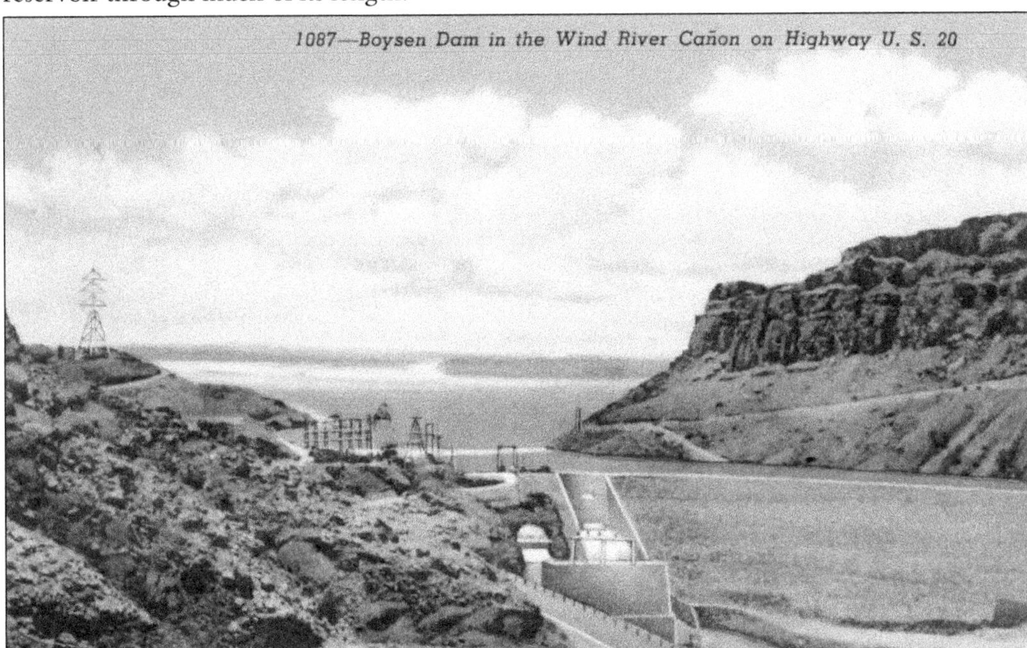

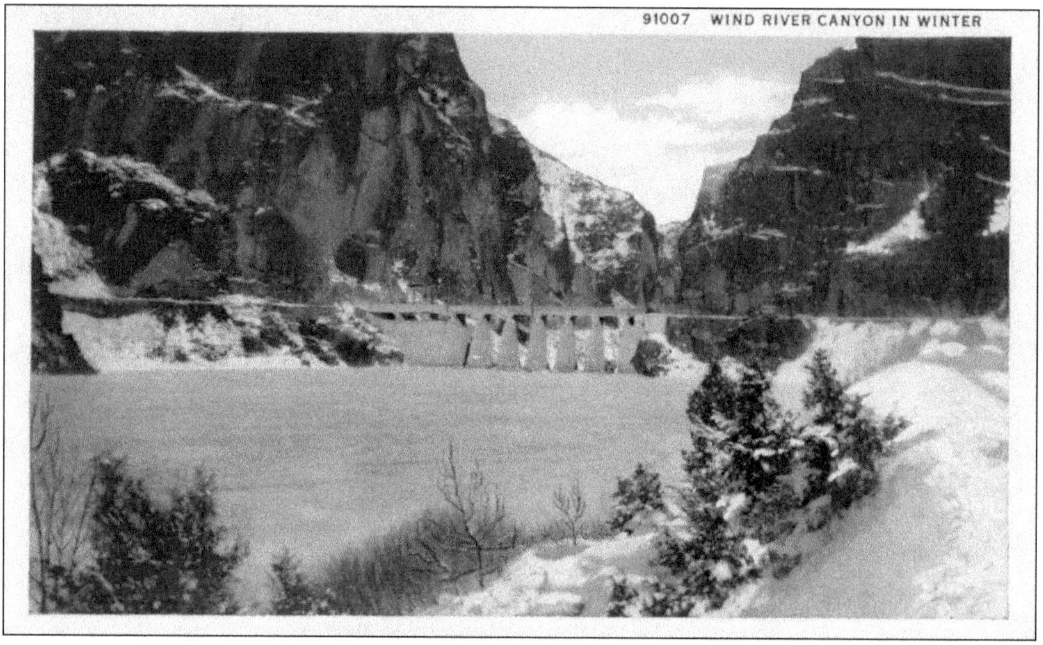

WIND RIVER CANYON IN WINTER, SHOSHONI. Views in Wind River Canyon change dramatically throughout the seasons. The scene on this card is typical of the winter months when the white snow contrasts with the multicolored walls of the cliffs and the foliage of evergreen trees and shrubs. Sparkling water dashing over riverbed rocks completes the view and provides a scene of natural beauty to remember.

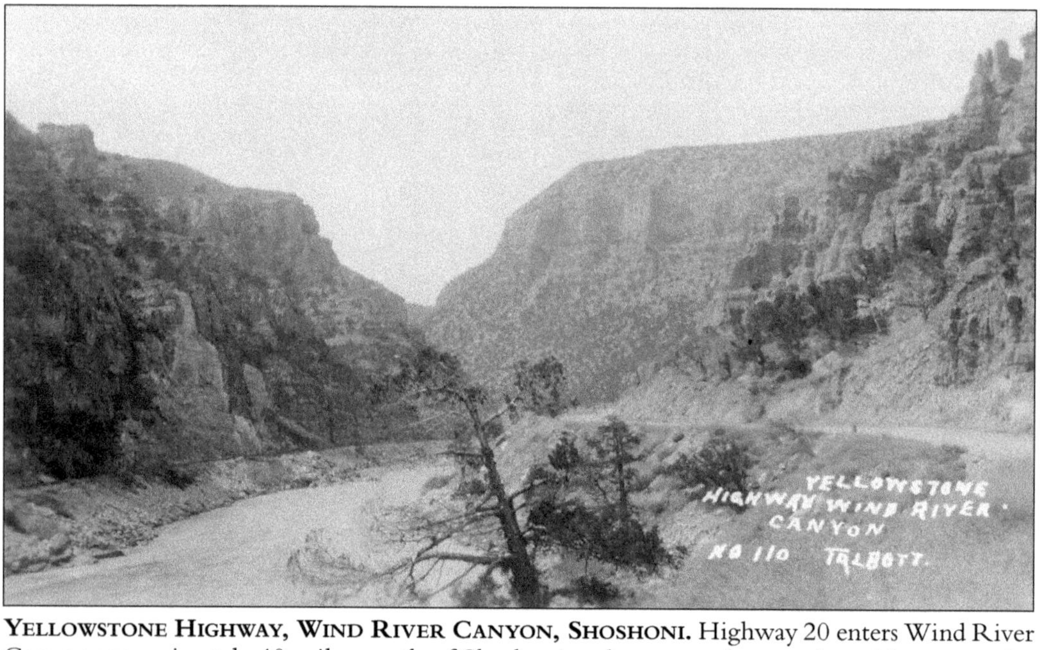

YELLOWSTONE HIGHWAY, WIND RIVER CANYON, SHOSHONI. Highway 20 enters Wind River Canyon approximately 10 miles north of Shoshoni and presents the traveler with spectacular scenery. The road follows the river before arriving in Thermopolis, passing through several tunnels and below cliffs reaching 2,500 feet in height. Geologically, the canyon ranges from 300 million to 3 billion years old. This postcard from the 1930s shows the still unpaved road surface.

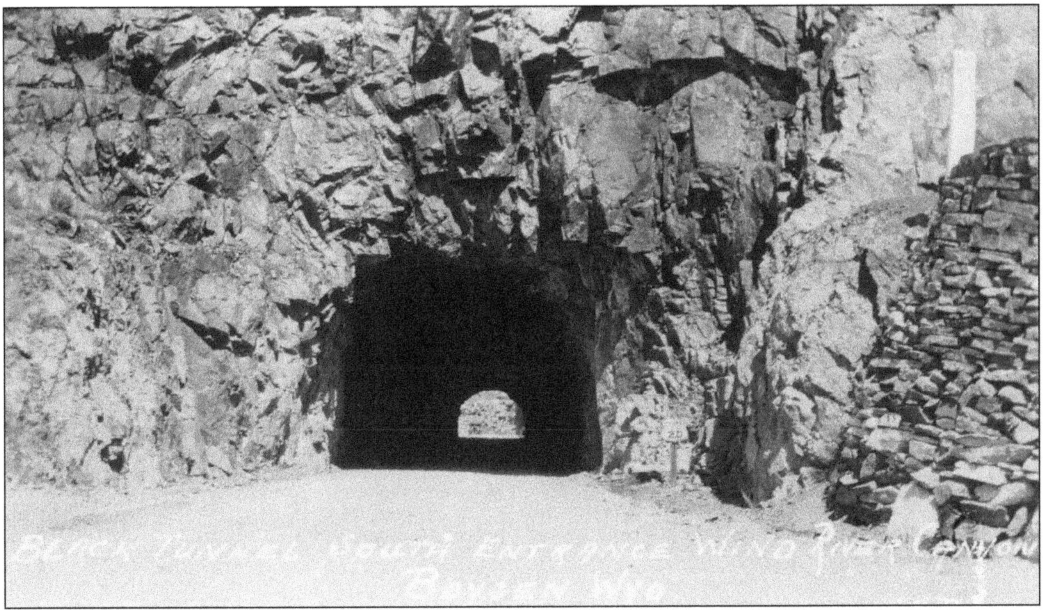

BLACK TUNNEL, AND THE DAM BAR, CAFE, AND PRIVY, SHOSHONI. Historic Highway 20 passes through three tunnels as it courses through the Wind River Canyon. Although these tunnels were not long, they required considerable engineering skill to accomplish; all three were blasted through solid rock. Seen above is the first tunnel, the Black Tunnel, which was named because of the dark appearance it presented to early motorists. It was not lighted, and even on the brightest day the approach looked like a black hole. The photograph below shows a similar tunnel only a short distance farther on. This location featured a bar and cafe, where travelers could rest and buy refreshments. The card points out that a privy was available for their use.

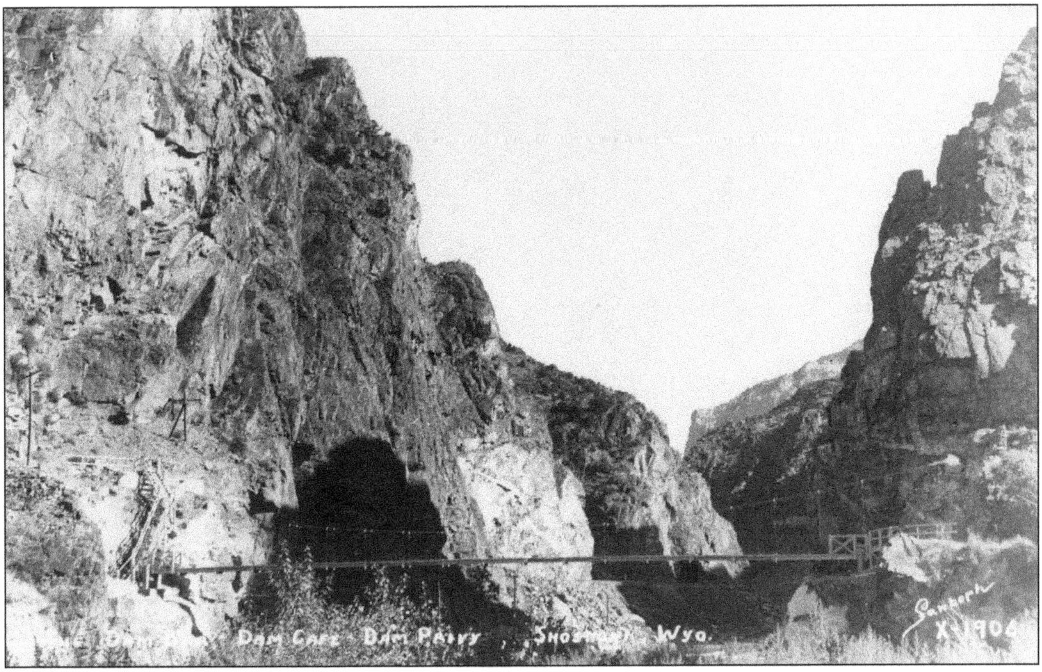

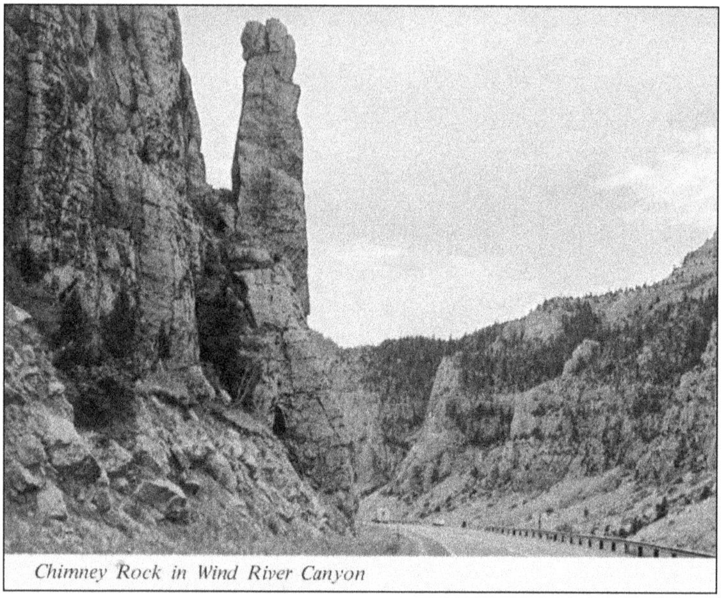

Chimney Rock in Wind River Canyon, Thermopolis. Although not as famous as its counterpart on Cody Road near Yellowstone National Park, the Chimney Rock in Wind River Canyon is actually a larger and more prominent roadside attraction. It owes its origin to the same combination of erosive conditions over several millennia. Going north on historic Highway 20, this geologic formation is located beside Highway 20 south of Thermopolis.

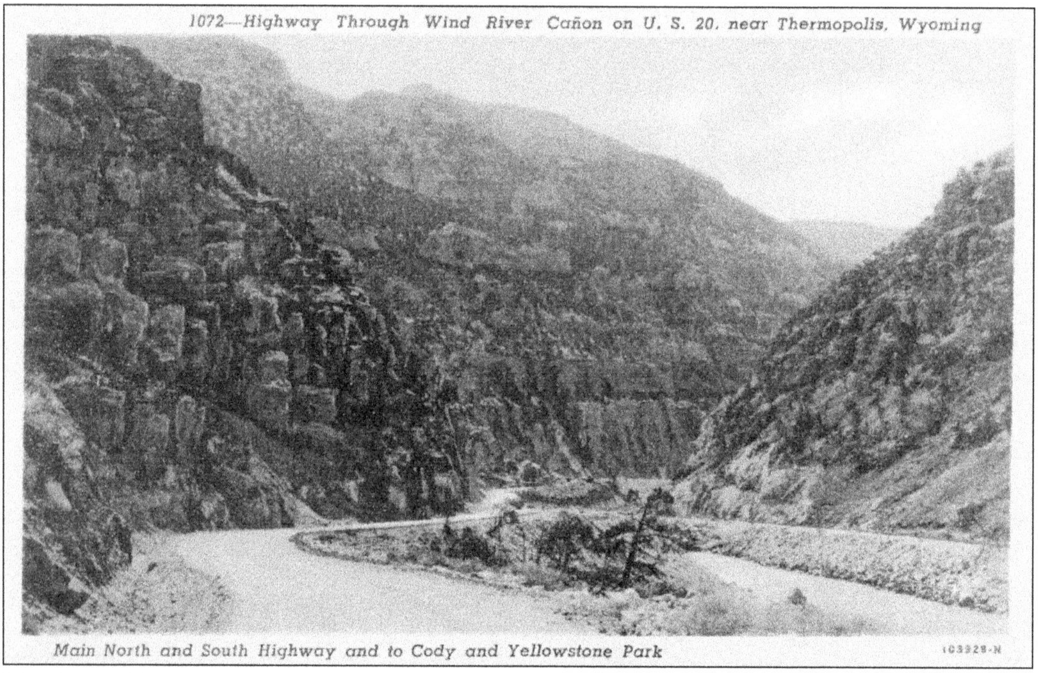

The Main North and South Highway to Cody and Yellowstone Park. Approximately 10 miles south of Thermopolis, historic Highway 20 crosses the Bighorn River and proceeds along the west bank into the town. Interestingly, the back of the card points out that this is the main road to Cody, Wyoming, and Yellowstone Park rather than focusing on the outstanding terrain in the road's immediate location.

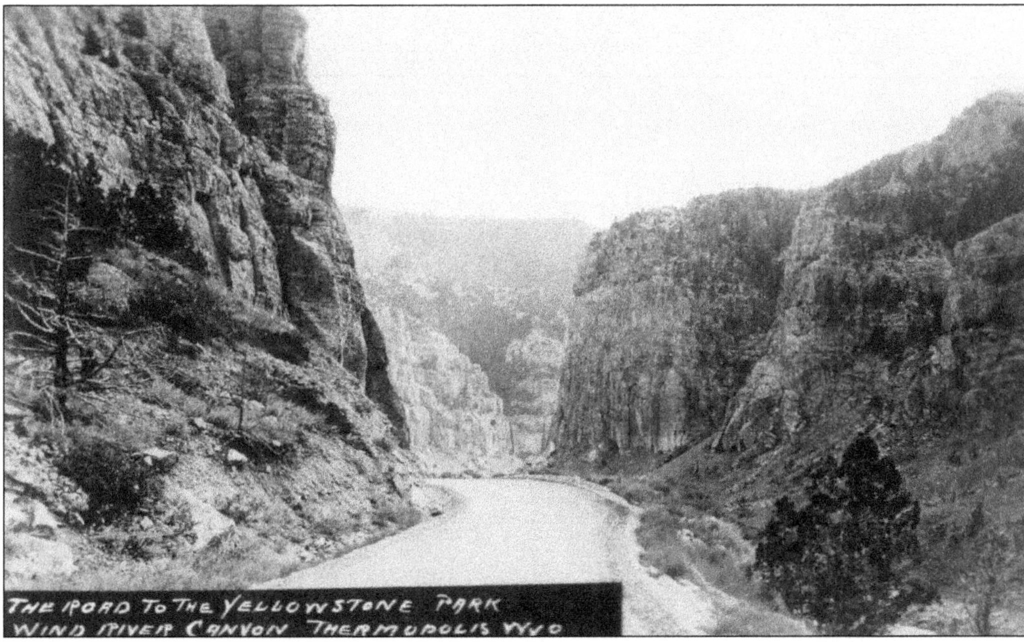

THE ROAD TO YELLOWSTONE PARK, WIND RIVER CANYON. This image, looking north, was taken closer to Thermopolis where Highway 20 was on the west side of the river. Striking features of the road were the mountain cliffs that lined the road on either side. As they drove along, sharp-eyed travelers could spot Bighorn sheep and other wildlife.

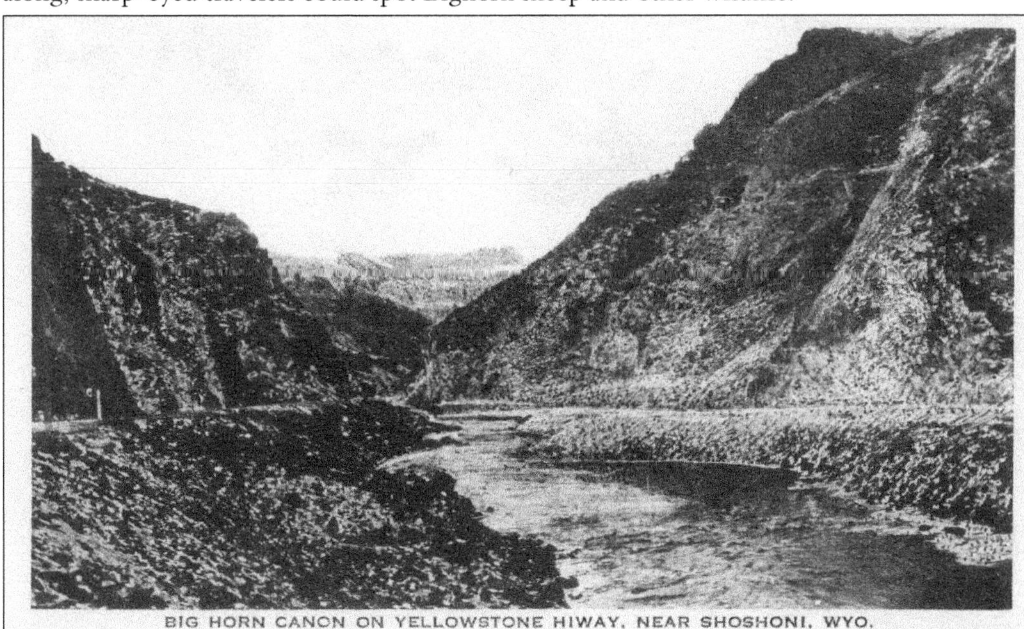

BIG HORN CAÑON. Big Horn Cañon on the Yellowstone Highway (Highway 20), between Shoshoni and Thermopolis, was the primary eastern route to Yellowstone Park through this section of Wyoming. At approximately this location, the name of the Wind River changed to the Bighorn, causing some postcard publishers to identify the canyon as Big Horn; most continued to use Wind River Canyon throughout the entire distance to Thermopolis.

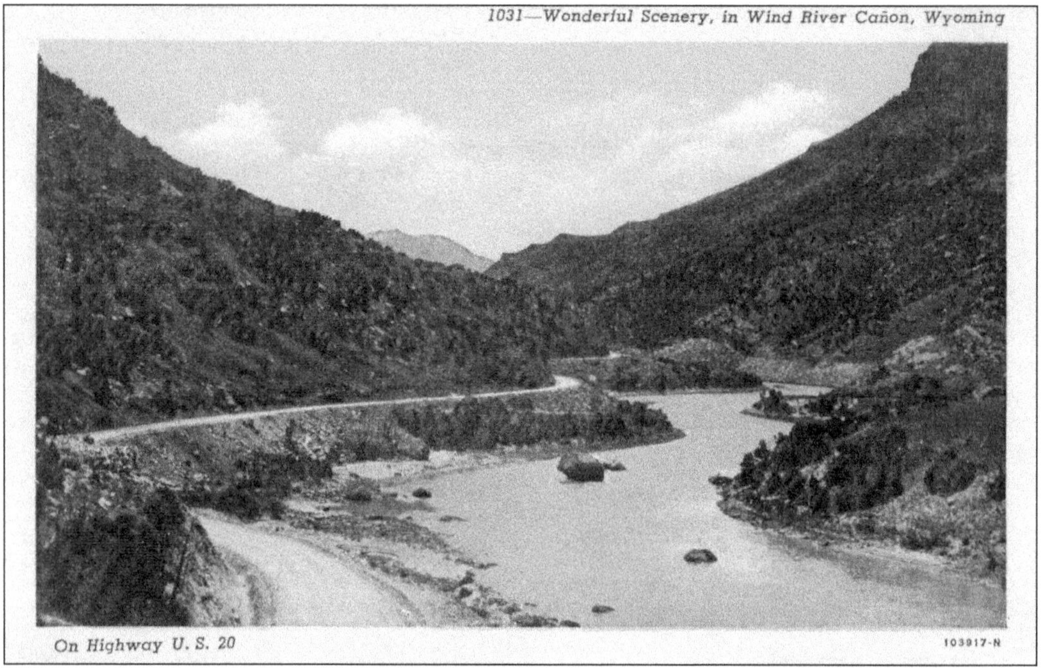

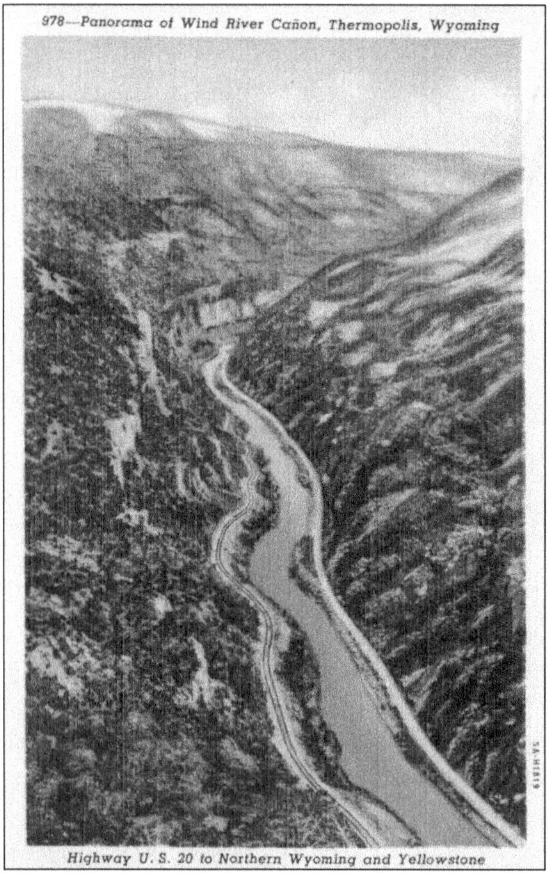

WONDERFUL SCENERY IN WIND RIVER CANYON, THERMOPOLIS. Although Yellowstone National Park may have been their destination, first-time visitors were surprised by the beauty of the Wind River Canyon, and most compared it favorably with views encountered farther along on their trip. The scenery along Highway 20 in this area could hold its own with any road in the country.

PANORAMA OF WIND RIVER CAÑON, SOUTH OF THERMOPOLIS. This view shows the northern extremity of Wind River Canyon south of Thermopolis. The river at this point was called the Bighorn. Historic Highway 20 is on the right side of the river heading south into Wind River Canyon and on to Shoshoni, about 30 miles farther south. The Burlington Railroad was to the left of the river.

Three

Hot Springs and Washakie Counties

Hot Springs County was created in 1911 and named for the famous mineral springs located near Thermopolis, the county seat. It is the smallest county in Wyoming and the second-least populous. In the late 1800s, this entire area was part of the Wind River Indian Reservation, and the healing capacity of the hot springs was well know to the Native Americans in the area. In 1896, a treaty between the United States and the Shoshone and Arapahoe tribes was signed so the healing waters of the mineral hot springs would be available in perpetuity to all people. The generous act is known as the "Gift of the Waters" and is memorialized annually by a pageant held the first weekend in August in which the treaty signing is reenacted.

Another historical location is known as Wedding of the Waters, which lies at the north end of the Wind River Canyon, just south of Thermopolis. The name does not denote the union of two separate rivers but rather refers to the point where the name of the river changes. In the early 1800s, two groups of explorers entered the canyon, one from the south and the other from the north. Although they both were following the same river, the southern group had called the stream Wind River and the northern group the Bighorn River. The place where the name of the river changes is the Wedding of the Waters. From here, the name of the river became Bighorn, which flowed north until it joined the Yellowstone River near the Montana border.

Washakie County also was created by the Wyoming Legislature in 1911. The county was named for Chief Washakie, whose Shoshone tribe was indigenous to the Bighorn Basin and who was friendly to the newly arrived white settlers. Worland is the county seat. Although surrounded by the Absaroka, Owl Creek, and Bighorn Mountains, the county lies in the basin and is relatively flat; thus, the economy is derived mostly from ranching and farming.

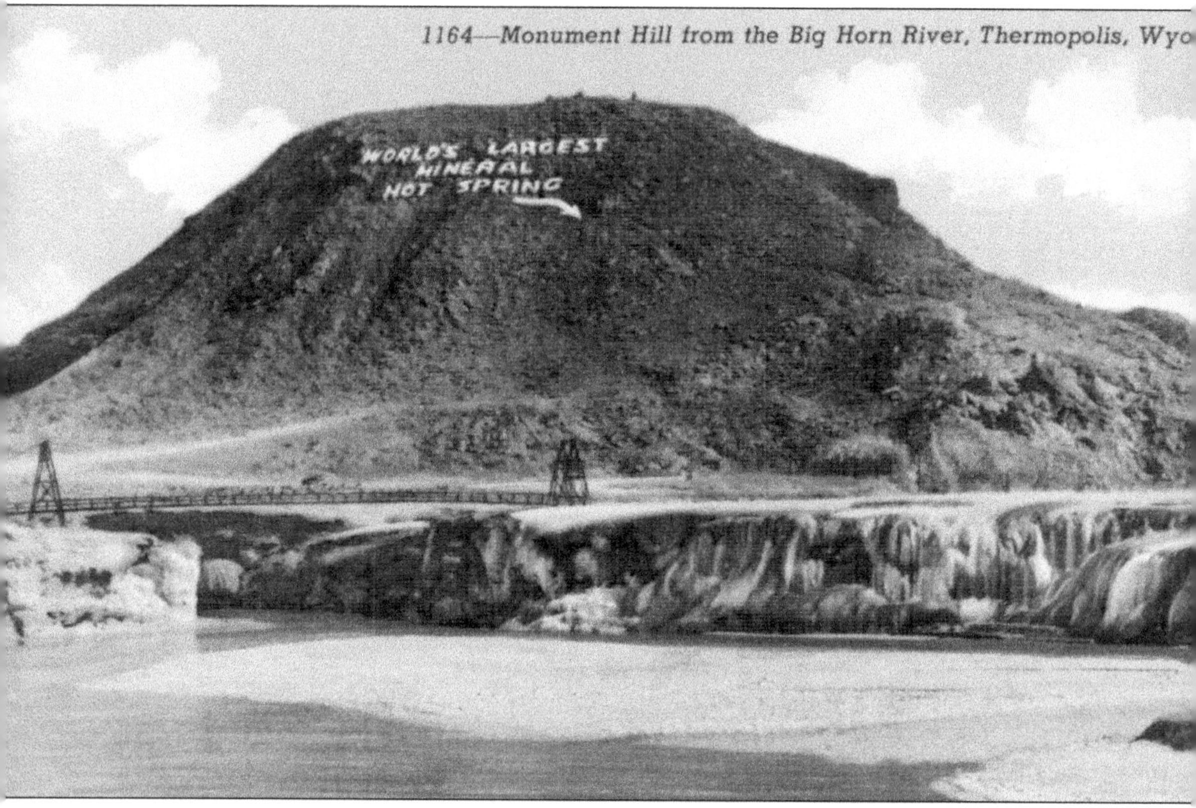

MONUMENT HILL, THERMOPOLIS. This huge mountain looms over the city of Thermopolis and can be viewed when entering the town from almost any direction. The official name is Roundtop Mountain, but it commonly is referred to as Monument Hill. As the sign indicates, Thermopolis is famous for being the home of the world's largest mineral hot springs. The city is located only a short distance north of the Wind River Canyon in the foothills of the Owl Creek, Bridger, and Bighorn Mountains. Thermopolis in Greek means "Hot City," which is derived from the hot mineral water that pours from springs at a temperature of 135 degrees. The mineral waters were thought to be curative for a variety of ailments, both when consumed and by bathing in it.

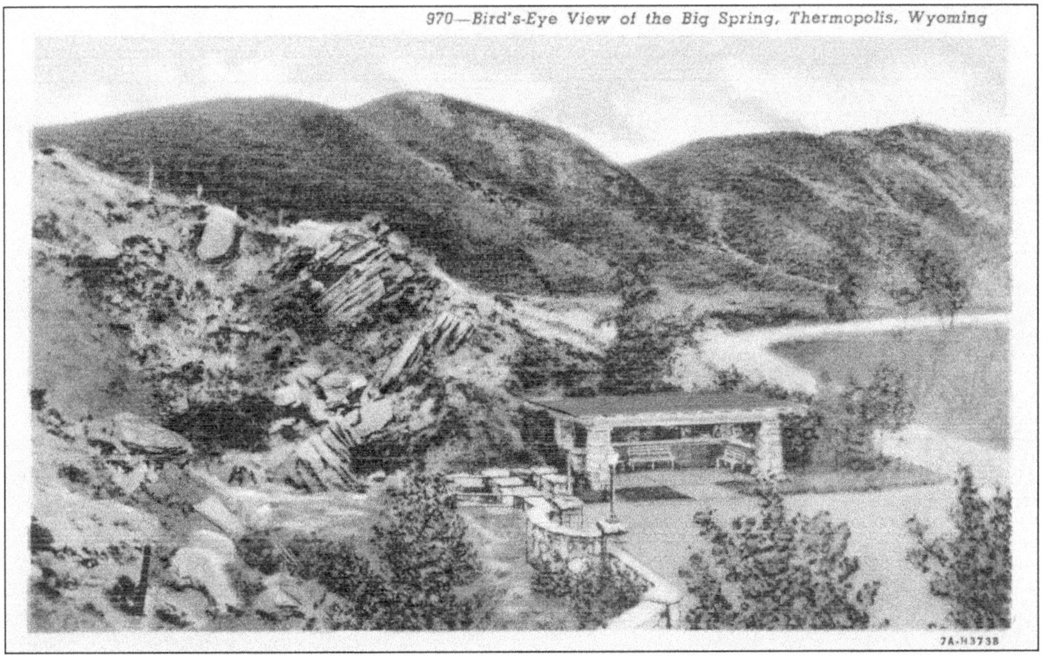

BIRD'S-EYE AND CLOSE-UP VIEWS OF BIG HORN HOT SPRINGS, THERMOPOLIS. The back of both cards on this page state that the hot springs were the largest known in the world, discharging millions of gallons of water every 24 hours. The water contained many mineral properties that were thought at the time to be beneficial for sufferers of rheumatism and similar disorders. Some bathers preferred the outdoor venues rather than the indoor spas. Among the most popular was the Big Spring shown on these cards; the curved wall of the outdoor pool is visible in both views. Water was maintained at 104 degrees for therapeutic bathing. The spectacular scenery throughout the park and surrounding area added to the enjoyment of the healing waters.

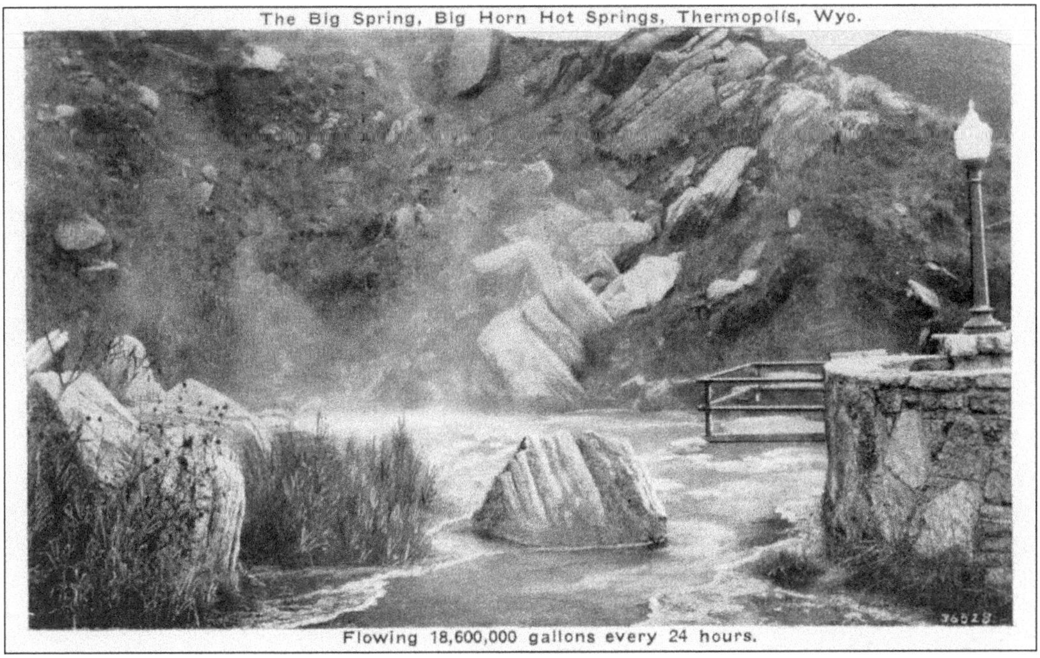

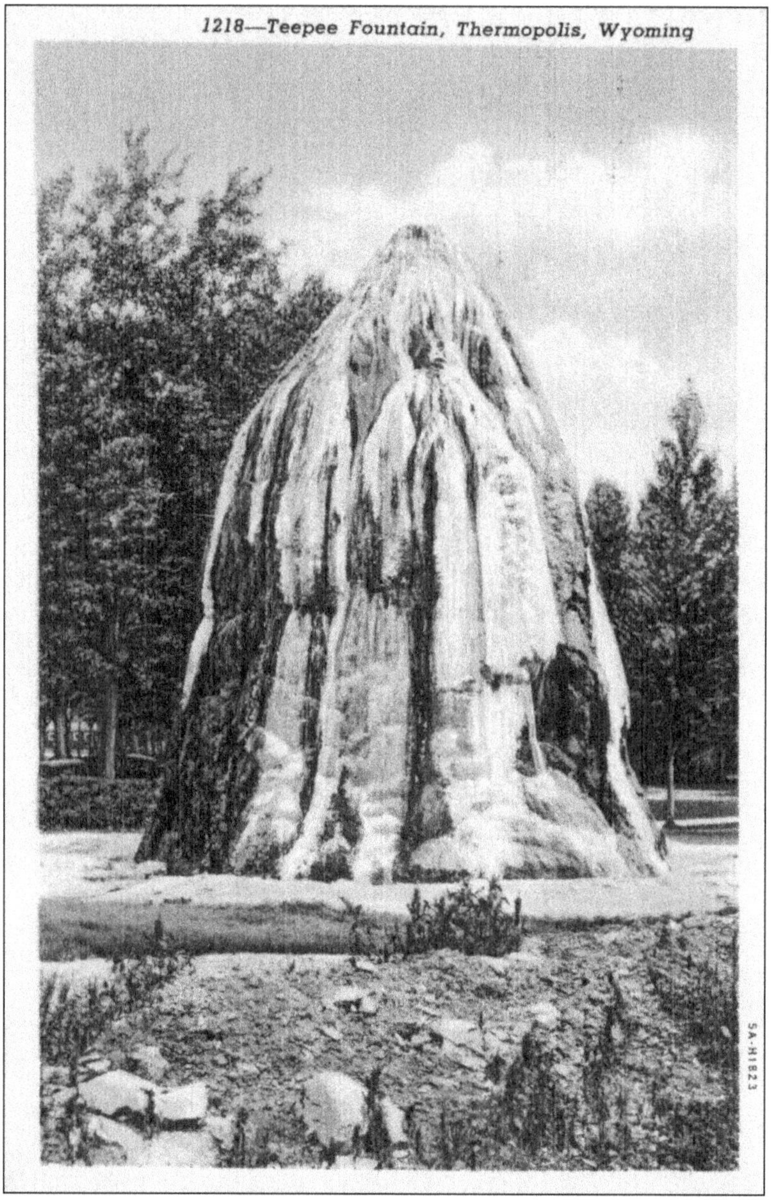

TEPEE FOUNTAIN, HOT SPRINGS STATE PARK, THERMOPOLIS. The land for Hot Springs State Park Reserve, the forerunner of Hot Springs State Park, was purchased from the Arapaho and Shoshone tribes in 1896. It was the first state park in Wyoming. The treaty ensured that the curative waters would be available to all people in perpetuity, and for more than 100 years natives from the area and visitors from around the world have taken advantage of this natural wonder. During the first half of the 20th century, several hotels, sanitariums, and spas were developed around the springs. The beautifully landscaped grounds, especially the water park, continue to attract many visitors. Few travelers pass through Thermopolis without making a side trip to Hot Springs State Park, where this huge mineral cone is one of the most unique attractions. Man-made rather than natural, the cone was formed from a pipe driven into a mineral spring in 1903. Since then, minerals in the water flowing from the top have solidified into the colorful multilayered cone.

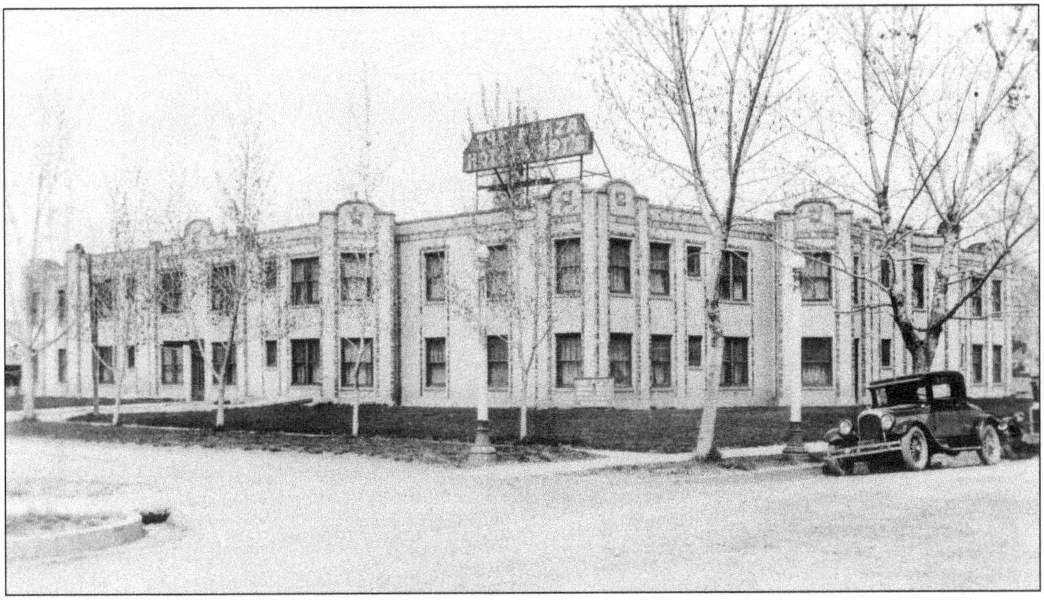

Plaza Hotel, Hot Springs State Park, Thermopolis. The Plaza Hotel, built in 1914, is the only remaining original hotel in the park. In the 1930s, it boasted of being "a home away from home," offering 42 completely furnished apartments. The latter included electricity, steam heat, bedding, and a heated garage at rates from $10 to $12 per week for two persons. A bath in the mineral spring cost 50¢.

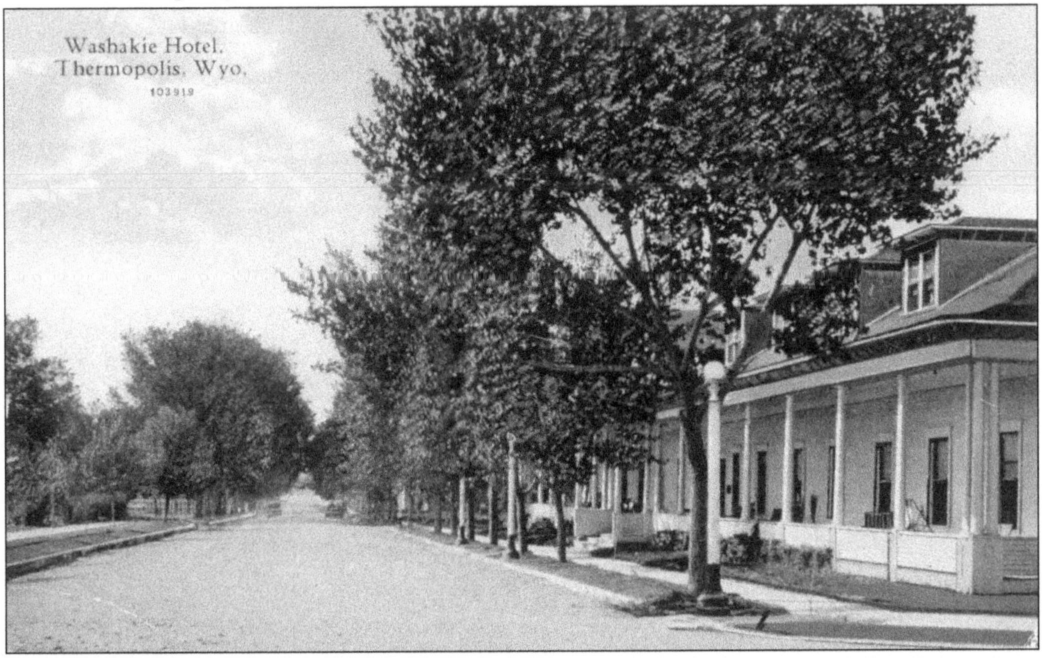

Washakie Hotel, Thermopolis. The Washakie served the dual purpose of a hotel for visitors in Thermopolis and a sanitarium where persons could live while undergoing treatment for various maladies. Depending on the patient's condition, some treatment was provided by local physicians and typically included immersion in the healing mineral waters. Guests who did not require specific medical supervision were welcome to use the mineral baths in the community.

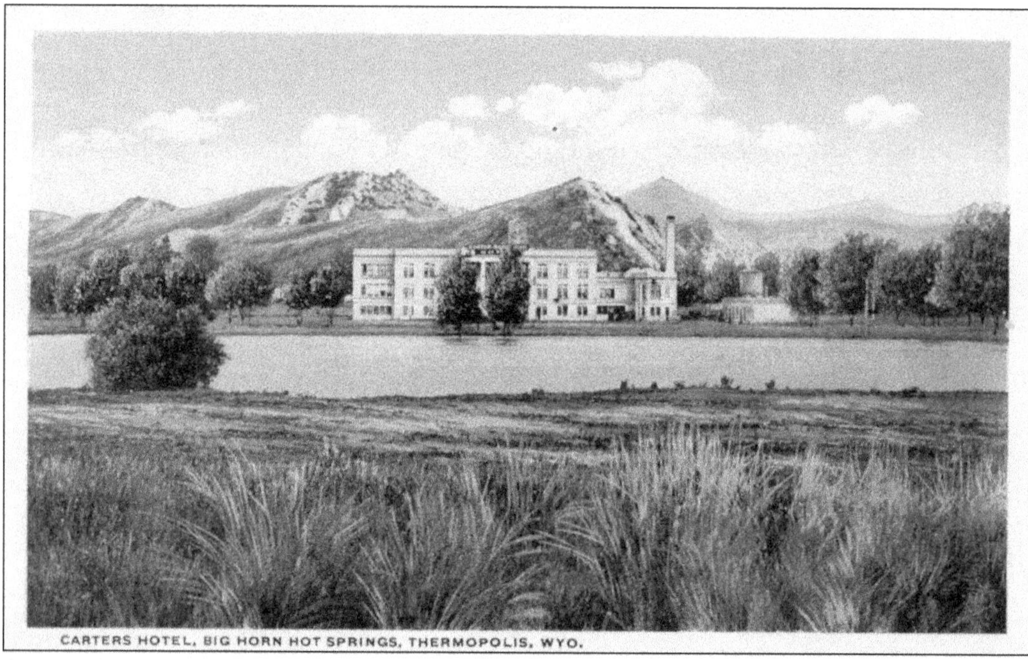

CARTER'S HOTEL, THERMOPOLIS. This hotel was formerly a hospital built by Dr. C. Dana Carter on the Hot Springs reservation in 1916 at a cost of $100,000. Dr. Carter was regarded as one of the most accomplished physicians in Wyoming. He is credited with performing the first Caesarean operation in Wyoming—alone and in a log cabin near Basin.

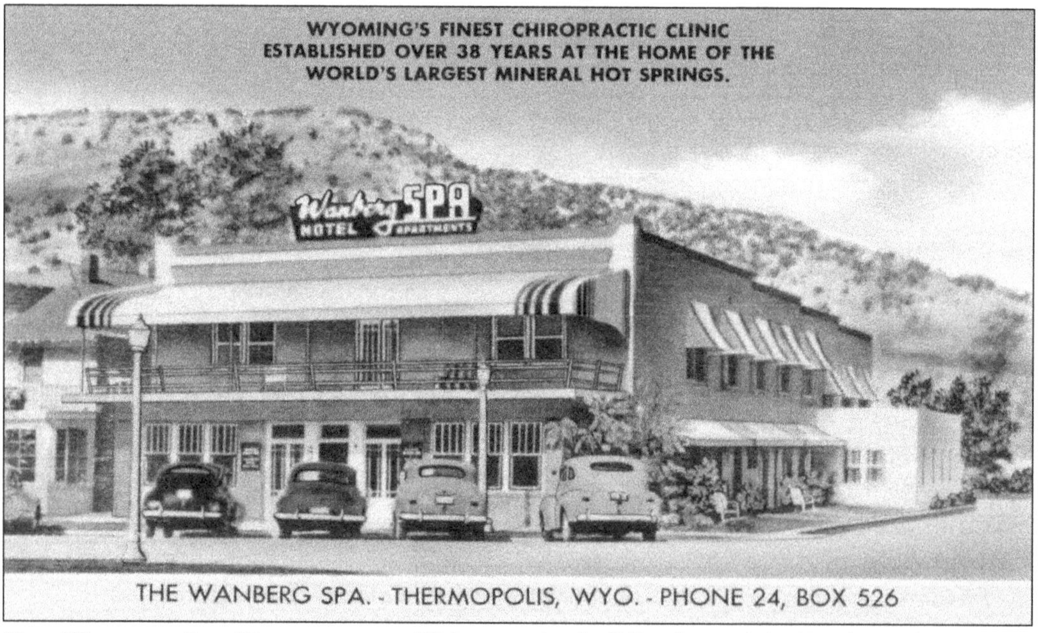

THE WANBERG SPA, THERMOPOLIS. This attractive building housed the Wanberg chiropractic clinic on the first floor that, according to the front of the card, had served patients for 38 years. The second floor was occupied by a hotel for daily visitors and apartments for longer-term guests. The back of the card states that the clinic was noted for its successful treatment of arthritis and associated diseases, including sciatica.

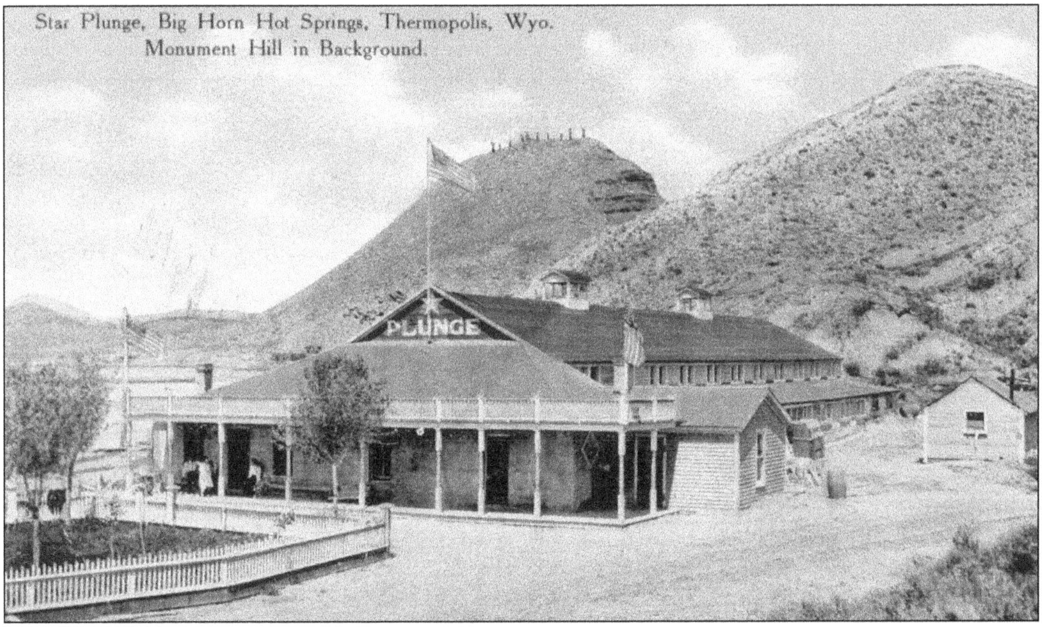

The Star Plunge, Hot Springs State Park, Thermopolis. The Star Plunge first opened in the late 1800s and has been an attraction in Thermopolis ever since. The facility offered both indoor and outdoor bathing in geothermal pools that were free and open to the public as part of the 1896 treaty with the Arapaho and Shoshone tribes. The Star Plunge is shown here as it appeared in the 1930s. The building above contained the indoor pool and the accompanying dressing rooms. The large screened-in porch was a popular place to relax after an invigorating swim. The view below is of the large indoor pool. The position of the swimmers might indicate that a class was in progress. Early visitors reputedly included Buffalo Bill Cody, Butch Cassidy, and the Hole in the Wall Gang.

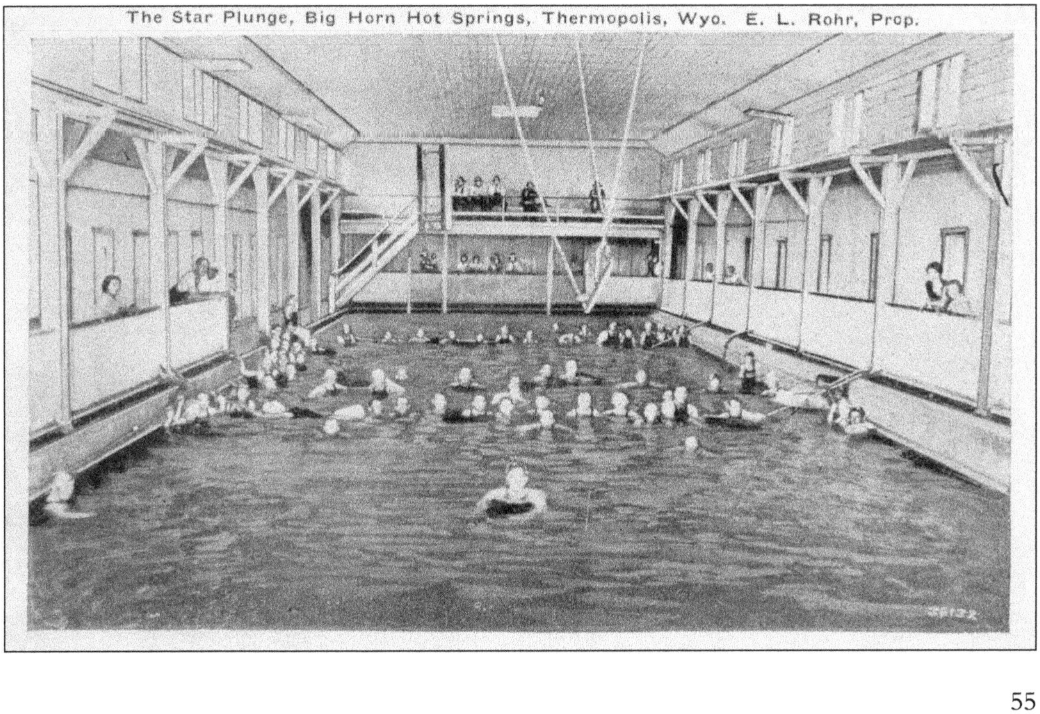

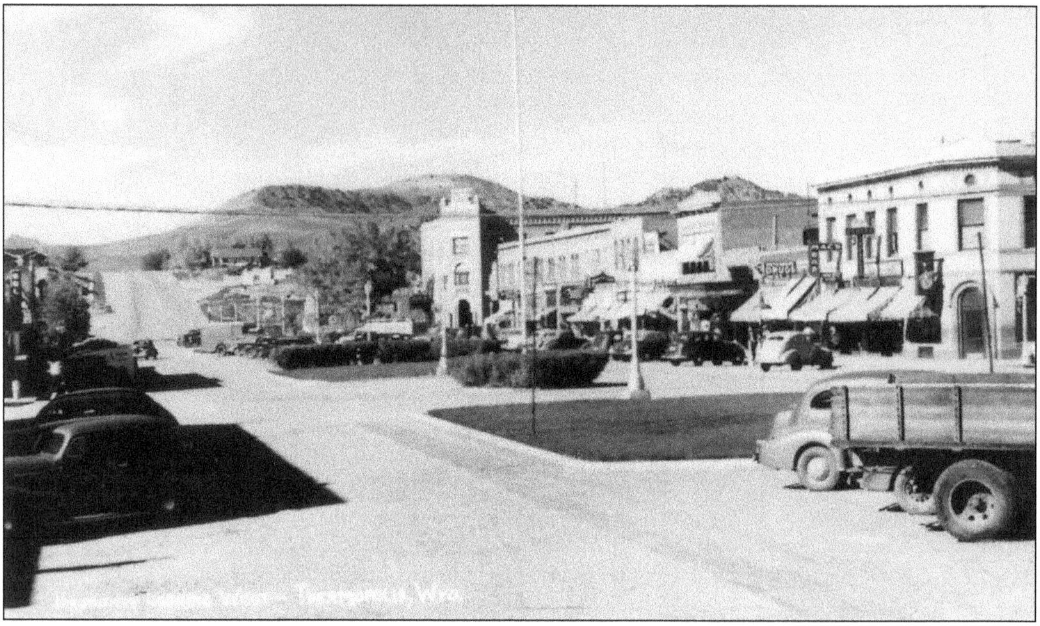

MAIN STREET, THERMOPOLIS. Historic Highway 20 runs north and south through Thermopolis, perpendicular to Broadway Street where the two views on this page illustrate the evolution of Thermopolis's business district over an approximately 20-year period. Notable in both photographs is the wide and attractive green space extending the length of the street and the typical Western vista in the distance. Parking was allowed adjacent to both the center islands and the curb, but in the image below, taken in the 1950s, parking meters had been installed. The city's population remained relatively steady at approximately 3,000 during the two-decade period. In addition to Mineral Hot Springs, the town was noted for its swimming, boating, fishing, hunting, and sightseeing. Visitors could observe the large herd of buffalo that roamed the prairies in the state park.

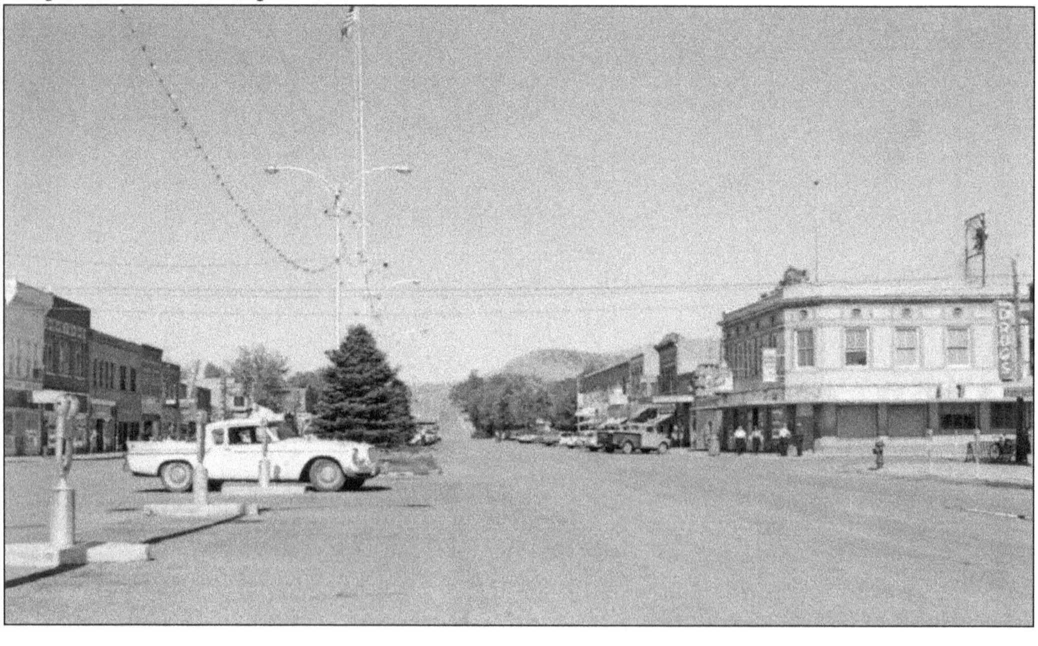

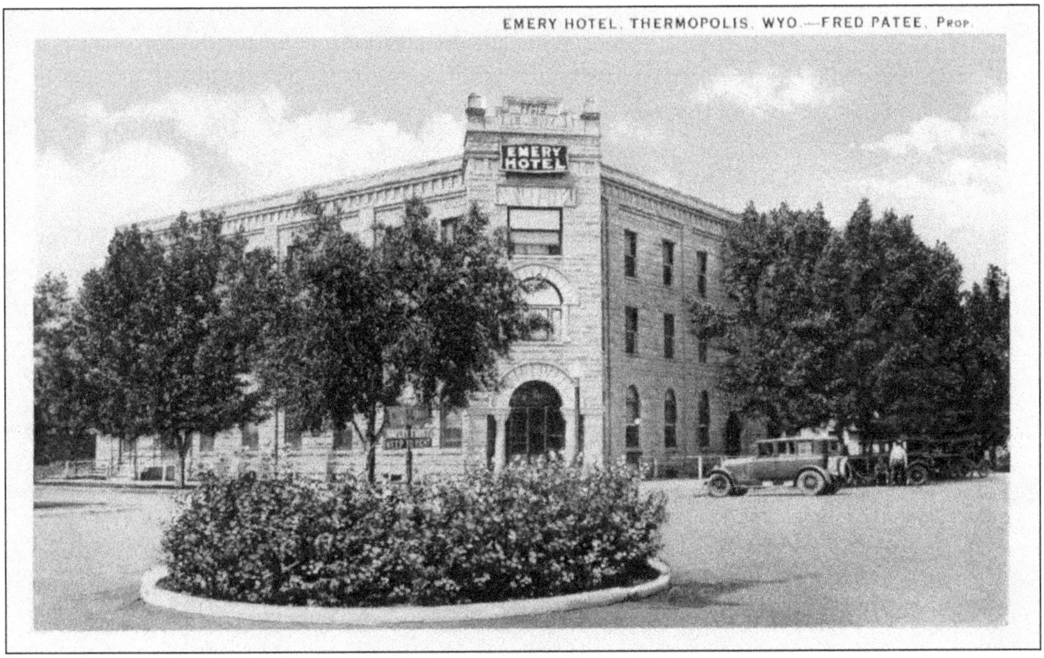

Emery Hotel, Highway 20, Thermopolis. The classic facade and graceful arched front entrance added to the attractiveness of the Emery Hotel. Located in the heart of the downtown business district, the three-story hotel offered all the latest amenities for guest comfort. Its coffee shop and colorful lounge were special attractions, as was the flower garden in the center of the intersection in front.

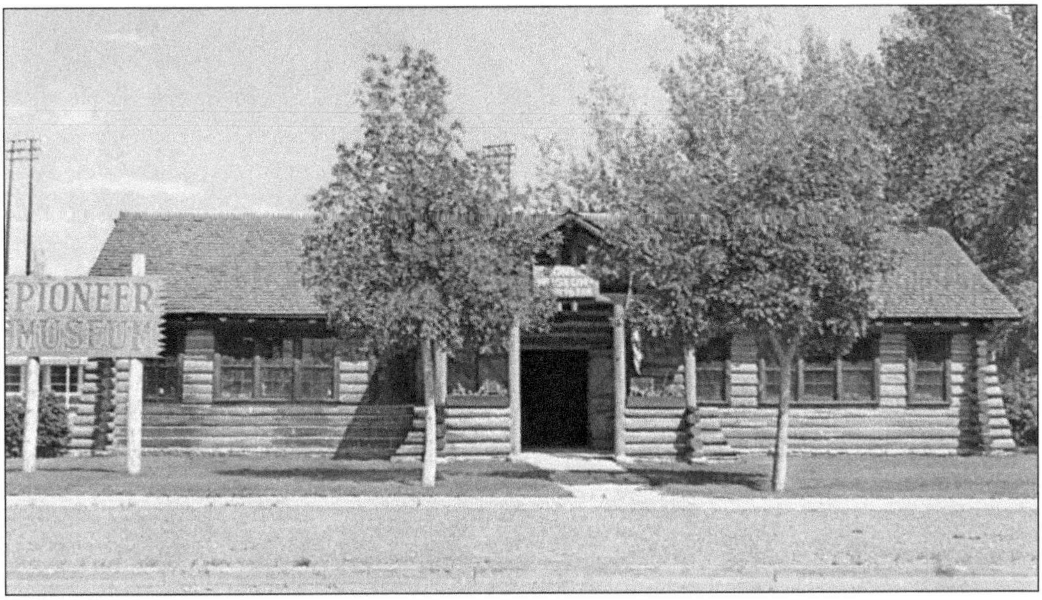

Pioneer Museum, Thermopolis. This log cabin, home of the Hot Springs Pioneer Museum, opened on July 4, 1941. Its mission was to preserve the history of the region's settlers. The museum's original collection included household items and implements used by early pioneers from the 1880s through the 1930s. The building burned down in 1967 and has been replaced by the Hot Springs County Museum and Cultural Center on Broadway Street.

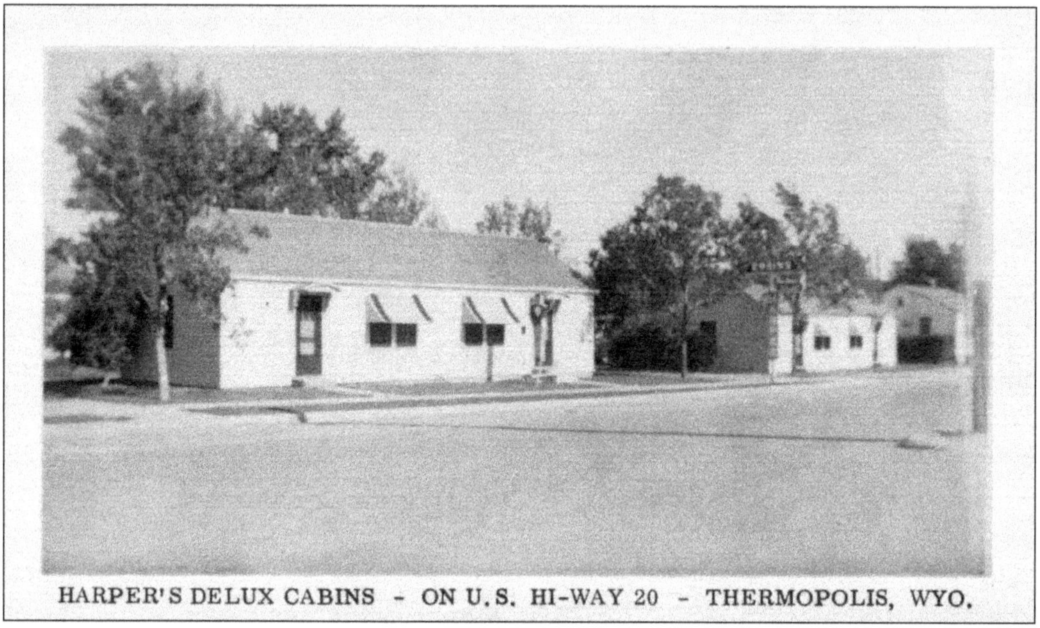

Harper's Delux Cabins, US Highway 20, Thermopolis. Noise from traffic on historic Highway 20 may have been a problem for guests at this motel, as the door to some units opened directly to the highway. Nothing on the card indicates if a parking lot was available or if guests were expected to park their cars on the street.

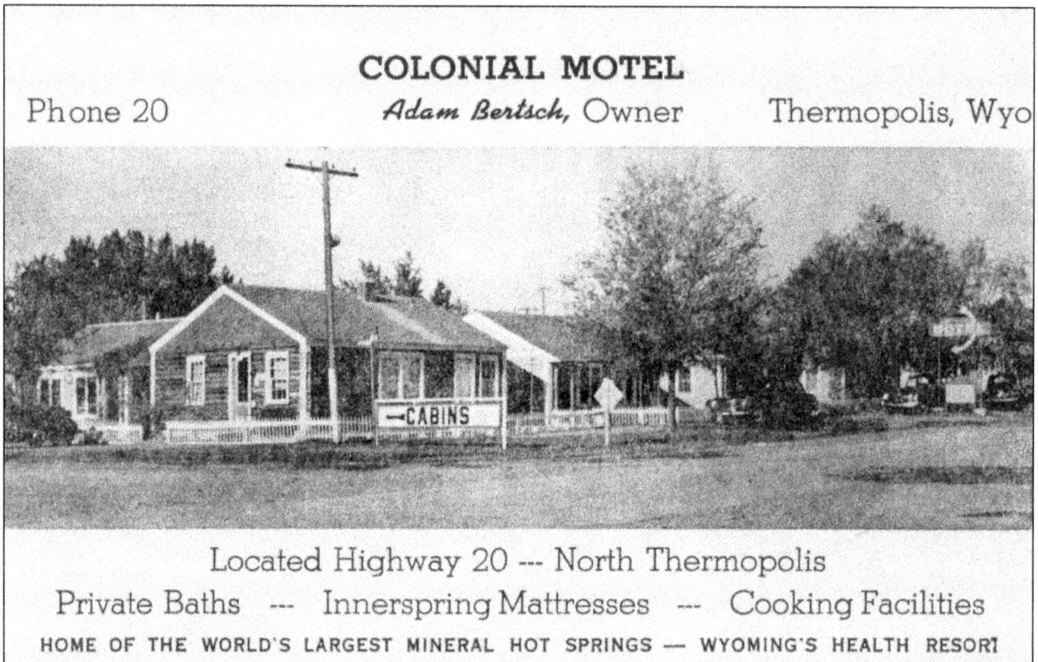

Colonial Motel, Highway 20, Thermopolis. The cars parked in front of this early motel and the two-digit telephone number indicate that this postcard was produced in the late 1930s or early 1940s. The sender of this card was typical of many travelers: they were on the way to Yellowstone National Park but had stopped in Thermopolis to experience the hot springs.

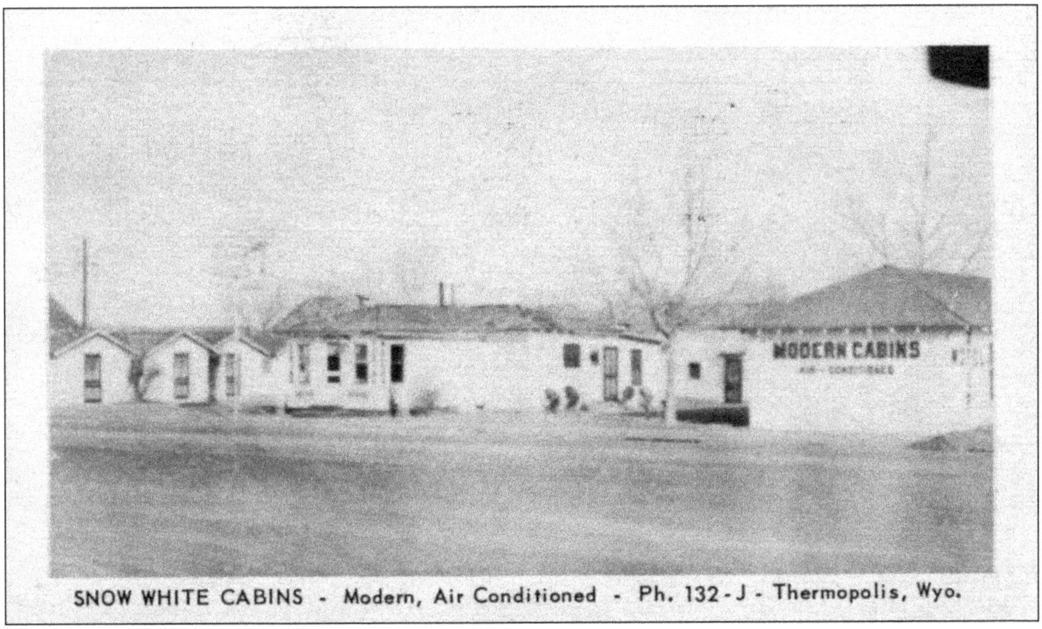

SNOW WHITE CABINS, THERMOPOLIS. This card was mailed in 1952. The sender reported leaving Sioux City, Iowa, at 3:00 a.m. the previous day and had just arrived in Thermopolis at 8:00 p.m., a distance of 982 miles. They had seen the mountains, no doubt through the Wind River Canyon, and intended to get to Yellowstone by noon the next day.

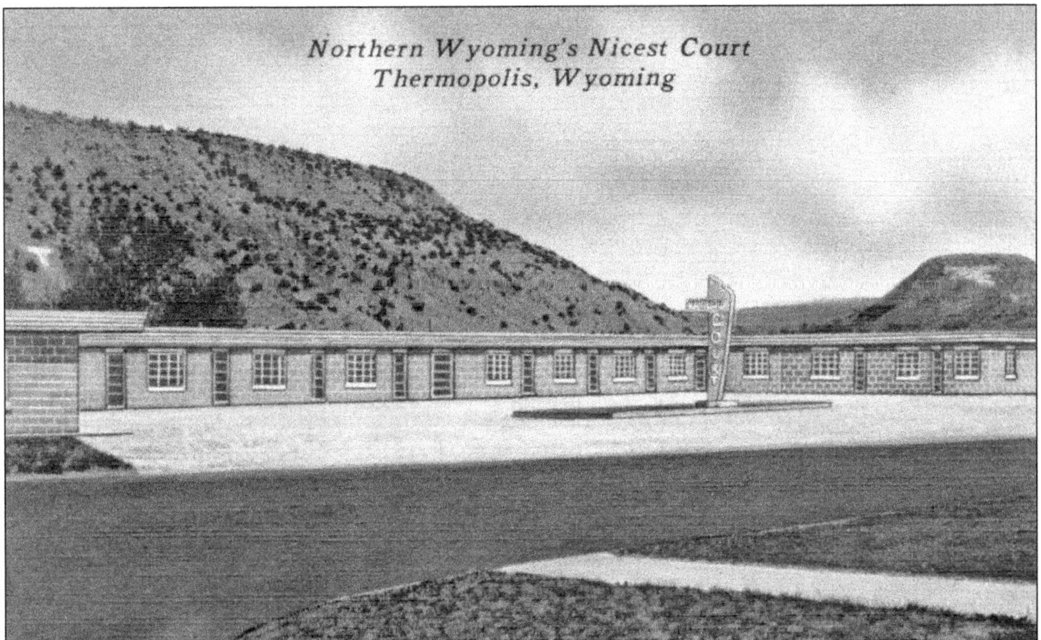

RAINBOW COURT, HIGHWAY 20, THERMOPOLIS. The design of this motel, which called itself "Northern Wyoming's Nicest," was characteristic of many small-town motels built in the 1940s and 1950s. It offered 19 strictly modern, carpeted units, some with electric kitchenettes, tub baths, thermostatic heat control, and reasonable rates. There is no mention of television, indicating that it probably was not available. Monument Hill can be seen in the background.

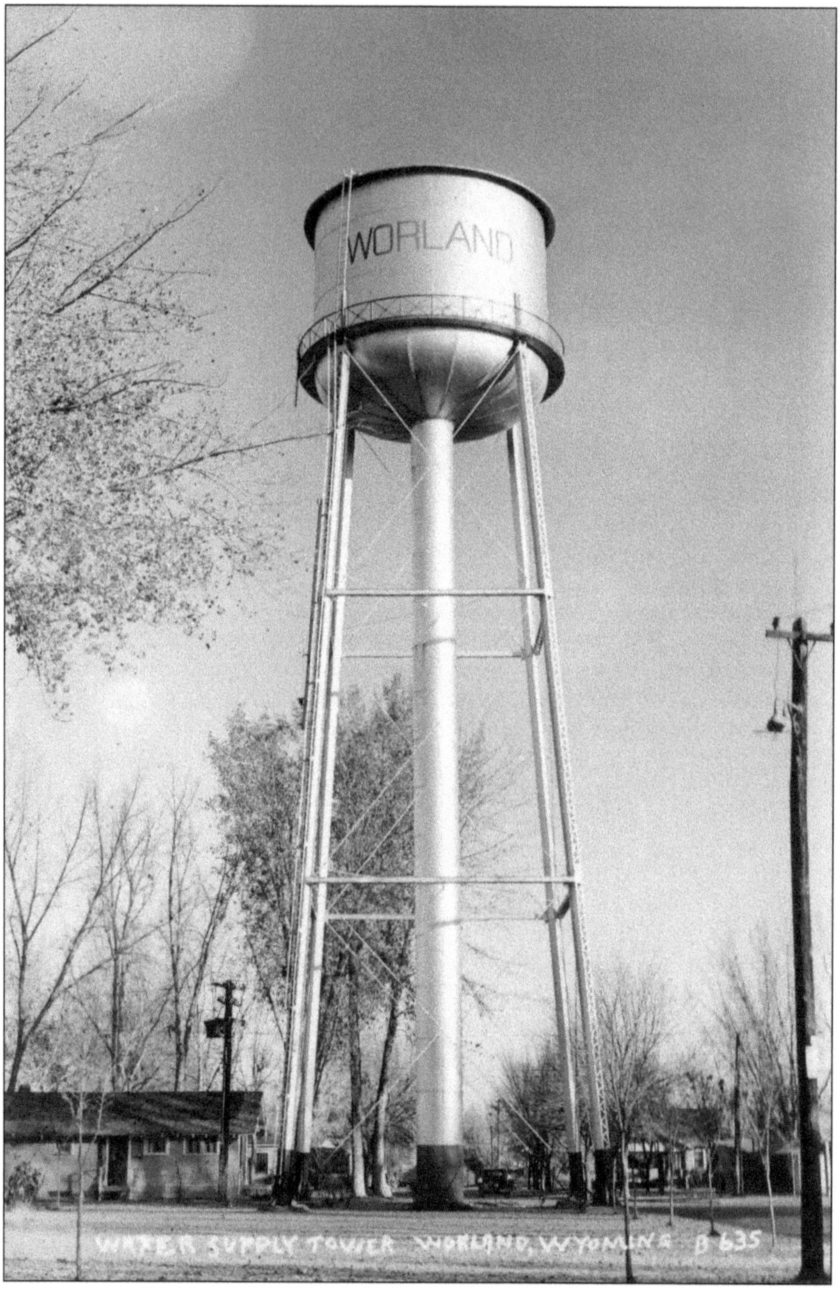

Water Tower, Worland. A 1930s-style water tower was standard in almost every small town across America. Typically it was the tallest structure in town, and it could be seen for miles. How many children were kept busy on a long journey by the challenge to see who could spot the next water tower down the road? In addition to its utilitarian function for citizens, the water tower also served the practical purpose of letting travelers know they would soon be driving down the town's main street. There they could eat, gas up, or possibly stop for the night. Present-day interstate highways no longer provide a close-up view of a community. The exit ramp sign, rather than the town name on the water tower, lets travelers know what town they are passing.

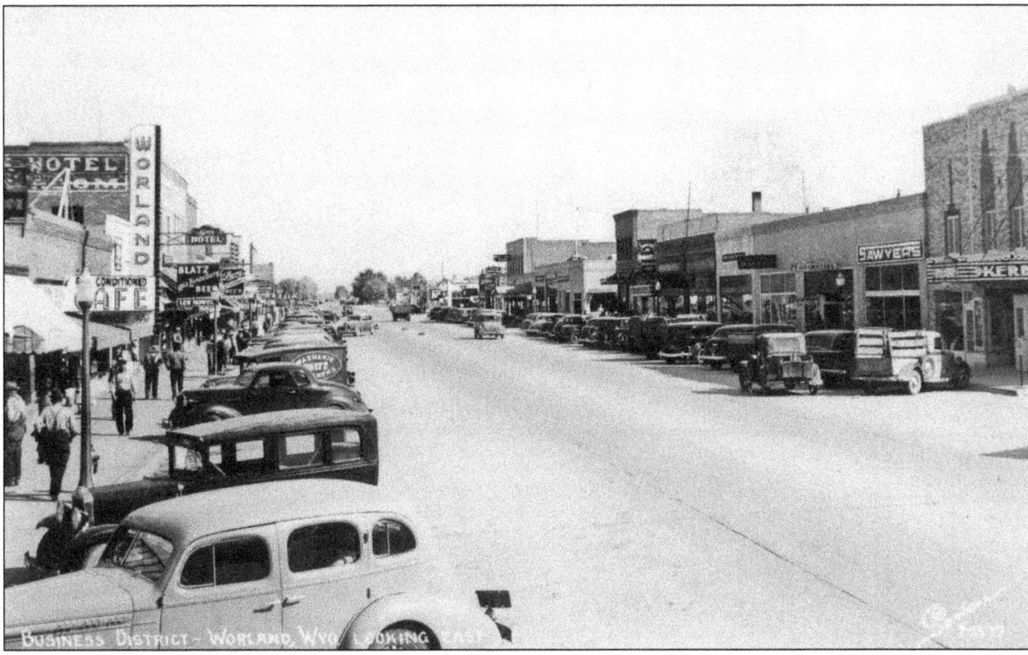

MAIN STREET AND BUSINESS DISTRICT, WORLAND. US Highway 20 passes through Worland on Big Horn Avenue. The two cards on this page depict similar views from the 1930s (above) and 1950s (below). Both photographs show that the community retained a dynamic business district complete with restaurants, bars, hotels, and retail establishments. The image above shows many pedestrians walking along the sidewalk or holding impromptu conversations with their friends. The autos seen below were directed by the traffic signal suspended on wires across the intersection. A Highway 20 sign can be identified on the lamppost at the extreme right of the photograph, and the Hotel Washakie sign dominates the skyline.

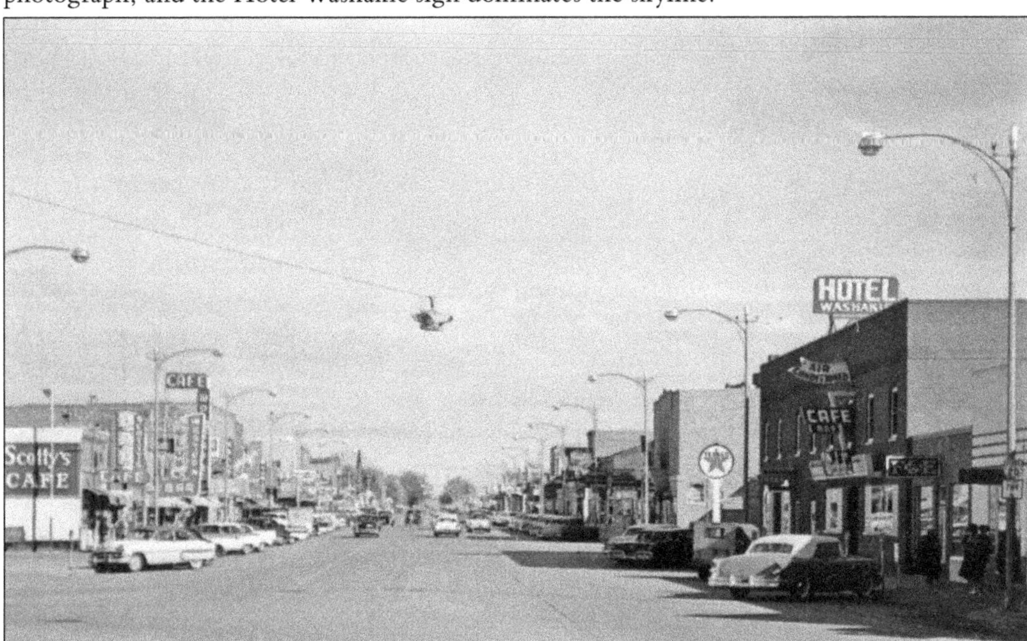

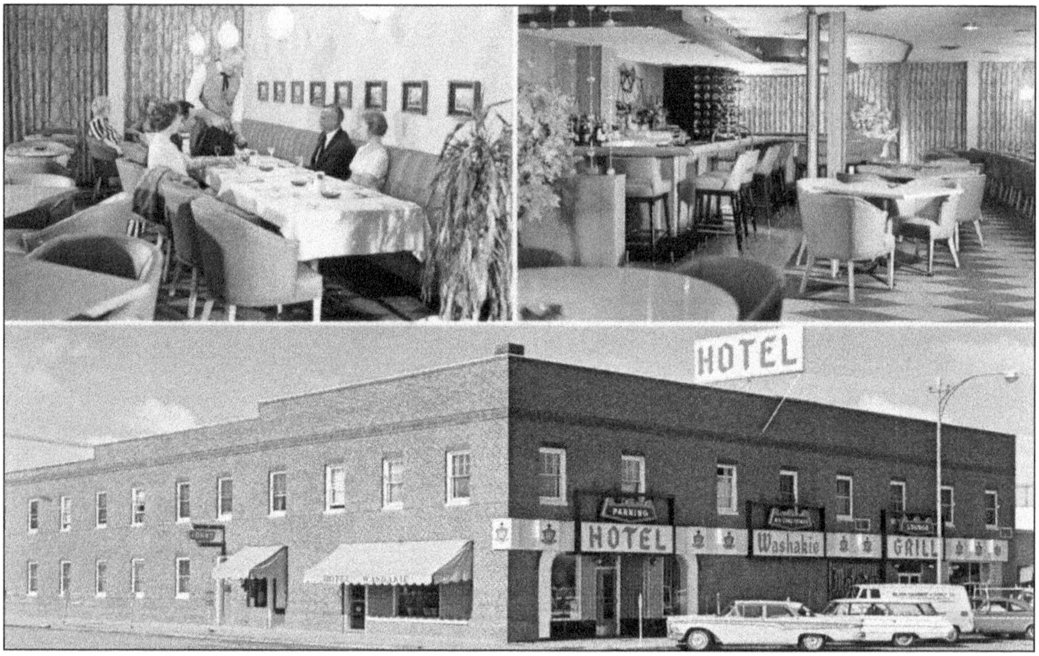

HOTEL WASHAKIE, HIGHWAYS 16 AND 20, WORLAND. In addition to showing the exterior of the hotel, this triple view postcard features two of the hotel's top attractions. The hotel's grill offered a full menu of favorite meat and fish dishes, and the Matador Lounge was famous for its drinks. Barber and beauty shops also were available.

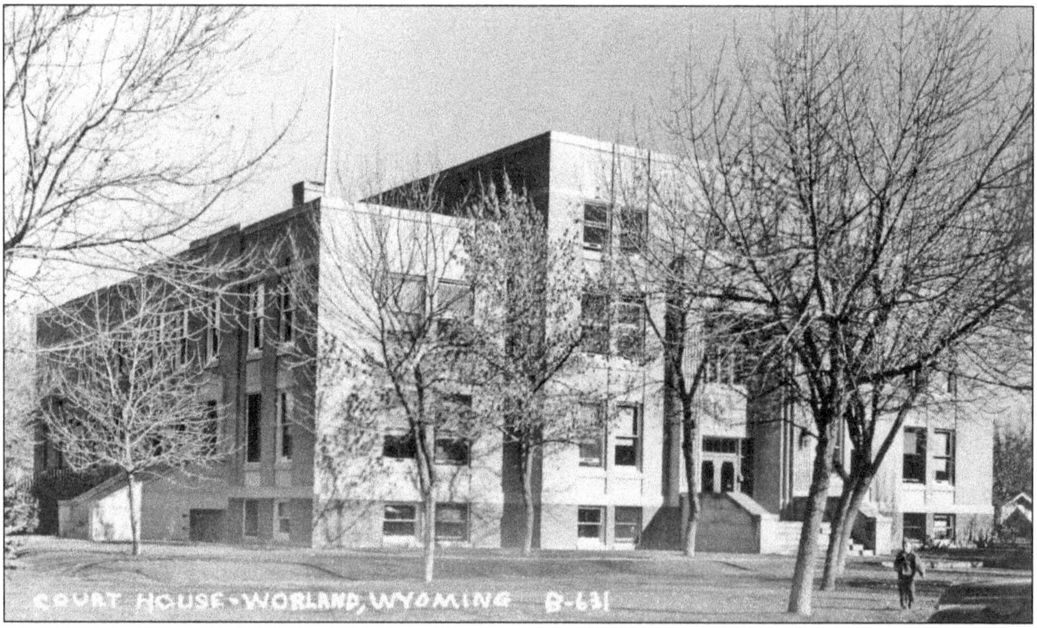

WASHAKIE COUNTY COURTHOUSE, HIGHWAYS 20 AND 16, WORLAND. This classic seat of government for Washakie County anchors the corner of Big Horn Avenue and Tenth Street at the east end of Worland's business district. Highways 20 and 16 meet at this intersection, where both routes turn north, passing directly in front of the courthouse. The building has a three-story central section flanked by symmetrical two-story wings on either side.

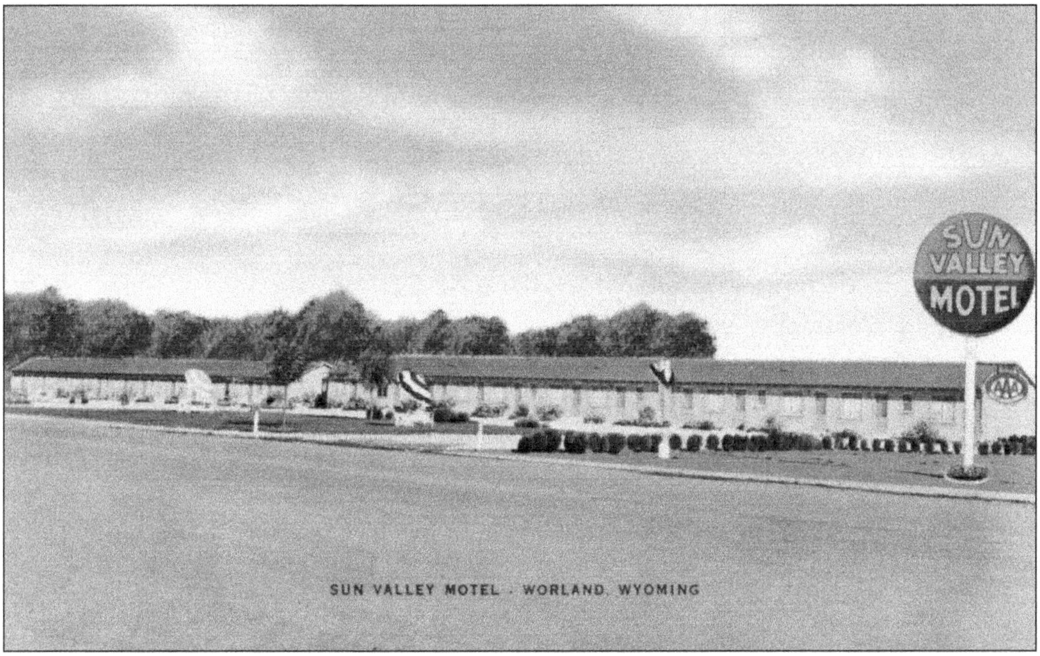

Sun Valley Motel, Highways 16 and 20, Worland. This 25-unit motel emphasized its location on the direct route between Yellowstone and the Black Hills National Parks. All guest rooms included ceramic tile showers and individually controlled heat. The motel provided its guests with complimentary morning coffee, and TV was available. There was no mention if the latter was in the room or in the motel's lounge.

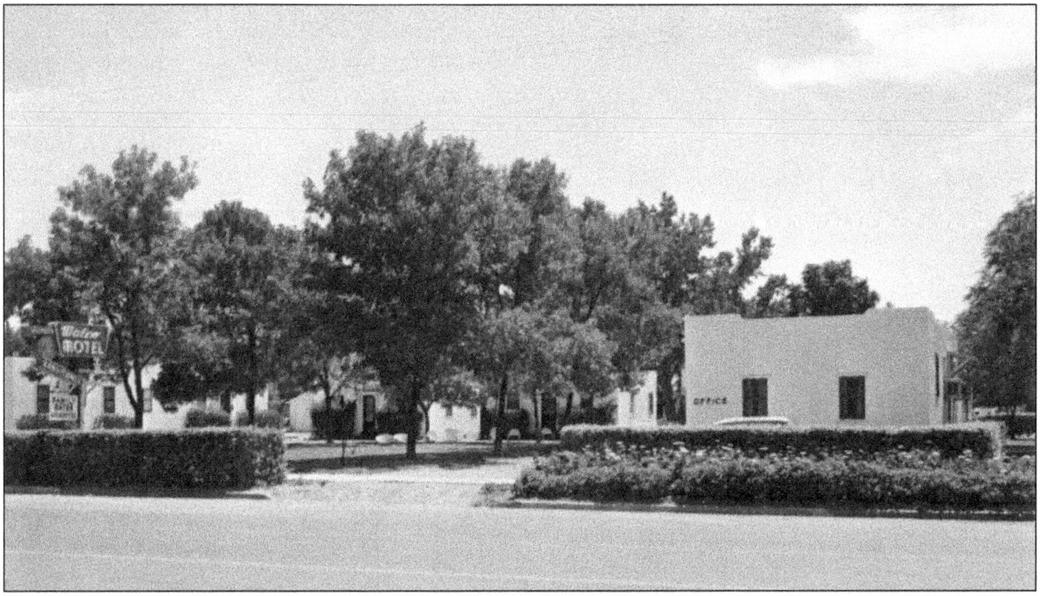

Watco Motel, 1300 Big Horn Avenue, Worland. No doubt this was another popular stopping point on the route between Yellowstone National Park and the Black Hills. The motel's attractive setting included well-trimmed hedges and shade on the large lawn where guests could relax in the fresh mountain air. Travelers on both Highways 20 and 16 had easy access to the modern cabins and proximity to Worland's restaurants and retail stores.

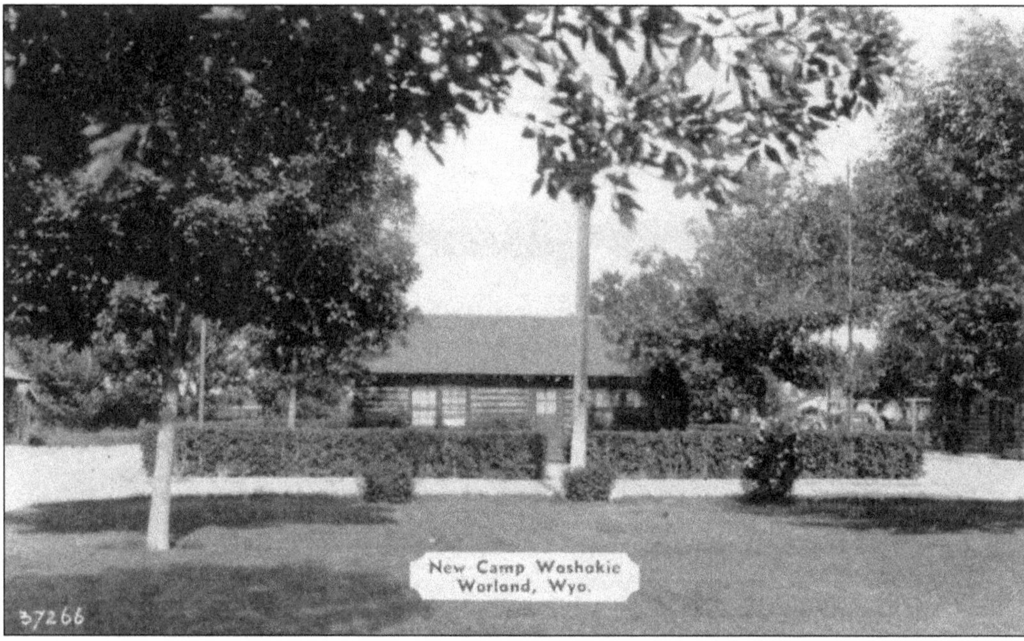

New Camp Washakie, Highways 16 and 20, Worland. The two views on this page show the New Camp Washakie's tourist accommodations (above) and the service station (below). The captions on both cards emphasize that this tourist camp is "located in the shadow of the Big Horns." The facility offered 20 modern rooms, all with private showers and baths and innerspring mattresses. It, too, featured well-manicured lawns, hedges, and plenty of shade. The service station provided not only gas and oil, but also tires and other automobile repair services. On the day the photograph below was taken in the 1930s, three cars were waiting for attention.

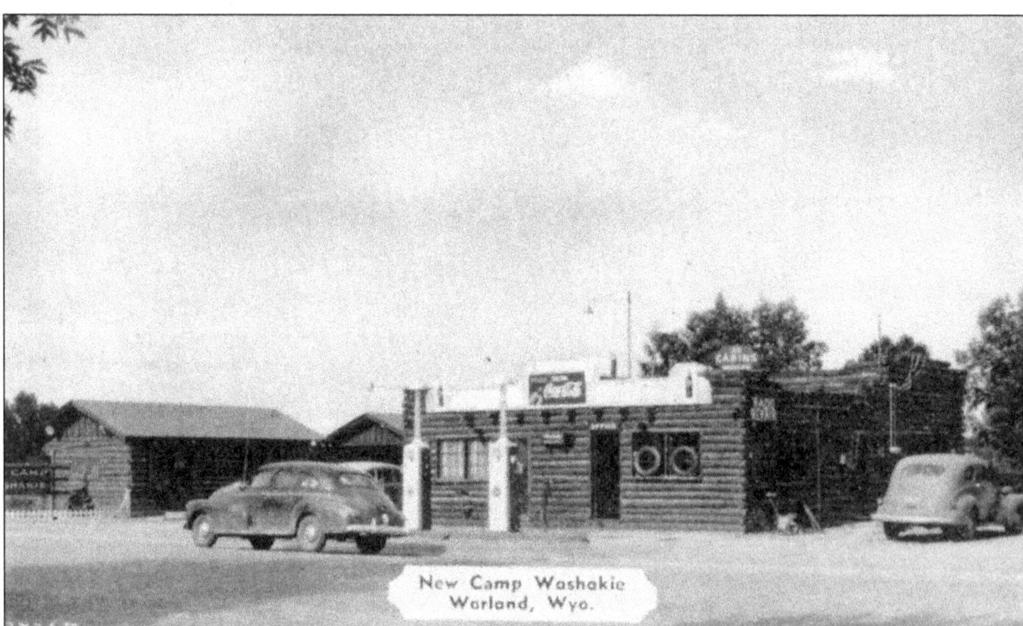

Four

Big Horn and Park Counties

Big Horn County was formed by the Wyoming Legislature in 1890 from land that formerly had been in adjoining Fremont, Johnson, and Sheridan Counties. In 1910, the legislature again altered the region and created Park County, giving both counties their present borders. Basin is the county seat of Big Horn County, and Cody is the seat of Park County. Big Horn County is named for the Bighorn Mountains, and Park County derives its name from adjacent Yellowstone National Park. Historic Highway 20 was the main federal highway to service both Big Horn and Park Counties from its inception in 1926 until the arrival of the present Interstate Highway System after World War II. As the name implies, Big Horn County is in the Bighorn Basin, an area between the Bighorn Mountains on the east and the Absaroka Range to the west. The Bighorn National Forest occupies the county's entire eastern border. Early white settlers were primarily ranchers who raised cattle and sheep. Later, conventional farming contributed to the economy. In the early 1900s, oil was discovered, and oil drilling and refineries soon followed.

Buffalo Bill Cody was an indefatigable champion for the Bighorn Basin and instrumental in founding both the town of Cody and the eventual Cody Road to Yellowstone National Park. Cody is the main community at the eastern gateway to Yellowstone National Park, although it is 53 miles from the gate. It evolved into a popular tourist town, and its location directly on historic Highway 20 has enabled persons on their way to Yellowstone National Park to experience its many attractions. Several hotels were opened, including the Irma Hotel owned by Buffalo Bill, whose name and personality virtually ensured the success of the establishment. The Irma is still a Main Street stalwart today. As tourism increased and the railroad brought visitors to Cody, many more tourist-related businesses evolved. The Buffalo Bill Center of the West displays artifacts from the early days of the community as well as memorabilia about Buffalo Bill.

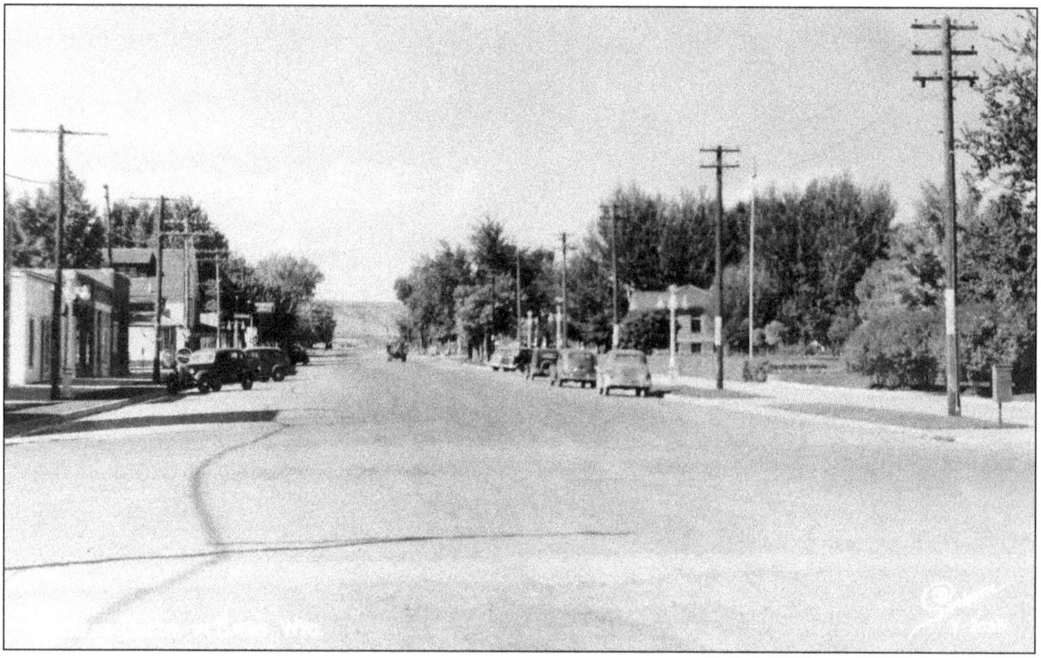

STREET SCENE IN BASIN. No name for this street is provided, but the businesses on the left side of the image indicate either a section of Main Street (Highway 20) or a street that intersected with Main Street and thus would have been visible from the highway. Interestingly, cars were parked diagonally on the business side and parallel on the residential side.

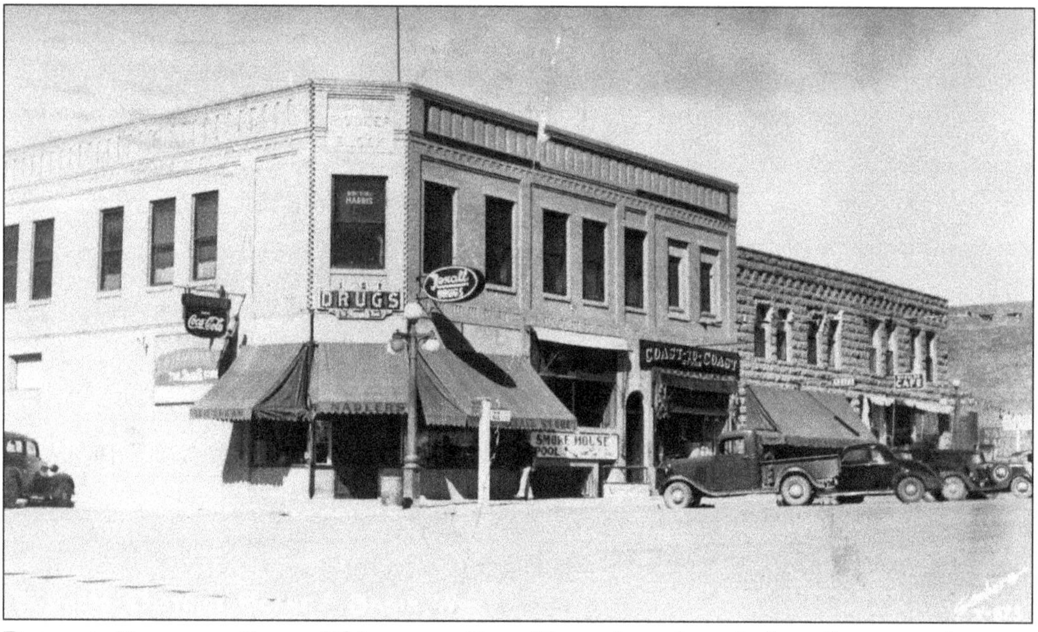

BUSINESS DISTRICT, BASIN. This postcard is an illustration of a typical small-town main street in the 1930s. The corner drugstore featuring Rexall products and Coca-Cola, a Coast-to-Coast Hardware Store, and the cafe at the end of the street all are icons of this era. Dr. Harris, either a dentist or physician, occupied the second floor of the building. The Smoke House Pool Room also can be identified.

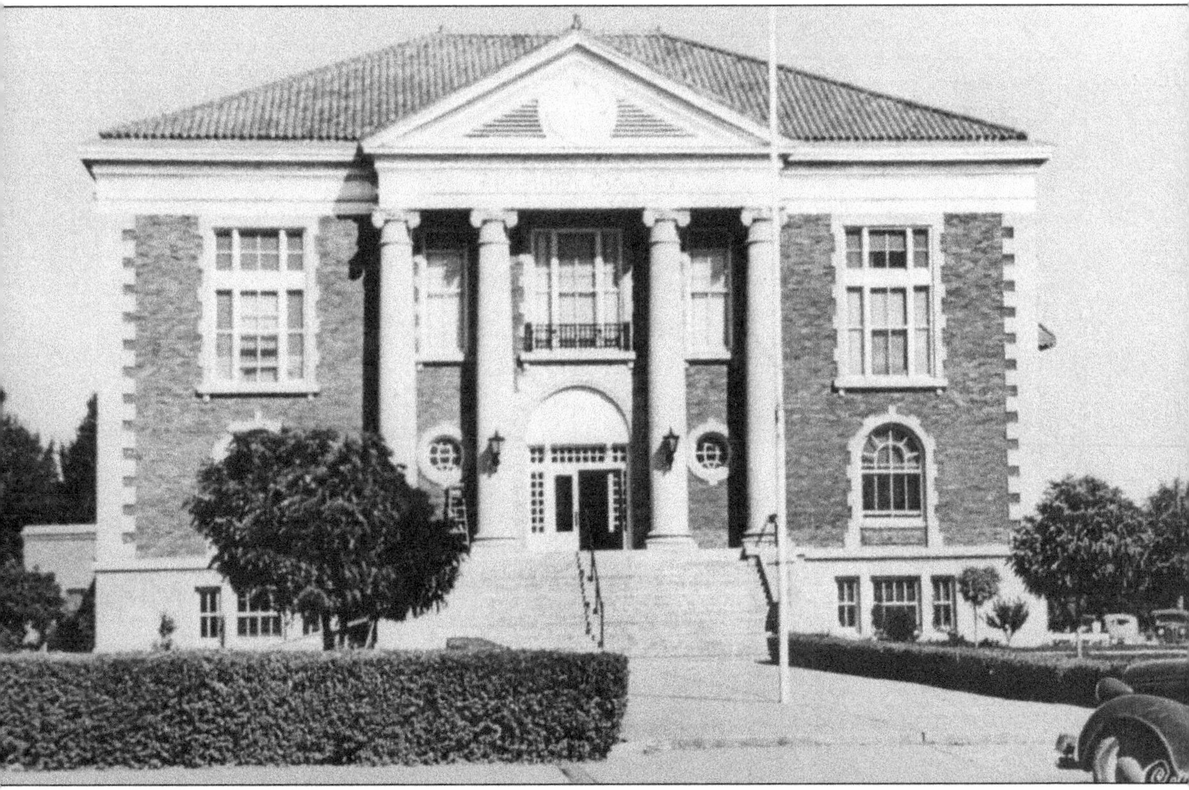

COUNTY COURTHOUSE, 420 WEST C STREET, BASIN. The Wyoming Legislature approved the formation of Big Horn County in 1890, but the county was not formally organized with Basin as its seat until 1897. The county was named for the Bighorn Mountain Range, which in turn was named for the bighorn sheep that populate the region. Originally, Big Horn County encompassed approximately 12,500 square miles, but subsequently Park, Hot Springs, and Washakie Counties were incorporated separately, giving Big Horn County its present dimension. The courthouse shown here was built in 1918 and has served the county ever since. The four columns adorning the front portico, plus its symmetrical facade, give this civic building an aura of authority. The Wyoming-Montana border extends across the northern border of the county.

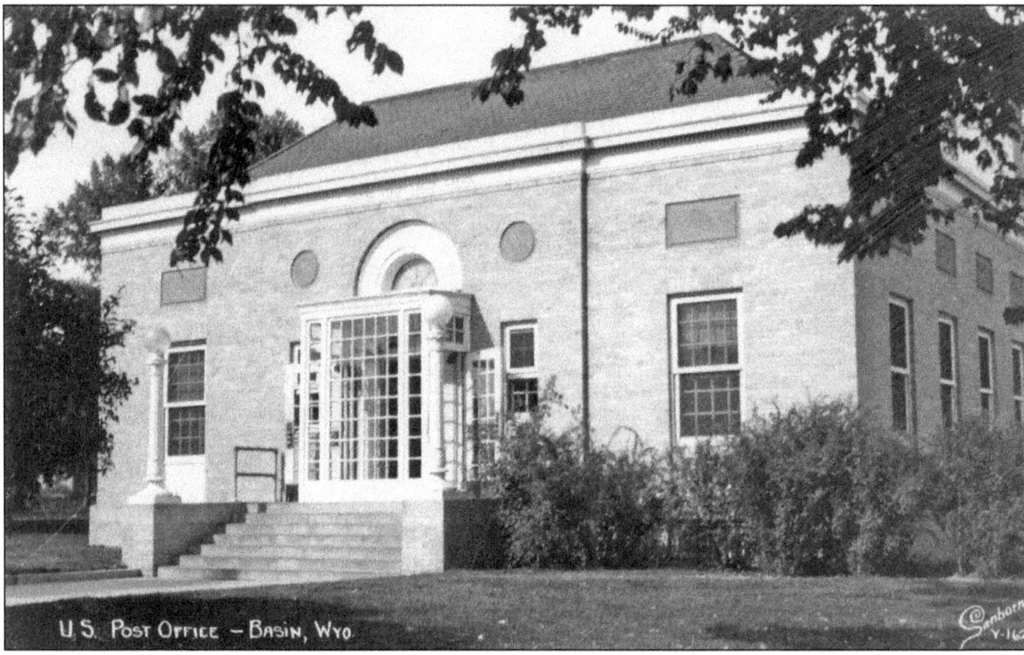

Post Office, 402 C Street, Basin. This classic 1930s post office is located within Basin's four-block civic center, which also contains the Big Horn County Courthouse, the library, and a park. In 1936, the town began a shrub-planting campaign, which has resulted in streets lined with perfumed hedges and shade trees. The post office is listed in the National Register of Historic Places.

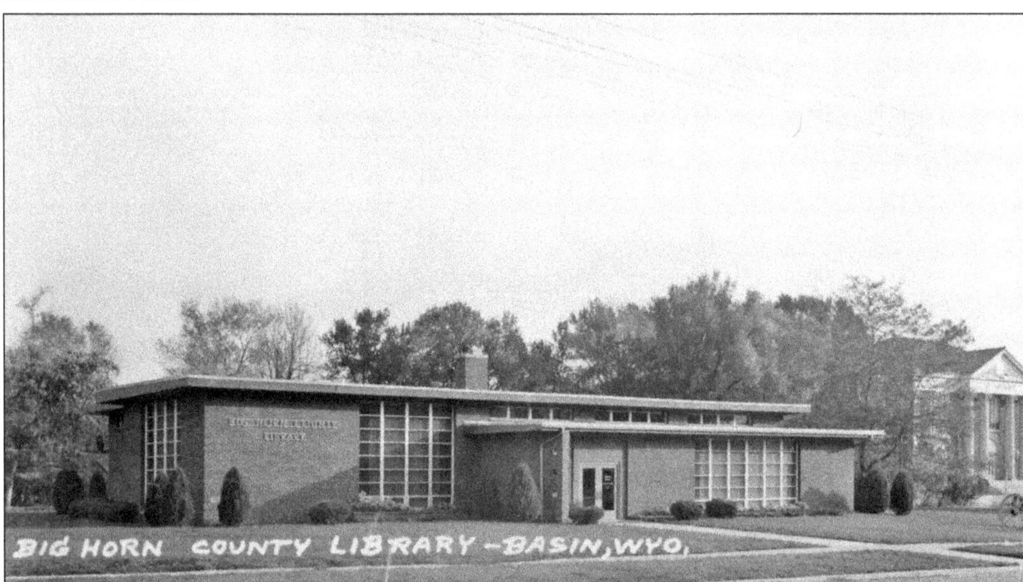

Big Horn County Library, Basin. Basin's first public library originated in 1907 because of the efforts of the town's Book Lovers' Club. A grant of $17,500 was awarded from the Carnegie Foundation, and in 1909 the permanent library opened. That library served until 1954, when the present library building was completed. Fortunately, a beautiful stained-glass window with "CL" in the center was retained and installed in the new library.

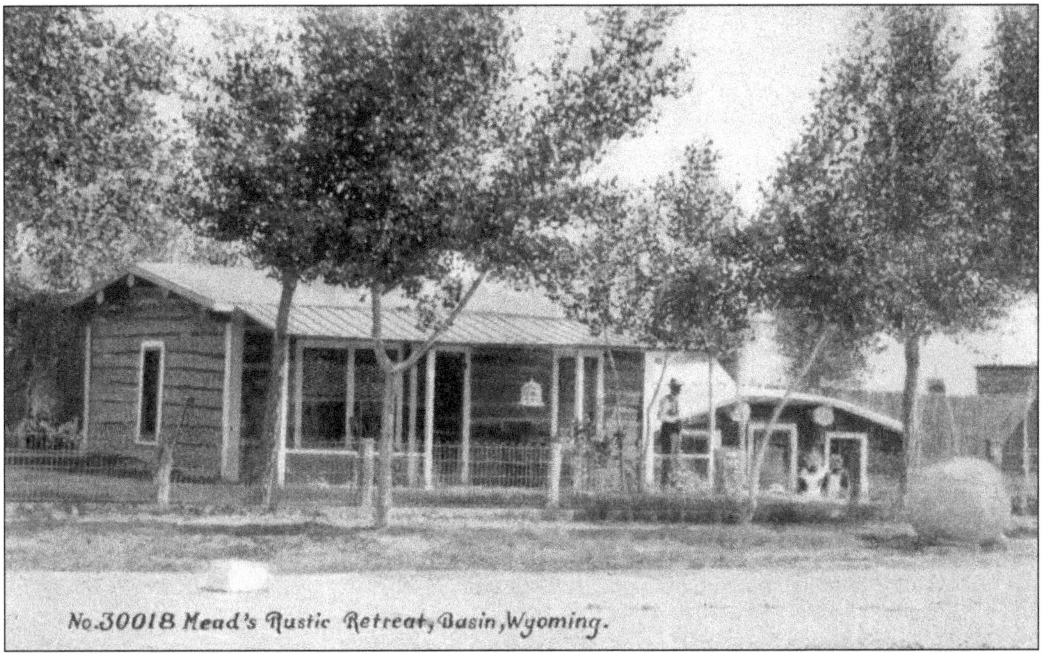

MEAD'S RUSTIC RETREAT, BASIN. The buildings and grounds of this early tourist camp lived up to the retreat's name. The setting was indeed rustic, with cabins interspersed among many trees on the green lawn. The parking lot was still gravel, which was common during the era in which travelers' accommodations were typically mom-and-pop establishments.

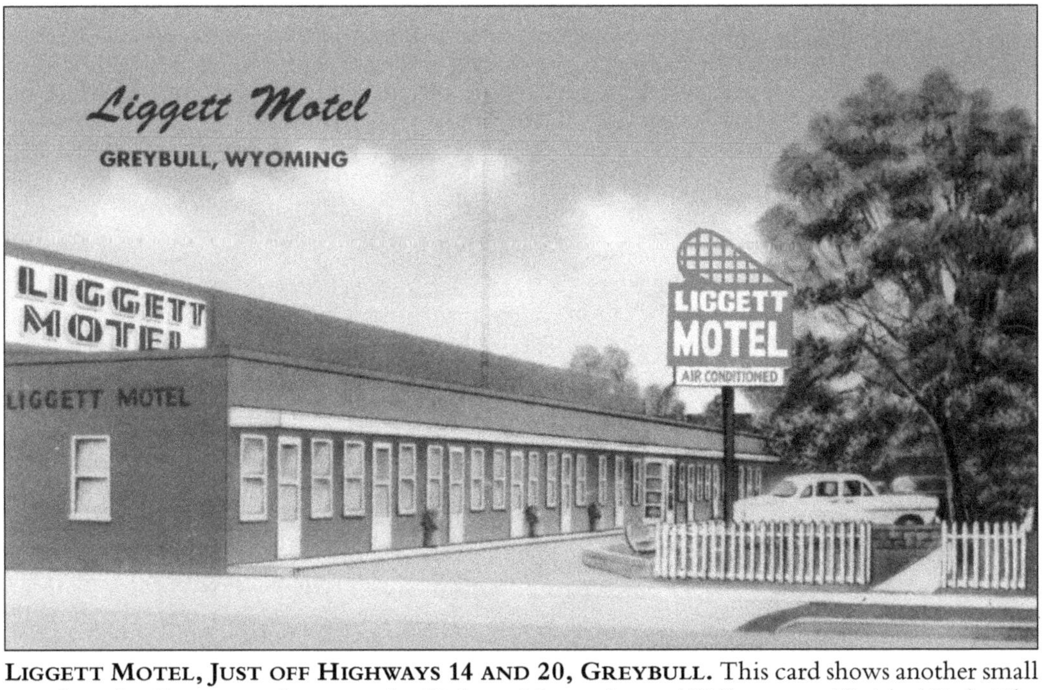

LIGGETT MOTEL, JUST OFF HIGHWAYS 14 AND 20, GREYBULL. This card shows another small motel on the direct route between the Bighorn Mountains and Yellowstone National Park. The 11-unit facility was located near downtown Greybull. A small outdoor sitting area was available for the guests' comfort.

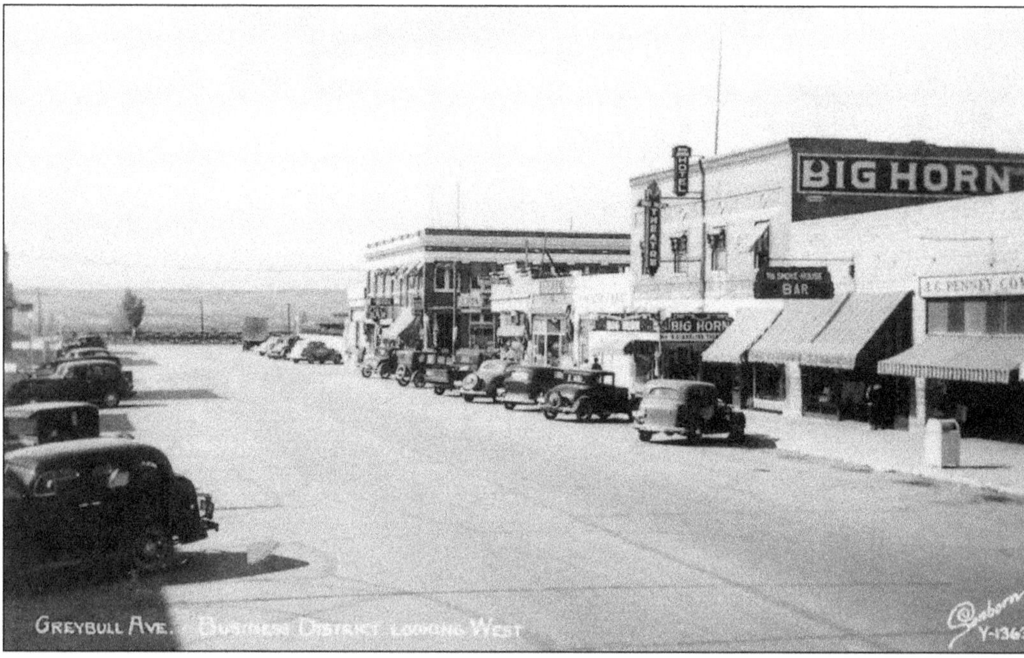

BUSINESS DISTRICT, GREYBULL. Greybull was described as a prosperous oil and ranch center in the Bighorn Basin. These two photographs give credence to this claim. The image above is from the 1930s, and the card below was produced in the 1950s. Notable changes include the aging of the Big Horn sign painted on the hotel and theater building and the addition of several new signs seen below. J.C. Penney and Rexall, two early Main Street stalwarts, are shown in both views, as is the Greybull Hotel, the striped building on the right side of the street. The most significant change appears to be at the end of the street. In the 1930s, the street terminated in open farmland, and only one small tree is evident. By 1950, several trees had matured, blocking the view.

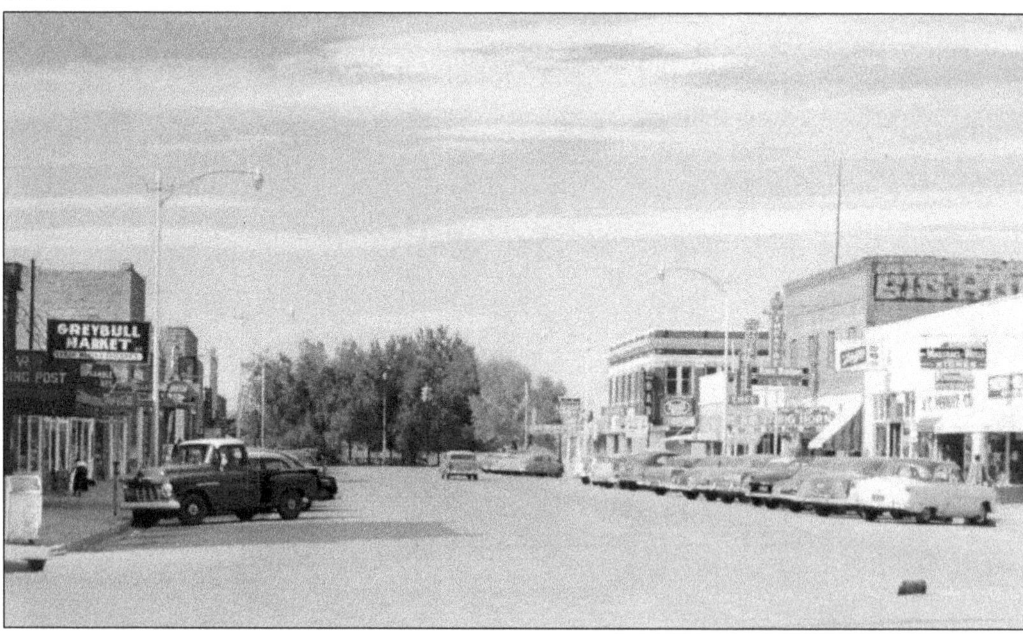

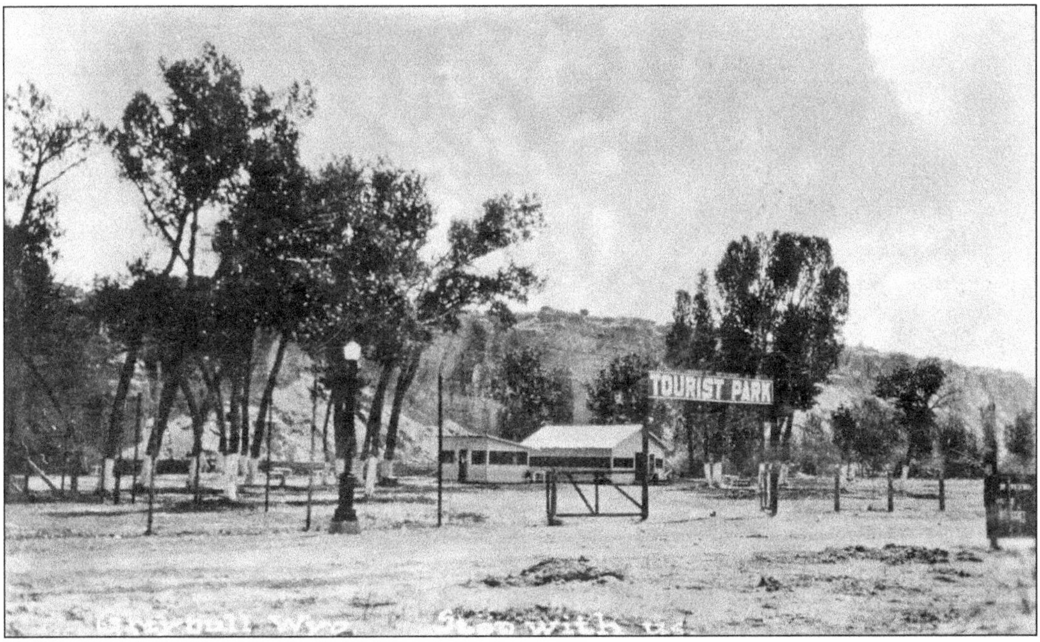

TOURIST PARK, GREYBULL. No address is given, but no doubt this tourist park was close to historic Highway 20 as travelers on that road were invited to "stop with us." Accommodations consisted of two small buildings, one of which housed the restrooms. Visitors provided their own shelter and could pitch tents wherever they wished in the park. Lawn chairs and picnic tables were available for guests.

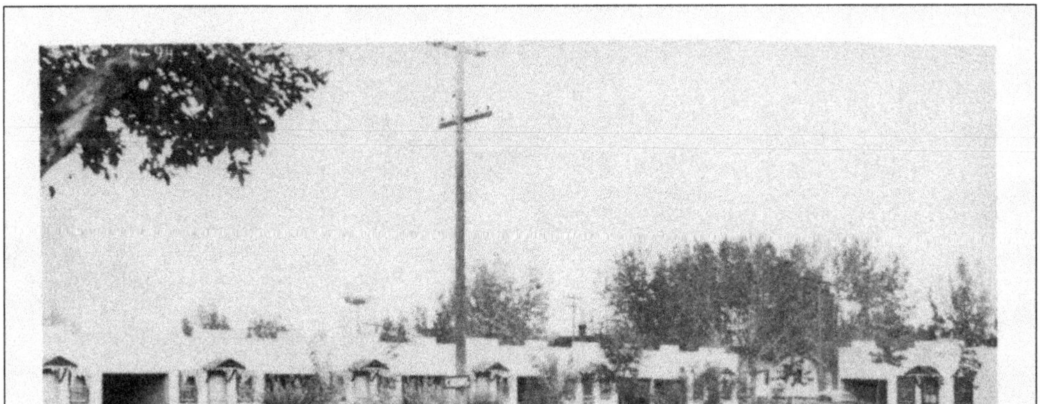

HOLLYWOOD COURT, HIGHWAYS 14 AND 20, GREYBULL. Roadside motels gradually replaced tourist parks and cabin courts as the favored places to spend a night. Many early motels incorporated garages into their designs. Here, a covered carport joins each two-unit facility. This trend lasted only a few years before the garage space was taken over for additional sleeping units.

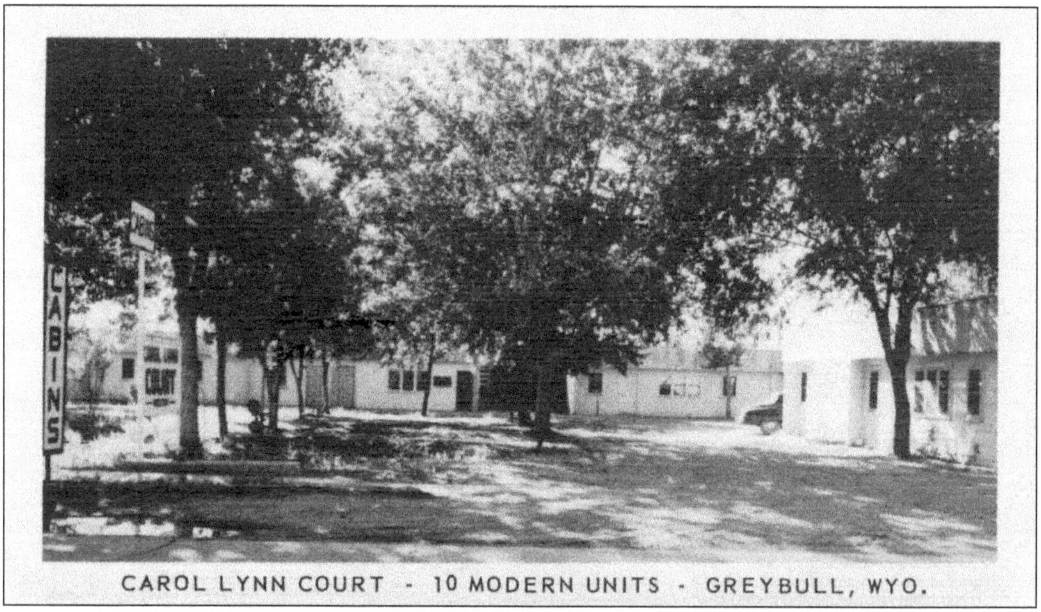

CAROL LYNN COURT, GREYBULL. Many visitors to Yellowstone National Park preferred to take a break before making the last leg of their journey. The Carol Lynn Court provided the ideal location to get ready for the exciting drive ahead. The motel's setting in a quiet grove, where guests could relax on the green lawn followed by a good night's sleep, virtually assured an outstanding experience the next day.

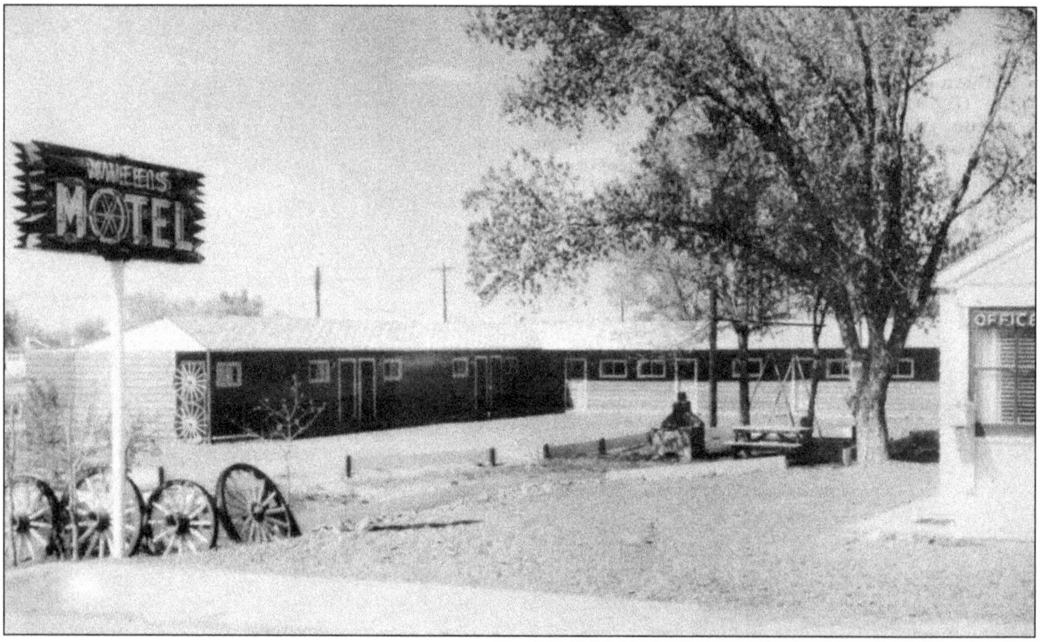

WHEELS MOTEL, HIGHWAYS 14 AND 20, GREYBULL. Old wagon wheels surrounding the motel sign were intended to attract the attention of motorists on historic Highway 20. This motel promoted its location in the Bighorn Basin to hunters, fishermen, and vacationers on their way to Yellowstone National Park, 100 miles farther west. Guests could take advantage of the picnic tables and playground equipment provided by the motel.

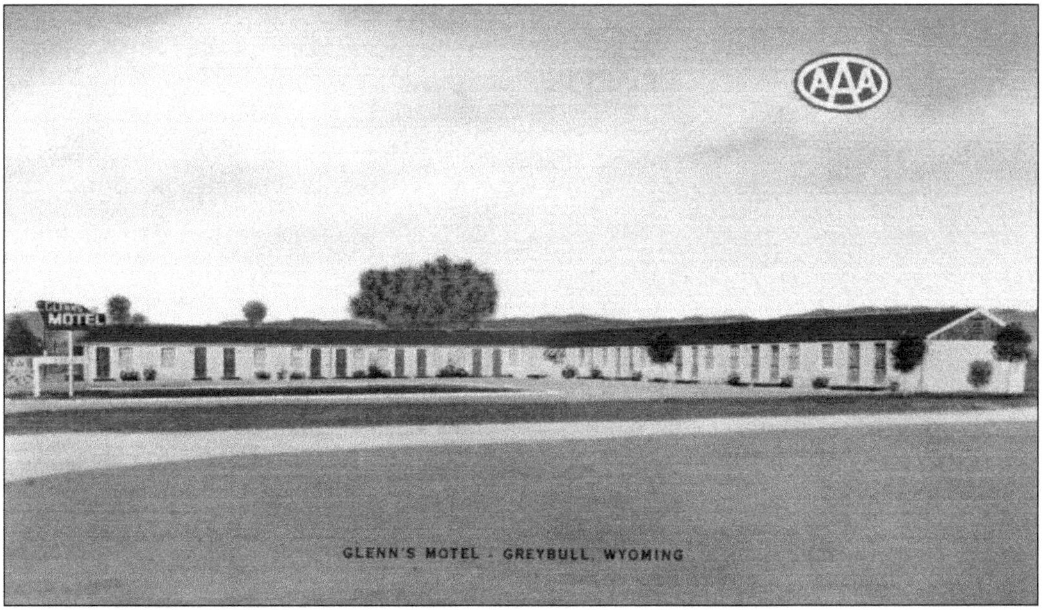

GLENN'S MOTEL, HIGHWAYS 14 AND 20, GREYBULL. This motel illustrated the evolution in motel design in the 1940s and 1950s from individual cabins to a single building with adjoining units. Named after owner Glenn Sutherland, the motel had 15 deluxe units, with air-conditioning and wall-to-wall carpeting. It was a three-hour scenic drive to the east entrance of Yellowstone National Park.

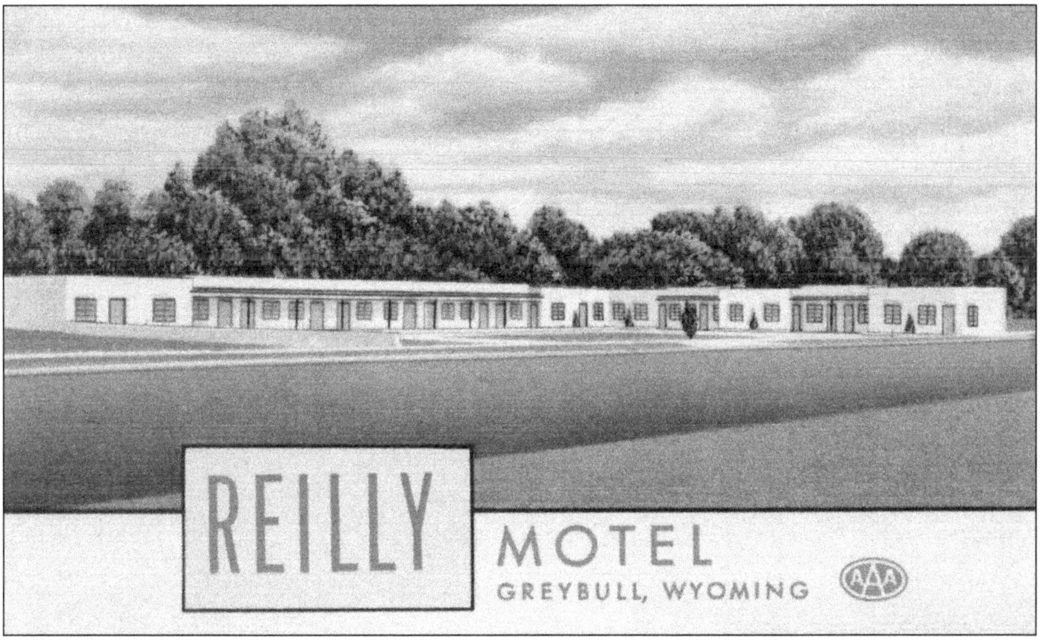

REILLY MOTEL, GREYBULL, WYOMING. Although located three blocks from US 20, the owner took advantage of the highway's popularity by featuring it prominently in the caption on the back of the card. The motel contained 21 strictly modern units, some with tub and shower combinations, vented wall heaters, and innerspring mattresses. The sender of this card wrote that her family of three had occupied Cabin 14 at a cost of $8.50.

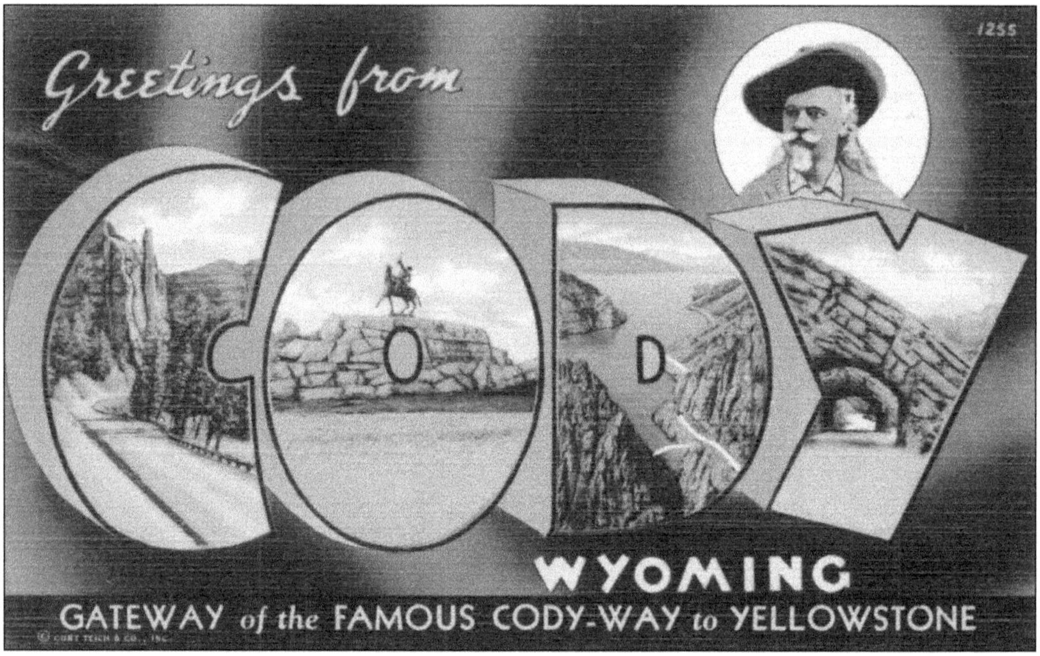

Greetings from Cody Wyoming. Cody had a population of approximately 2,200 during the period covered in this book. For those arriving from the east, it was the closest town to Yellowstone National Park, offering many tourist accommodations, restaurants, and shopping. The card emphasizes the warm greeting that Cody extended to visitors. Each of the scenes on the card is featured in more detail later in the chapter.

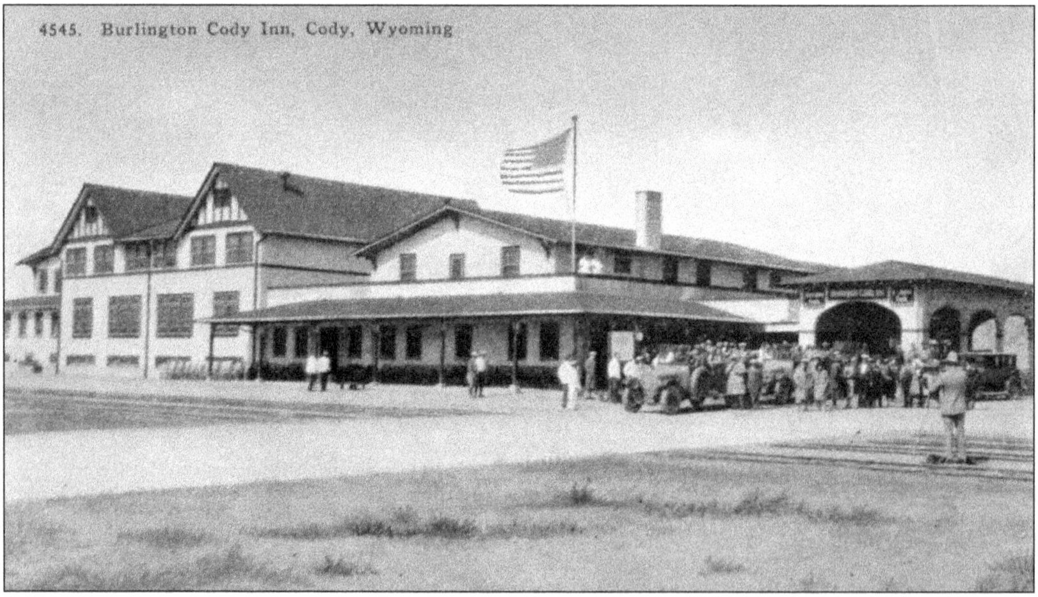

Cody Inn, Cody. This inn contributed greatly to the early success of Cody. Located adjacent to the Chicago, Burlington and Quincy Railroad Depot two miles north of town, it was popular with tourists when Cody was the railroad's western terminus. The inn could accommodate 400 to 500 guests in spacious, comfortable rooms. Guests received first-class service in the restaurants and Shoshone Lounge. The Cody Inn was torn down in 1947.

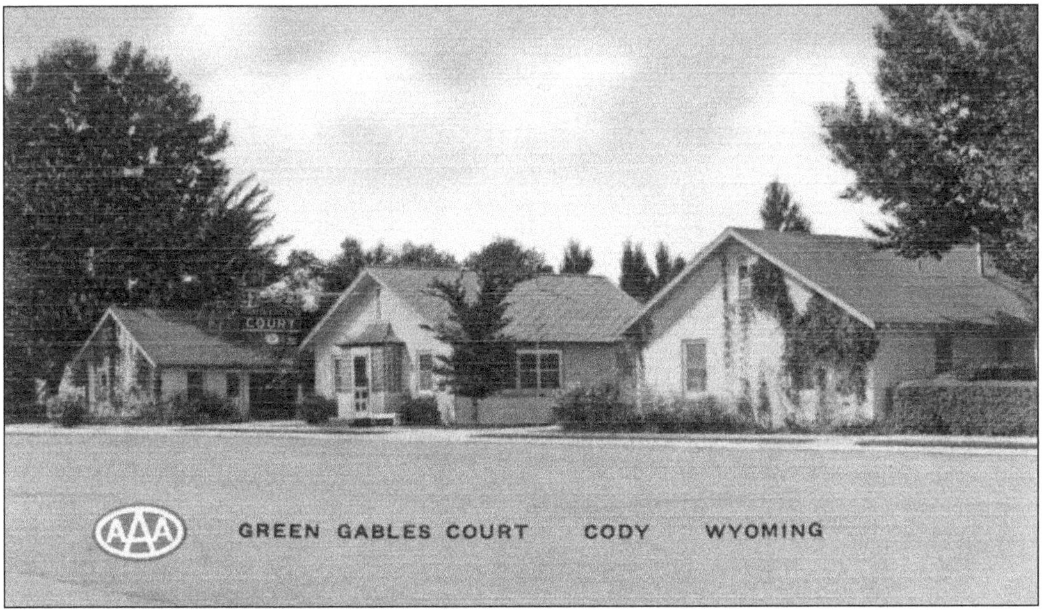

Green Gables Court, Highways 14 and 20, Cody. Guests of the Green Gables were greeted with frontier vernacular on the back of the card: "Howdy, stranger! Hankerin' for some western hospitality? We're rigged out with A-1 fixings, topnotch sleeping and a flower garden for your sitting pleasure. Hold your horses when you get to Cody." The court's comfortable, furnished rooms, all with private baths, were offered at reasonable rates.

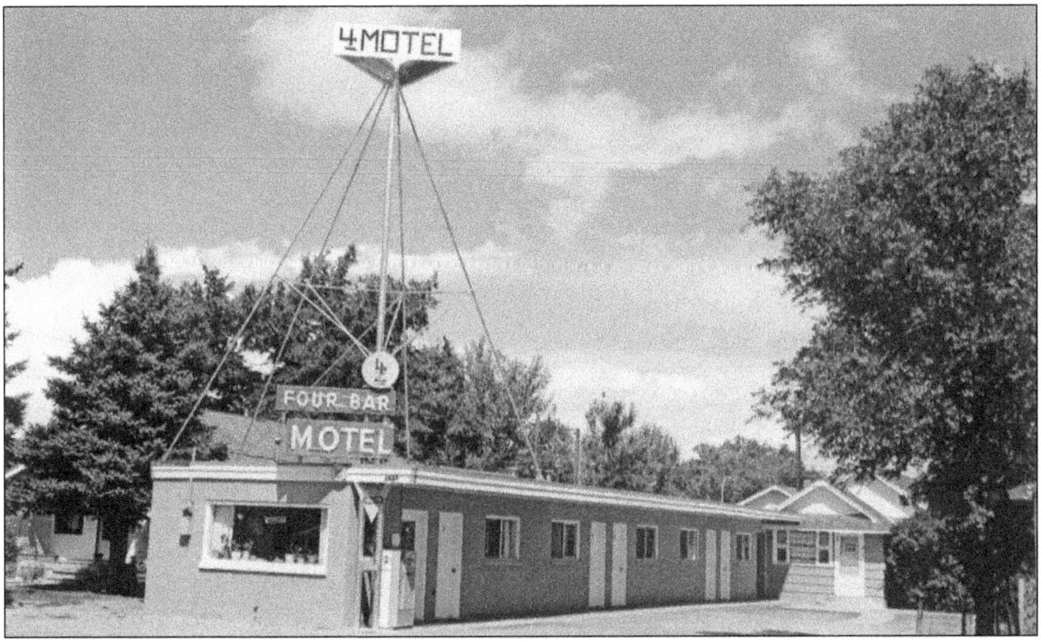

Four Bar Motel, 1637 Alger Avenue, Cody. Western names were frequently attached to local establishments. The owners of the Four Bar Motel chose a typical cattle brand to identify their business. This motel was located close to Highways 14, 16, and 20, and its tall sign was visible to travelers on each of those highways. The motel catered to family vacationers and featured larger units to accommodate multiple guests.

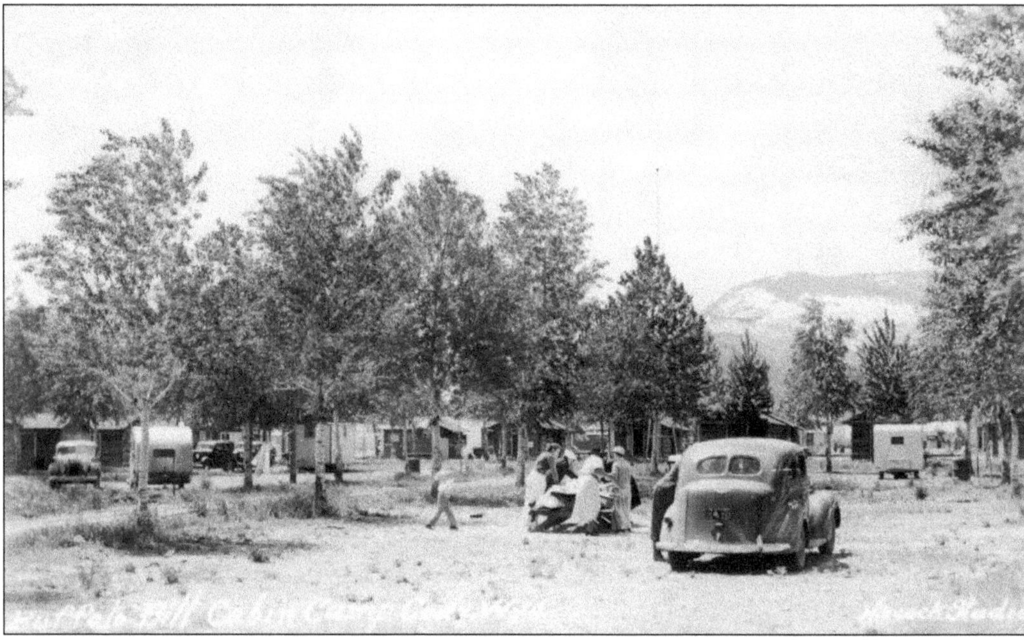

BUFFALO BILL COURT, 1701 SHERIDAN AVENUE, CODY. The Buffalo Bill Court was one of Cody's larger facilities and was a busy place when this photograph was taken in the mid-1930s. Tourists had arrived in automobiles, some pulling vintage house trailers, while others were using tents or making camp in the cabins. In addition to overnight accommodations, the court's gift shop featured curios, Indian jewelry, moccasins, and other local handicrafts.

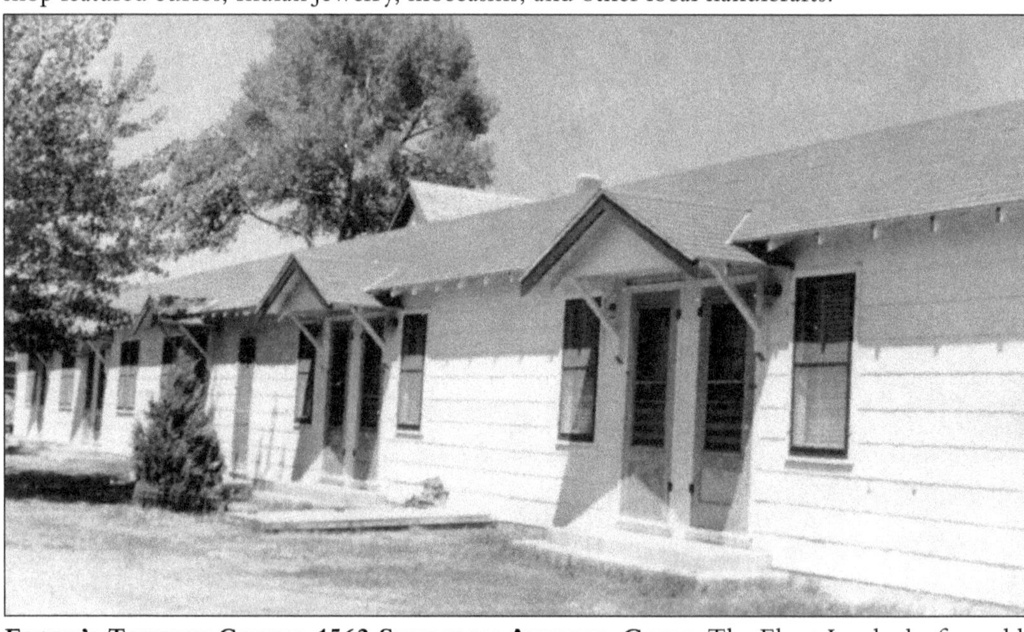

EBERT'S TOURIST COURT, 1562 SHERIDAN AVENUE, CODY. The Ebert Inn had a favorable location near the eastern end of Sheridan Avenue. It would have been one of the first tourist courts that motorists could choose as they entered the town from the east. Its location directly on Highways 14 and 20 ensured a steady flow of customers on their way to Yellowstone National Park.

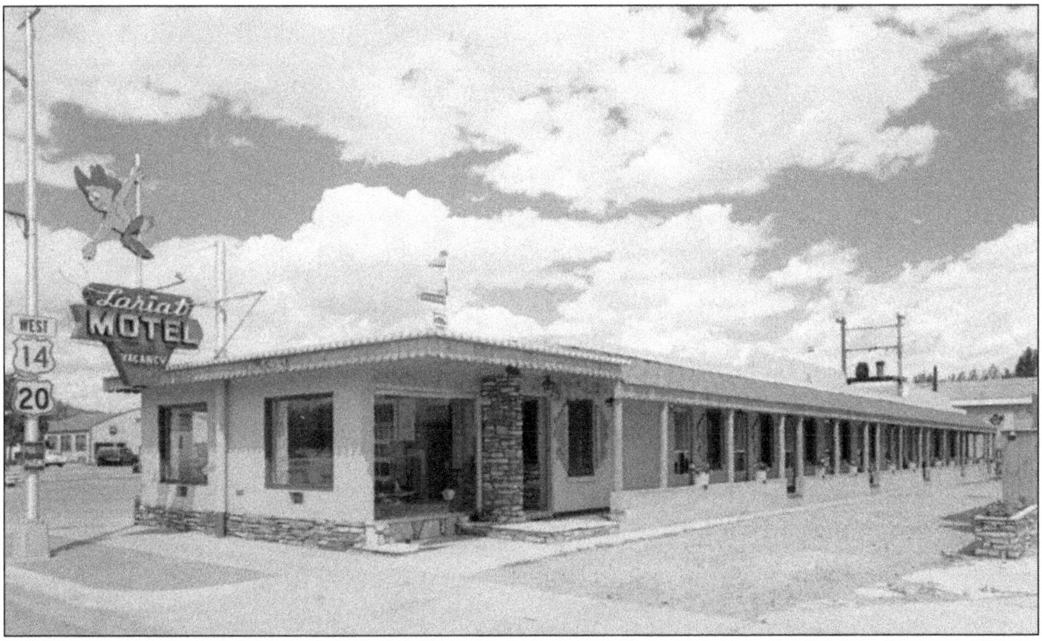

Lariat Motel, 1535 Sheridan Avenue, Cody. The US 20 shield on the left side of the card shows that this motel was located directly on historic Highway 20. The Lariat was more modest than some of other accommodations in Cody, but nonetheless it offered modern rooms, controlled heat, and wall-to-wall carpets. An early perk was a free radio, which was included in each unit.

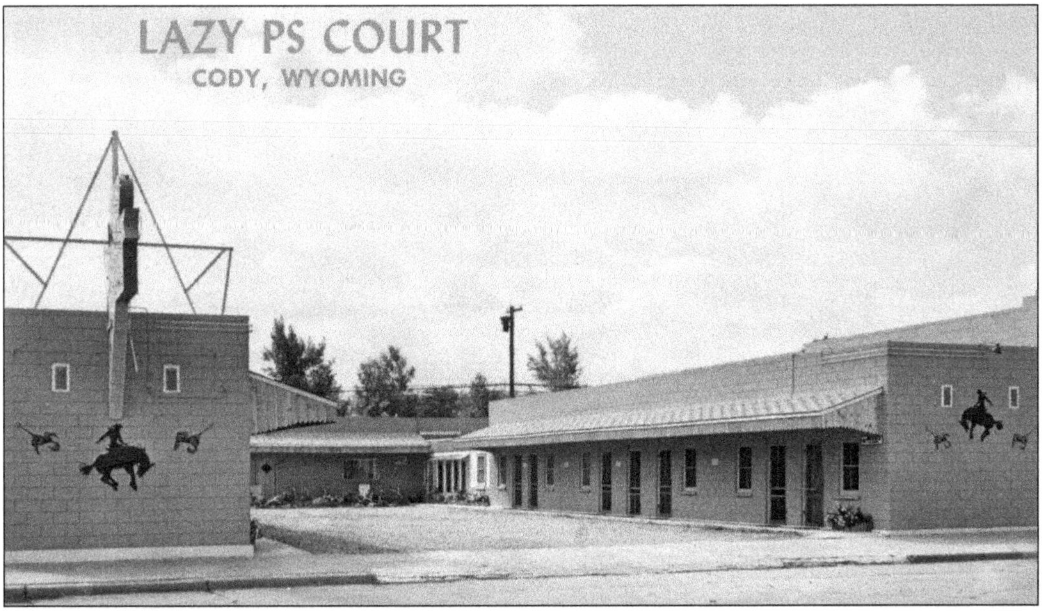

Lazy PS Court, 1456 Sheridan Avenue, Cody. Historic US 20 followed Sheridan Avenue through downtown Cody, where many of the early motels in the community were located. The Lazy PS Court offered 14 strictly modern units close to the business district and the tourist attractions in the city. The unique name Lazy PS probably was an indication owner Pete Shultz's sense of humor.

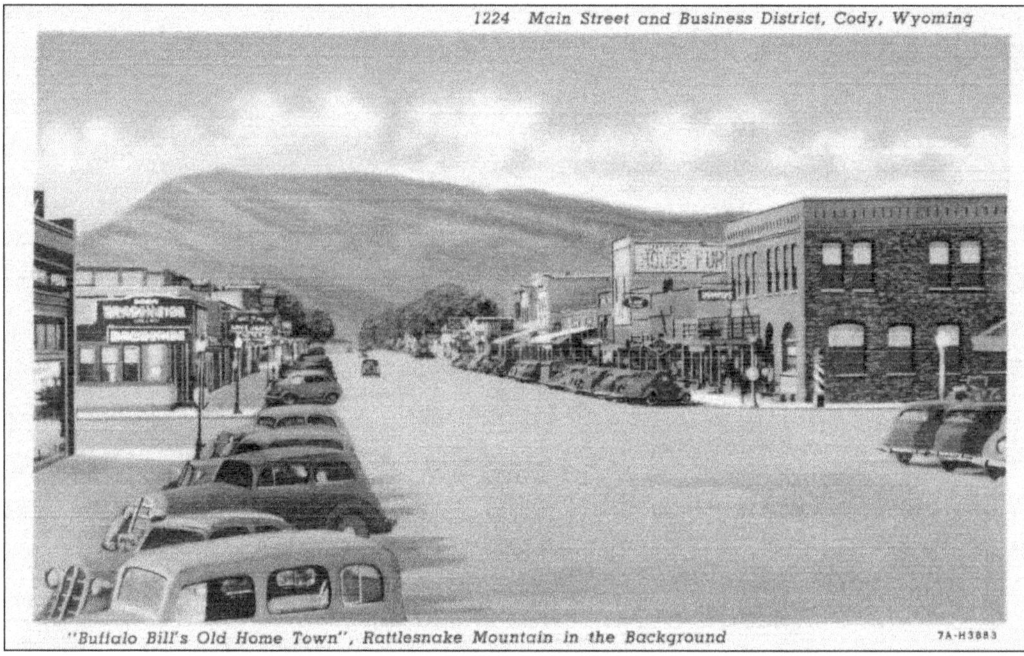

SHERIDAN AVENUE, CODY. For most towns on the road leading to Yellowstone National Park, the period from 1930 to 1950 was a time of evolution, most often illustrated on their main streets. Such was the case in Cody. The 1930s card above shows the street when Highway 20 was in its infancy. Cars line the street, but many tourists still would have arrived by train. In the 1950s view below, trains were no longer a factor and cars are the predominant mode of transportation. Fast-food restaurants and big box stores were many years in the future. Grocery, drug, and clothing stores were main street regulars, as were taverns, restaurants, and hotels. Cody had a larger than average number of stores that featured Western jewelry and attire. Rattlesnake Mountain, at an elevation of 9,116 feet, dominates the background in both images.

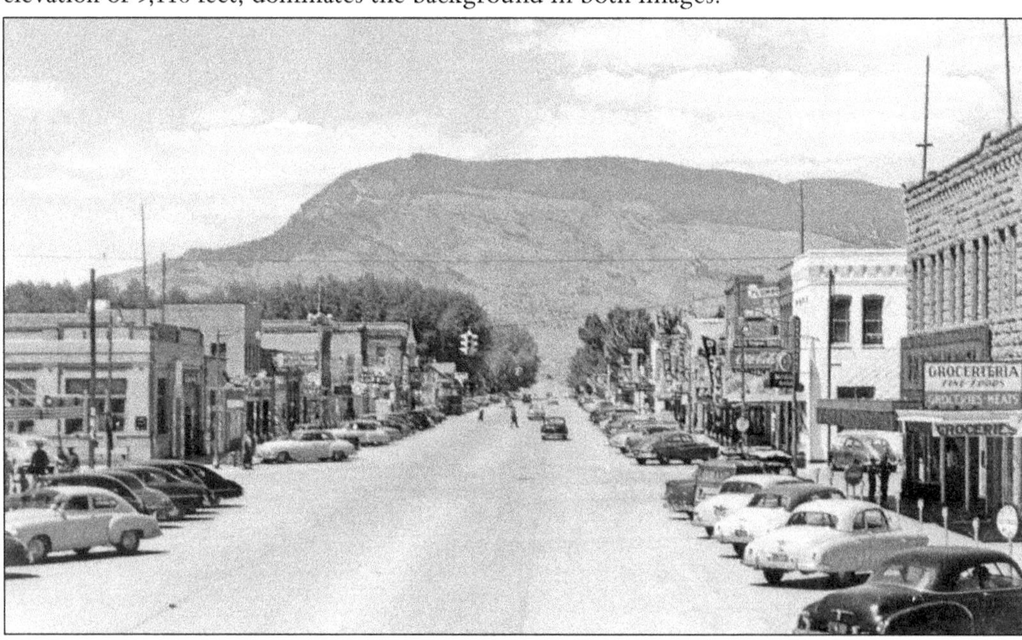

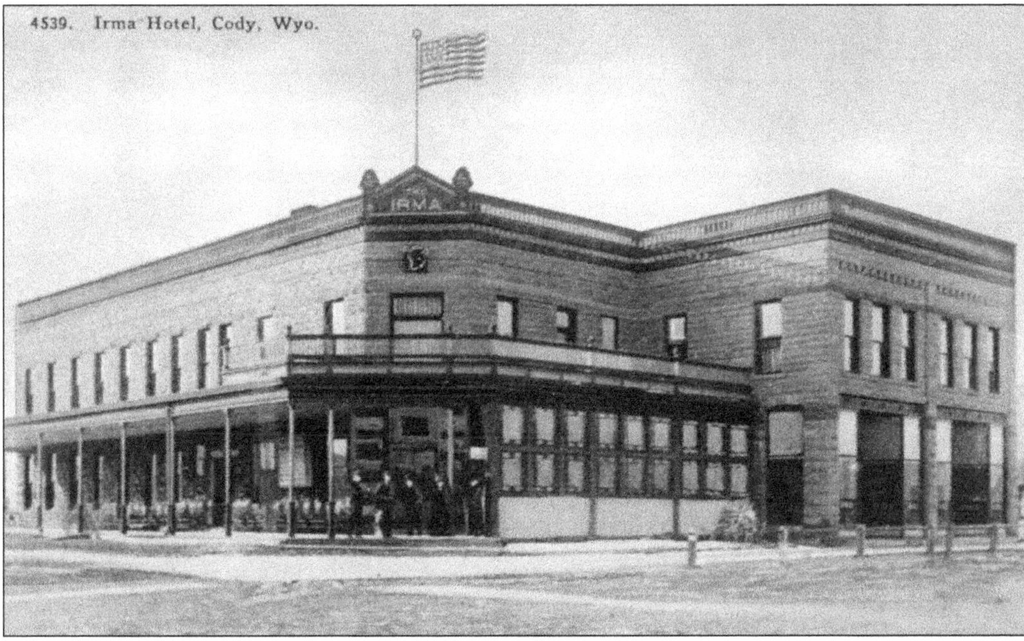

Irma Hotel, 1192 Sheridan Avenue, Cody. The Irma Hotel was built in 1902 by Buffalo Bill Cody and named after his daughter. He called it "the sweetest hotel that ever was." Two suites and an office were reserved for his personal use. It was constructed of river rock and sandstone quarried in nearby areas. The Irma was one of three facilities Buffalo Bill established to accommodate travelers to Yellowstone Park.

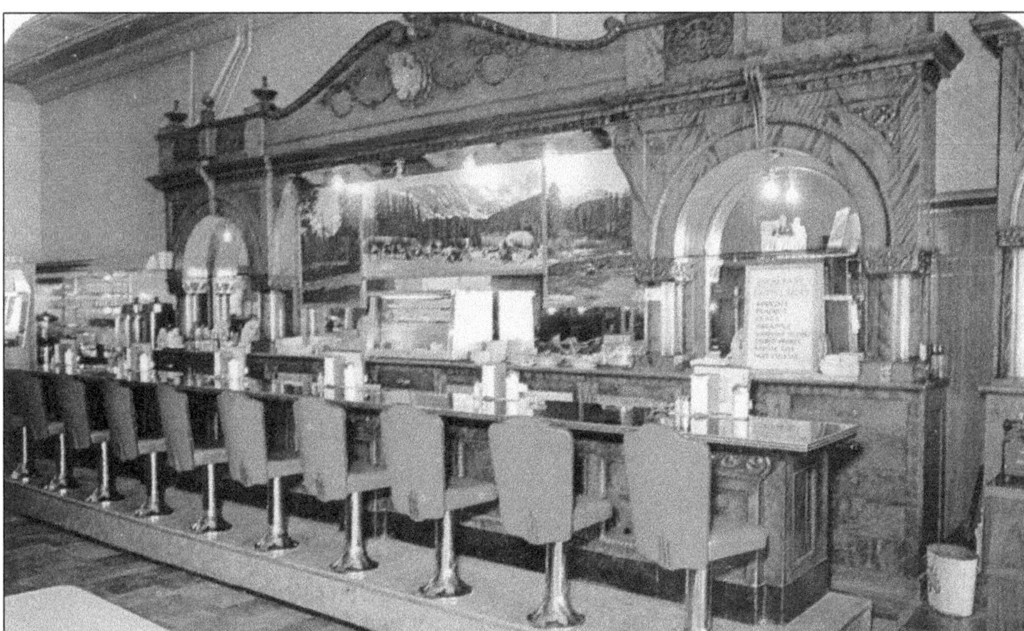

Irma Grill, 1192 Sheridan Avenue, Cody. The ornate cherry wood back bar shown on this postcard is original to the Irma Hotel. It was installed during the construction of the hotel in 1902. This room is reputed to be one of the most photographed locations in all of Cody.

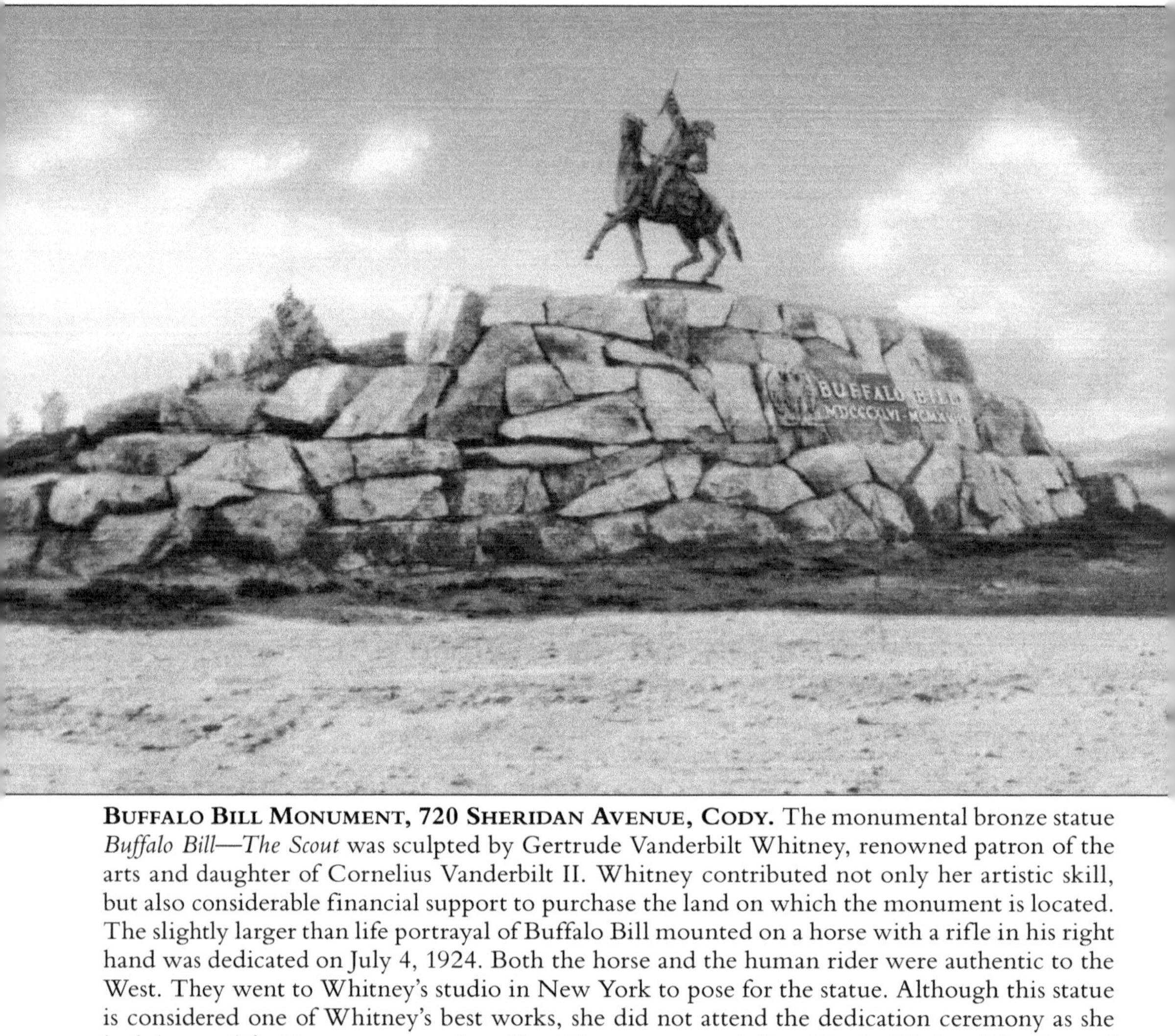

BUFFALO BILL MONUMENT, 720 SHERIDAN AVENUE, CODY. The monumental bronze statue *Buffalo Bill—The Scout* was sculpted by Gertrude Vanderbilt Whitney, renowned patron of the arts and daughter of Cornelius Vanderbilt II. Whitney contributed not only her artistic skill, but also considerable financial support to purchase the land on which the monument is located. The slightly larger than life portrayal of Buffalo Bill mounted on a horse with a rifle in his right hand was dedicated on July 4, 1924. Both the horse and the human rider were authentic to the West. They went to Whitney's studio in New York to pose for the statue. Although this statue is considered one of Whitney's best works, she did not attend the dedication ceremony as she had departed for Europe one week earlier. The monument is listed in the National Register of Historic Places.

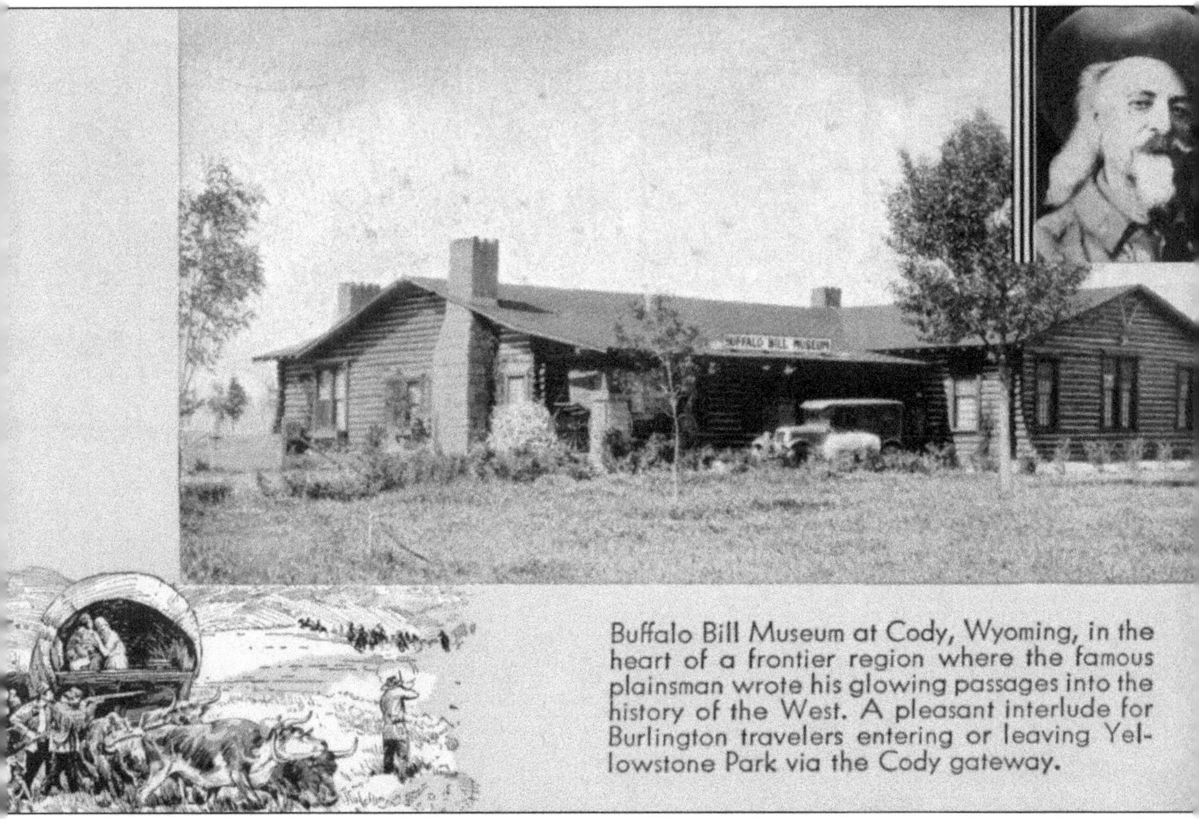

BUFFALO BILL MUSEUM, 720 SHERIDAN AVENUE, CODY. The Burlington Northern Railroad was a major promoter of tourism along its routes, especially in the Yellowstone National Park region. This postcard features the Buffalo Bill Museum in Cody. Buffalo Bill, a consummate entrepreneur, had been influential in bringing the railroad to Cody, which was a starting point for many tours to the park. Buffalo Bill recognized the area's potential for tourism and built its first hotel, the Irma, as well as two lodges on the road to Yellowstone. The museum shown on this card is a replica of the main building on Buffalo Bill's old ranch home. The museum was dedicated on July 4, 1927, where relics of the frontiersman were preserved, including a priceless collection of trophies and mementos depicting the life and exploits of the famous scout, hunter, and rider for the Pony Express. The museum has now been expanded into the much larger and more complete Buffalo Bill Center of the West.

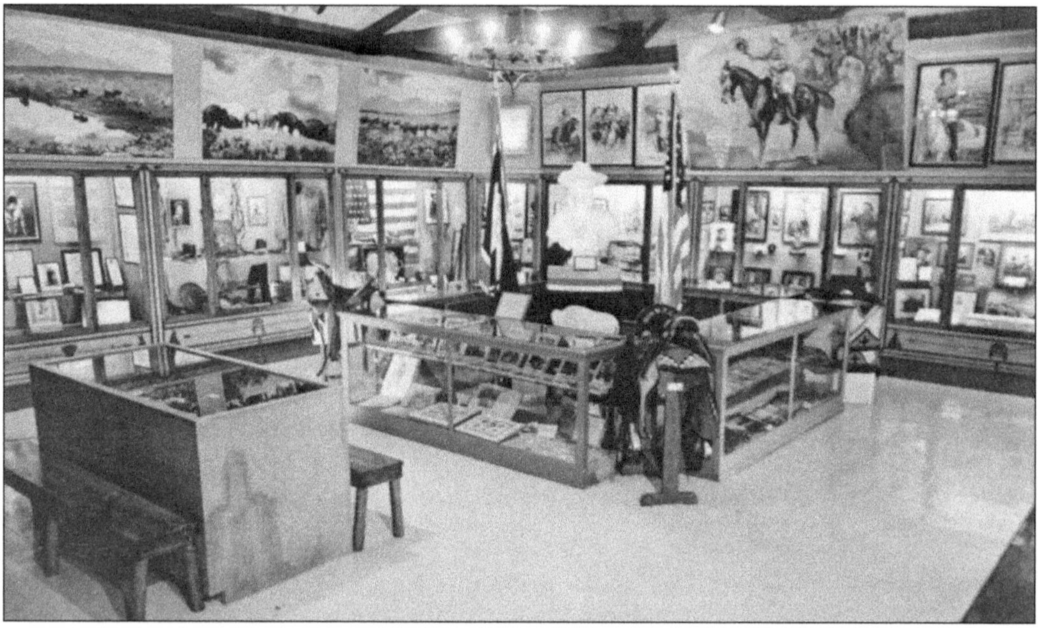

Trophy Room, Buffalo Bill Museum, Cody. Various rooms throughout the museum house artifacts collected by Buffalo Bill himself, and many were later donated to the museum in his memory. Some exhibits are from his national and world travels, whereas others are more local, including examples of Native American arts and crafts and wild game animals. Paintings illustrating Western life are contained in this room.

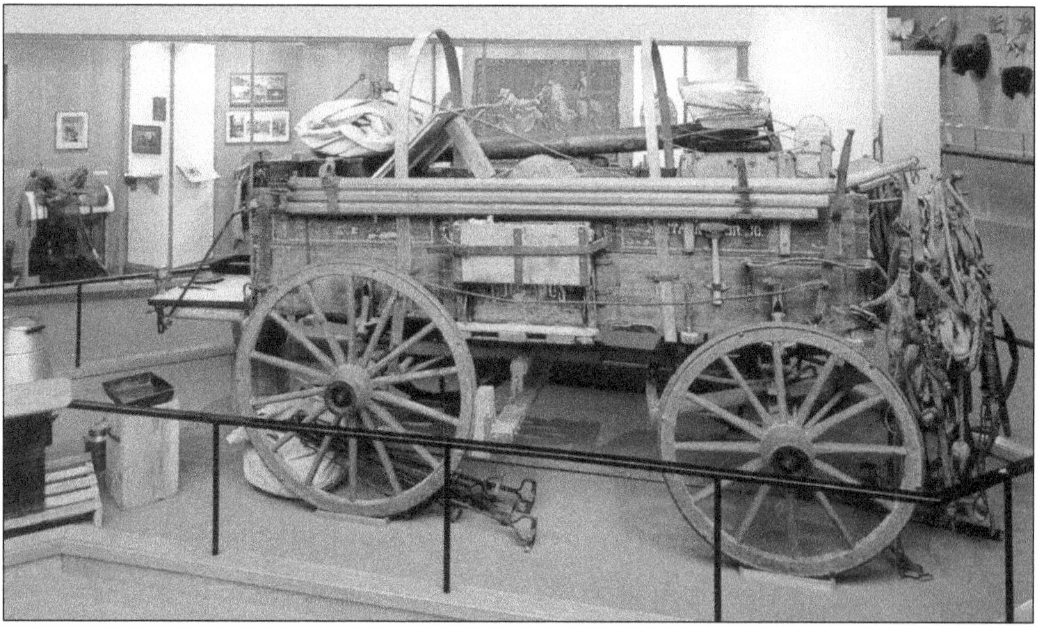

Mess and Roundup Wagon, Buffalo Bill Museum, Cody. The caption on this card describes the mess and roundup wagon as a cowboy's home away from home. The contents included a complete kitchen capable of feeding three meals a day to hungry cowboys. Note the branding irons, ropes, and other equipment needed to handle cattle at roundup time or on a long drive. The canvas top could be raised in inclement weather.

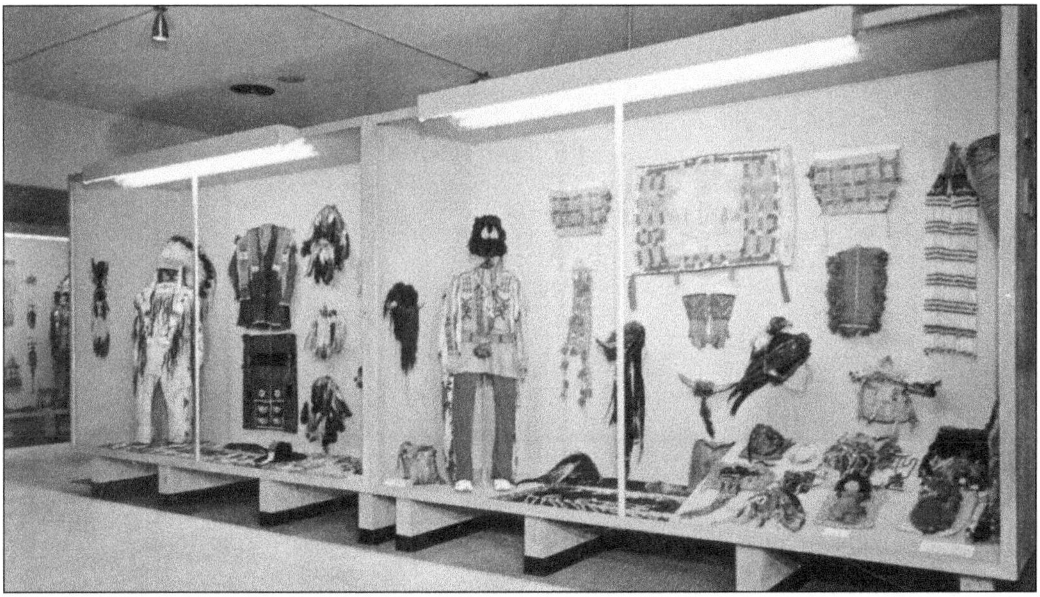

PLAINS INDIAN REGALIA, WHITNEY GALLERY OF WESTERN ART, CODY. The dedication of the bronze statue *Buffalo Bill—The Scout* in 1924 led to the formation of the Whitney Gallery that over the years has become a major component of the Buffalo Bill Center of the West. Officially established in 1959, the Whitney Gallery exhibits a large collection of Western art and regalia typical of the Native American tribes indigenous to the area.

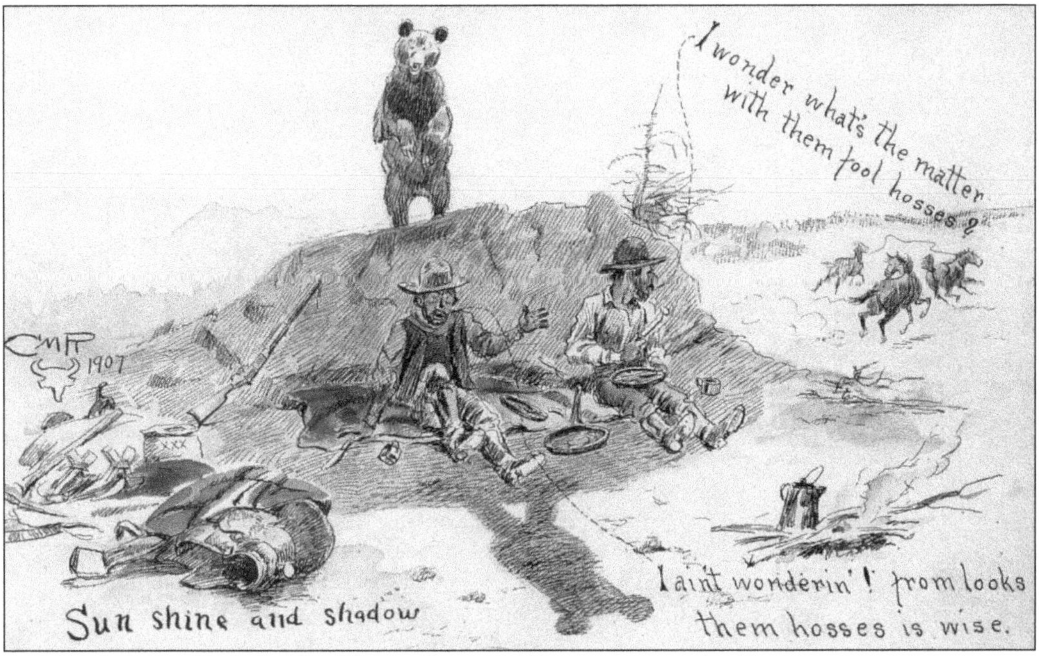

***SUNSHINE AND SHADOW*, WHITNEY GALLERY OF WESTERN ART, CODY.** Artist Charles M. Russell completed the original watercolor painting in 1907 from which this postcard was made. It was a gift to the Whitney Gallery from the Charles Ulrick and Josephine Bay Foundation, Inc. The horses were far ahead of the cowboys in recognizing the shadow of the huge bear looming over them.

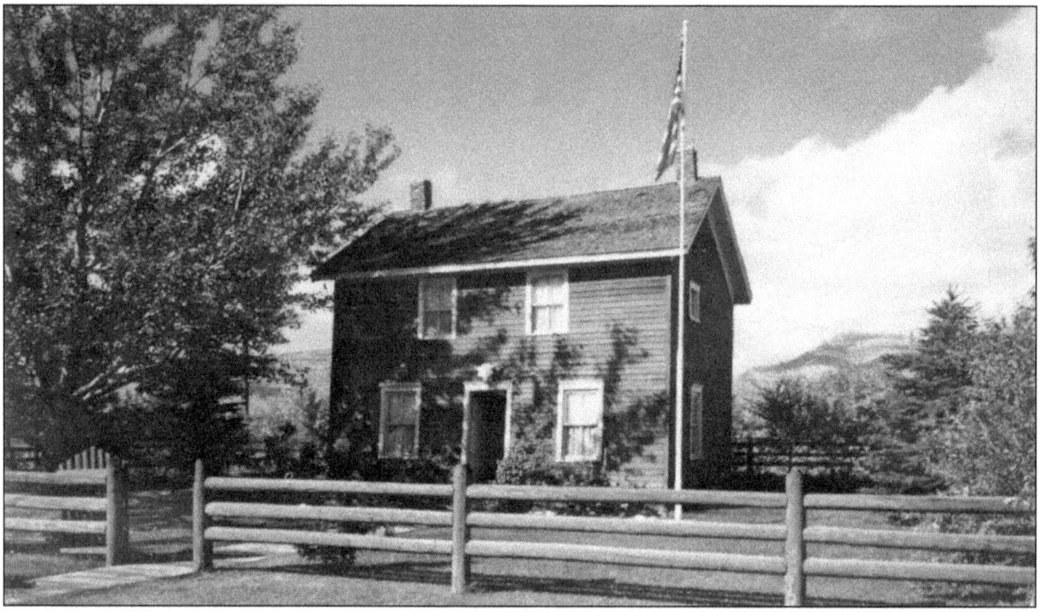

BUFFALO BILL'S BOYHOOD HOME, BUFFALO BILL MUSEUM, CODY. This house, where William Cody spent his early years, was built by his father in 1841. The Burlington Railroad moved the house from LeClaire, Iowa, to Cody in 1933, where it was a tourist attraction adjacent to the railroad's Cody Inn. The house was relocated to the Buffalo Bill Museum in 1947 and is reputed to be the oldest house in Cody.

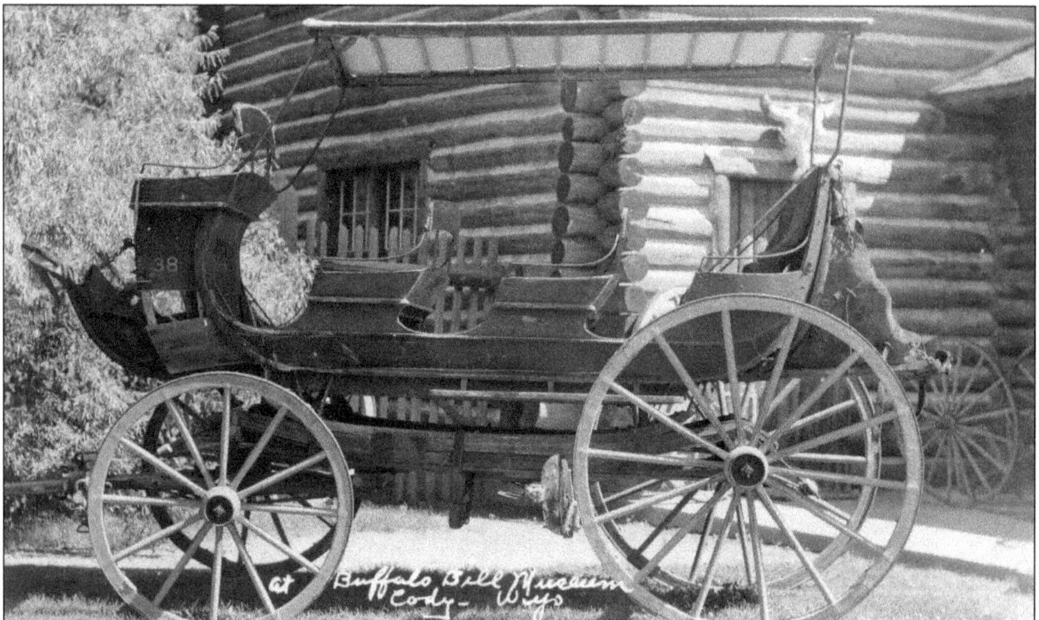

THREE-SEAT CARRIAGE, BUFFALO BILL MUSEUM, CODY. Before the arrival of automobiles, the primary means of transportation in Cody and the vicinity were open carriages pulled by horses. Carriages such as the one shown here conveyed visitors between the Burlington Railroad depot and the various hotels throughout the town. Closed stagecoaches offering protection from the weather were used for persons traveling on to Yellowstone National Park.

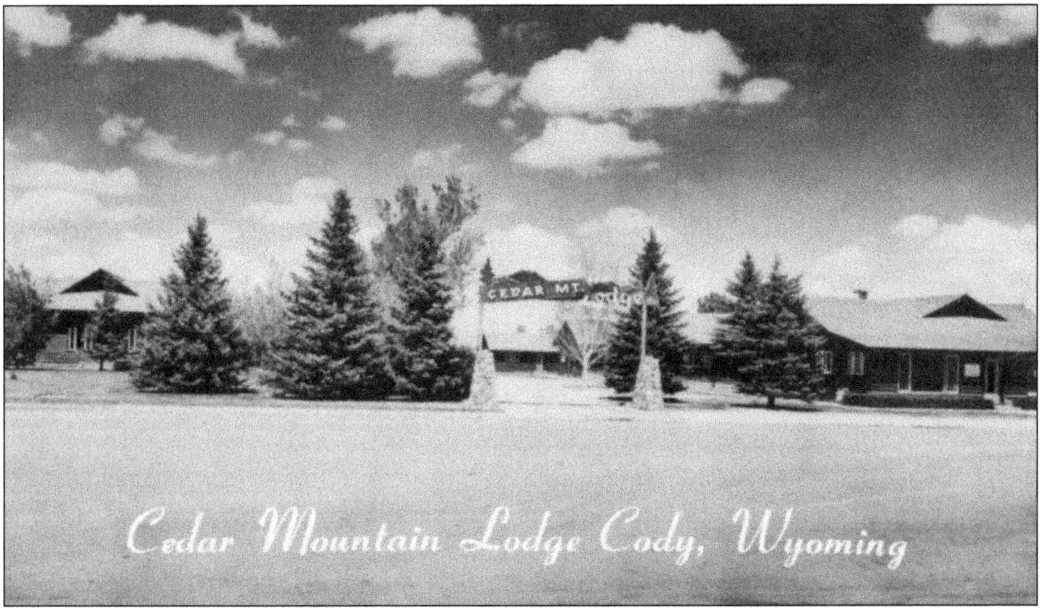

CEDAR MOUNTAIN LODGE, CODY. The address printed on the back of this card is simply "on Highways 14 and 20 across from the Buffalo Bill Museum." This ideal location close to downtown stores and restaurants, along with the attractive grounds, no doubt was inviting to travelers visiting Cody or on their way to Yellowstone National Park.

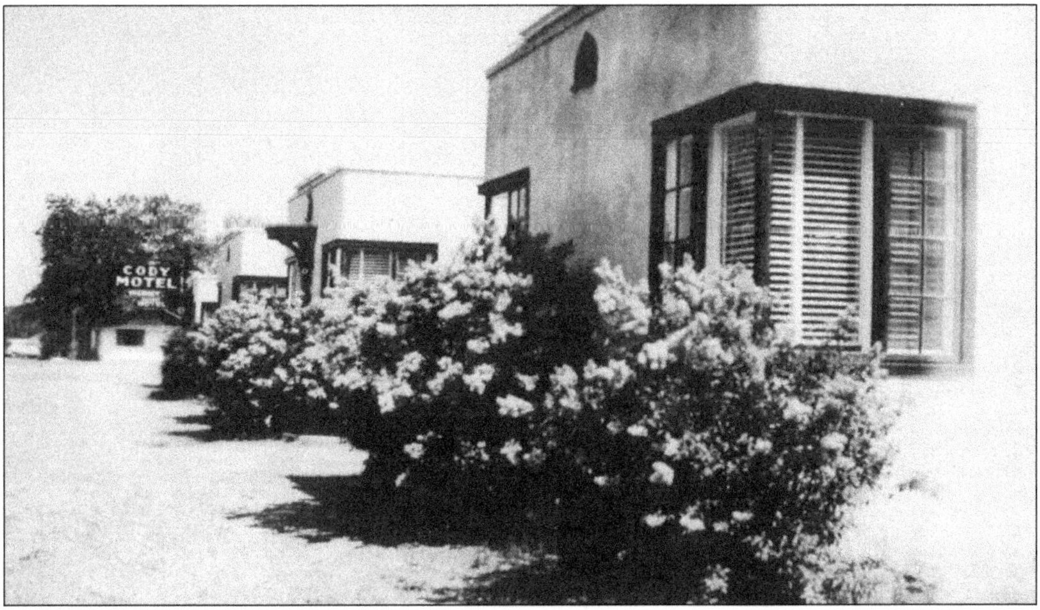

CODY MOTEL, HIGHWAYS 14 AND 20, CODY. This motel was newer than many of the other motels and cabin courts in Cody. Its Art Deco architectural style was popular during the 1920s–1940s. All units appear to have followed the same basic design. The windows forming the corners were indicative of the times. The back of the card described the motel simply as "modern and reasonable." A specific address was not provided.

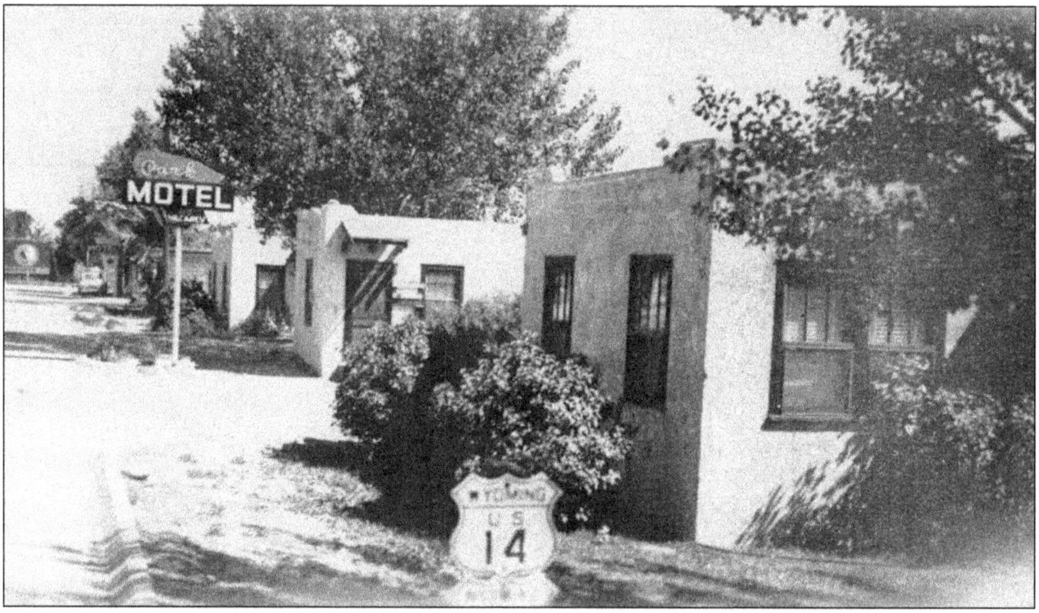

PARK MOTEL, HIGHWAYS 14 AND 20, CODY. The Park Motel appears similar to the motel in the previous photograph with the exception that the windows were not placed in the corners. The Highway 20 shield is below the Highway 14 shield in the center. The sender of this card explained to her friend, "We're staying here tonight and will be in Yellowstone tomorrow."

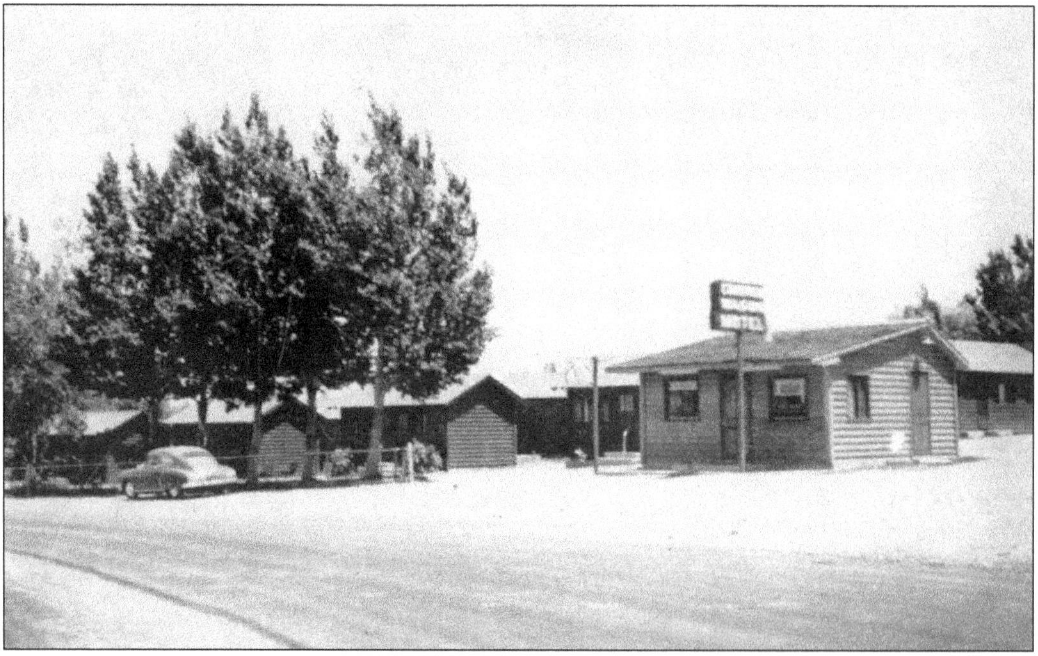

COVERED WAGON MOTEL, HIGHWAYS 14 AND 20, WEST CODY. This log cabin motel was one of the last tourist accommodations before travelers began the 53-mile drive to Yellowstone National Park. The motel was given a four-star rating by the American Travel Association. Sixteen one- and two-bedroom cabins were available at reasonable rates.

Five

Cody Highway

The road between Cody, Wyoming, and the east entrance to Yellowstone National Park deserves a special chapter even though it is entirely contained within Park County. Cody Highway, alternately called Cody Road, is named in honor of Buffalo Bill Cody. It opened in 1903 and in 1926 was incorporated into Federal Highway 20. Once described by Theodore Roosevelt as the 50 most scenic miles in America, the natural beauty and geologic features along its course are awe-inspiring. Travelers are struck by unique rock formations, broad canyons, sparking streams, and magnificent forests. Although each of the park's other four entrances present compelling views, the eastern portal lives up to its original slogan, "You don't see Yellowstone Park if you don't see Cody Road."

This unique highway has been blessed with many superlatives since it opened to motorized travel, but early pioneers were not so complementary. The river, which Cody Road follows through the canyon, was named Stinking Water in 1807 due to the sulfur springs nearby. It carried that name for almost 100 years before being officially pronounced the Shoshone River by the Wyoming Legislature, with the concurrence of the US Board of Geographic Names. The river is now called Shoshone, and the odors have been largely controlled. West of Cody, the road goes through a geyser basin and passes the largest geyser cone in the world. Since 1912, visitors have been treated to views of the Buffalo Bill Dam and Reservoir (originally named the Shoshone Dam and Reservoir) and the Shoshone National Forest, designated in 1891 as the first national forest in the United States.

Cody Highway is an engineering masterpiece, carved from solid rock on high cliffs and requiring the crossing of the Shoshone River and lesser creeks in the valleys below. In several places, passage was attained by boring tunnels though sold granite walls. Tourist lodges designed to accommodate visitors on their way to Yellowstone National Park sprang up along Cody Highway almost as soon as it opened. The historic Absaroka and Pahaska Tepee Lodges are products of Buffalo Bill's efforts.

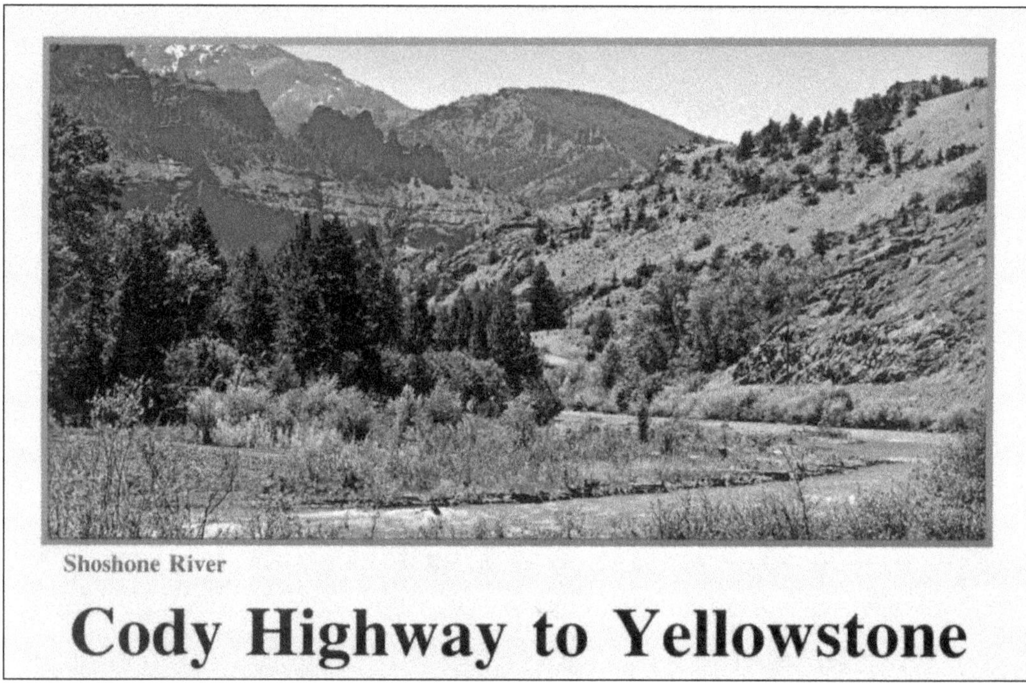

Cody Highway to Yellowstone, Promotional Card. US Highway 20 between Cody and Yellowstone National Park has not only carried the numbering system of federal and state highways, but also a variety of local names. The most popular were Cody Highway, Cody Road, Cody Way, and Buffalo Bill Scenic Byway. No matter what name was applied, the road provided a wealth of memories for motorists who traveled this route.

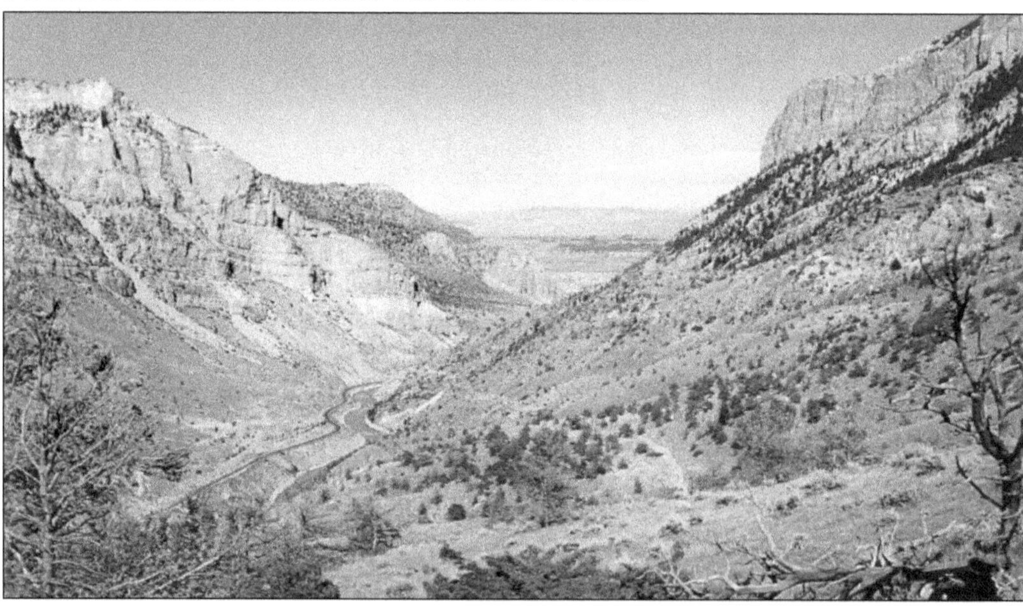

Shoshone Canyon Looking East, Cody Road. Historic Highway 20 and the Shoshone River are both barely visible in the depth of Shoshone Canyon a short distance west of Cody. At this point, the canyon is broad and the walls are more sloping as they ascend from the base. Farther west, the canyon becomes narrower with vertical walls.

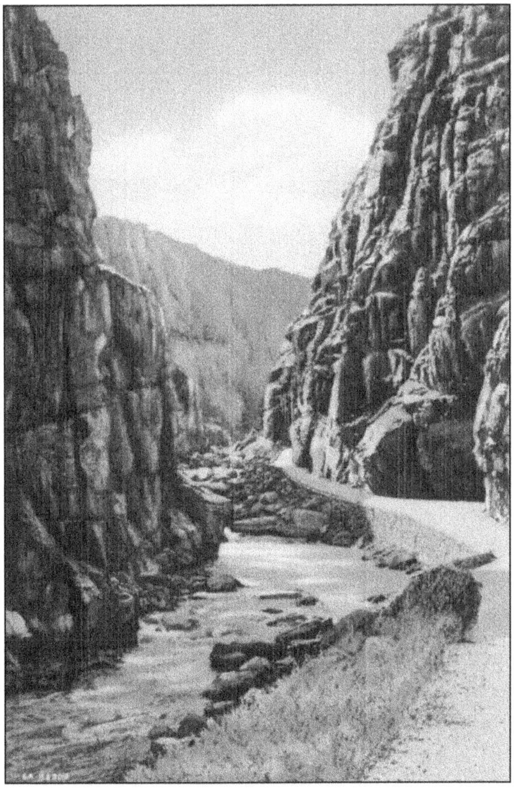

Shoshone Canyon Approaching the Dam from the East, Cody Road. Cody Road follows the course of the Shoshone River from the town of Cody to the Buffalo Bill Dam. Along this seven-mile span, the topography of the canyon changes from the broad expanse of the previous image to a narrow cut at river level. As shown at right, the initial path of the road was adjacent to the river. As the road progressed westward, it continued to follow the river but at a much higher elevation. The card also illustrates the exceptional skill of the surveyors, engineers, and construction workers who planned and built the road. The roadbed was carved out of the solid stone walls several feet above the river, resulting in a thrilling but harrowing drive.

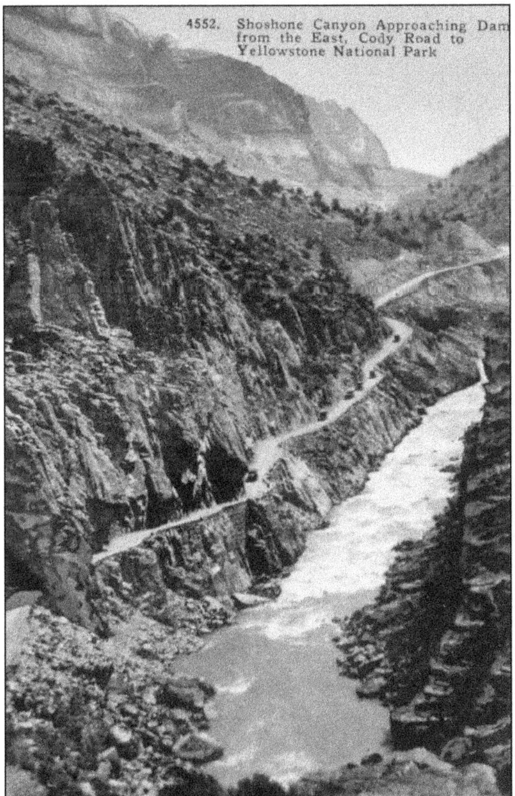

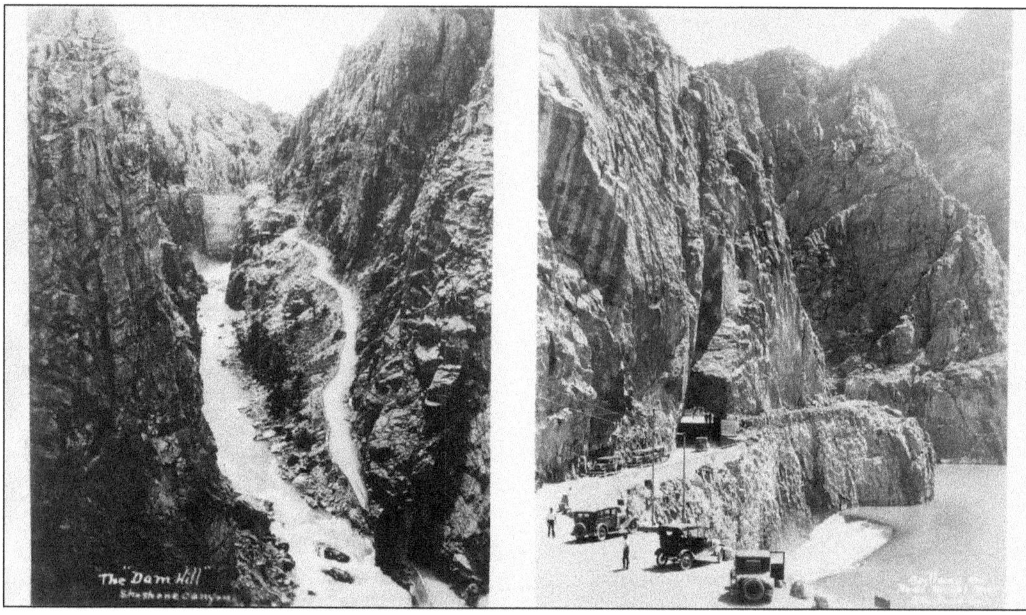

DAM HILL AND SCENIC OVERLOOK, CODY ROAD. Many drivers probably used the expletive form of the word while approaching the Buffalo Bill Dam. A 1930s brochure advised westbound drivers to shift into low gear to climb the hill and eastbound travelers to use low gear to control their speed of descent. The photograph on the right shows one of several overlooks where motorists could view the spectacular scenery.

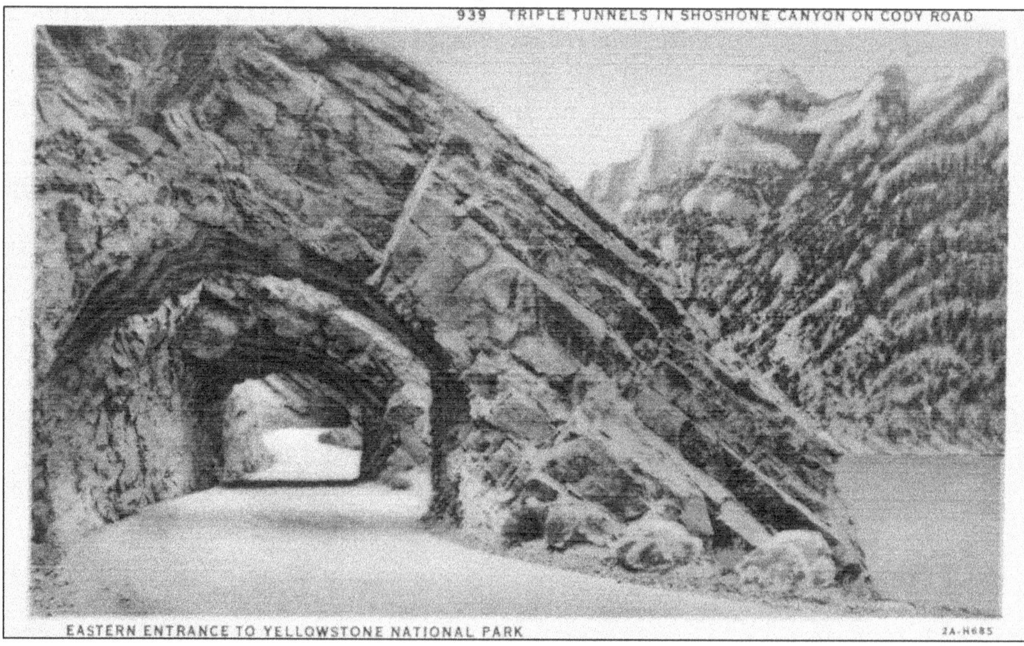

TRIPLE TUNNELS, CODY ROAD. The walls of the mighty gorge through which the Shoshone River passes are nearly perpendicular, and yet along the base of Rattlesnake Mountain a road had been blasted through solid rock, necessitating tunnels in several places. The triple tunnels shown on this card proved to be too narrow for modern traffic and have been removed in favor of a wider roadbed.

Shoshone Dam and Canyon, Cody Road. Shoshone Dam, named the Buffalo Bill Dam in 1946, is located approximately seven miles west of Cody. Construction was begun in 1904 and completed in 1910 at a total cost of $92,658. The dam was 325 feet high, and when completed it was the tallest dam in the world. Its top was 200 feet long and 10 feet thick. The base was 80 feet long and 108 feet thick. Steep steps and a catwalk (right) allowed construction workers and officials to have a close-up view of the front face of the dam. The walkway across the top of the dam (below) enabled inspections and easy communication between the mechanical structures at both abutments. The Buffalo Bill Dam is listed in the National Register of Historic Places.

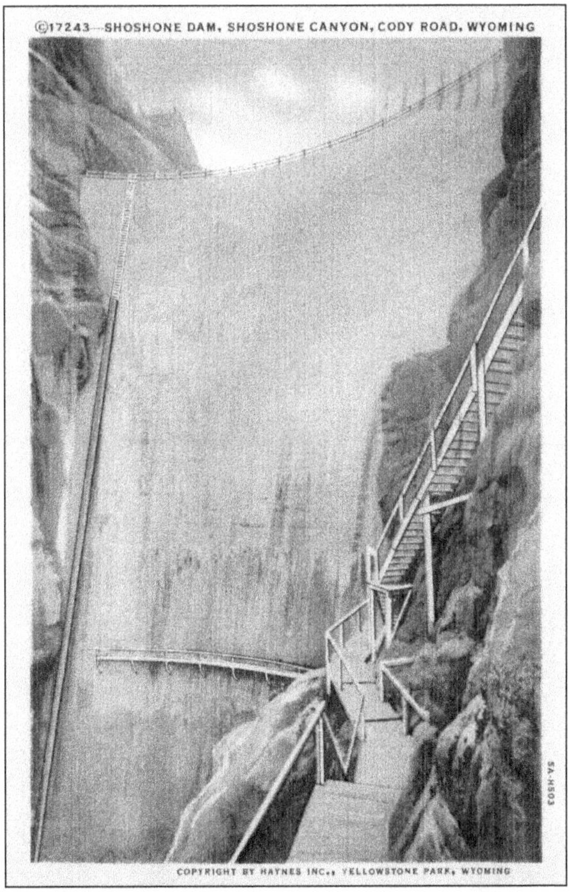

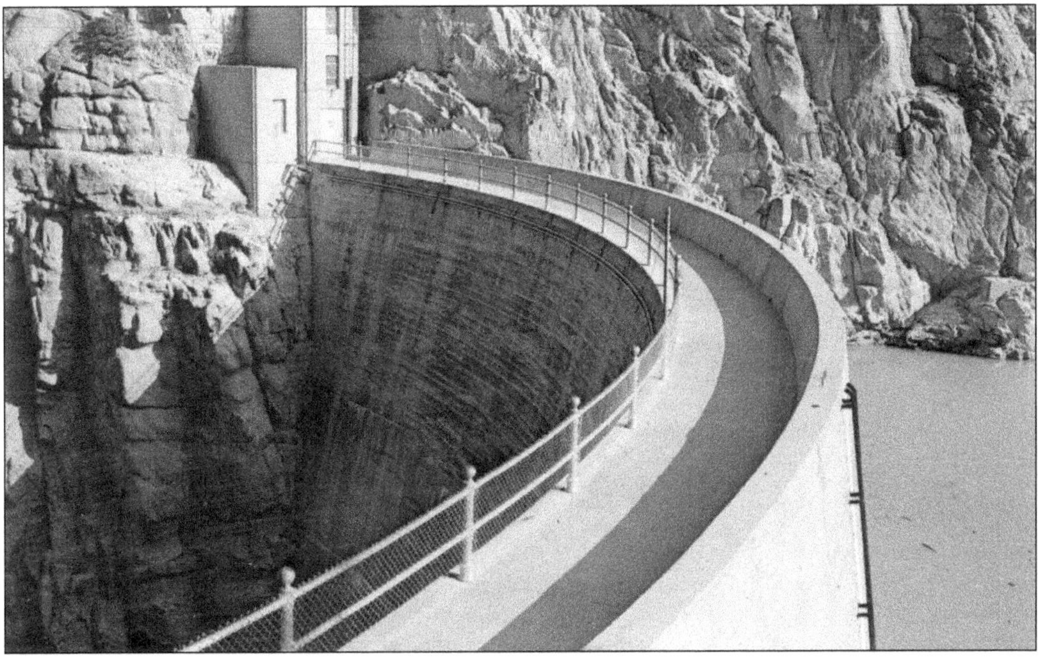

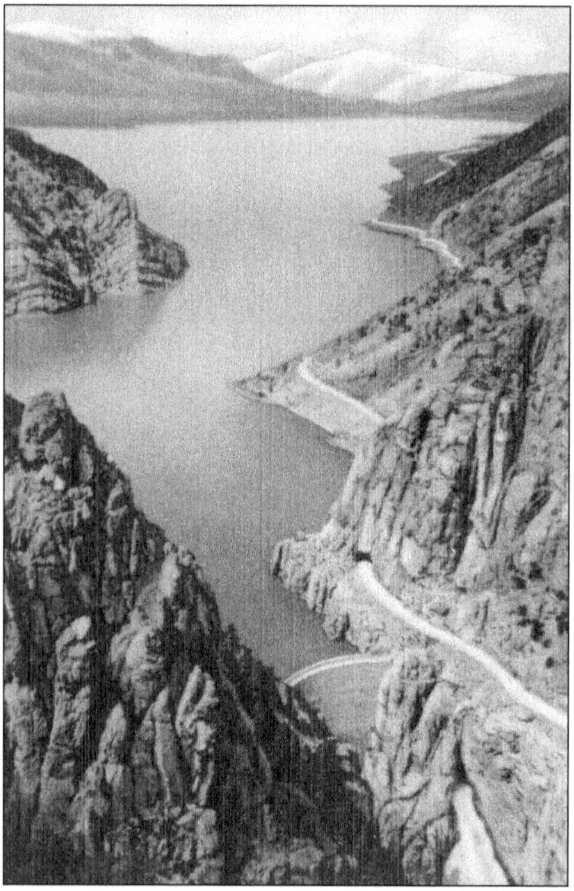

Shoshone Dam and Reservoir, Cody Road. The reservoir extends for more than 10 miles and involves both the North and South Forks of the Shoshone River. The cliffs of Rattlesnake and Cedar Mountains on the north and south sides of Shoshone Canyon dwarf the immense height of the dam. Cody Road clings to the edge of the reservoir through this section of the canyon.

The Wapiti Valley, between Cody and Yellowstone. Cody Road follows the north fork of the Shoshone River through the Wapiti Valley west of the Shoshone Reservoir. Here, the terrain is broad and flat but nonetheless provides outstanding scenery that offers a pleasing contrast to the high cliffs and deep crevices found elsewhere along the highway.

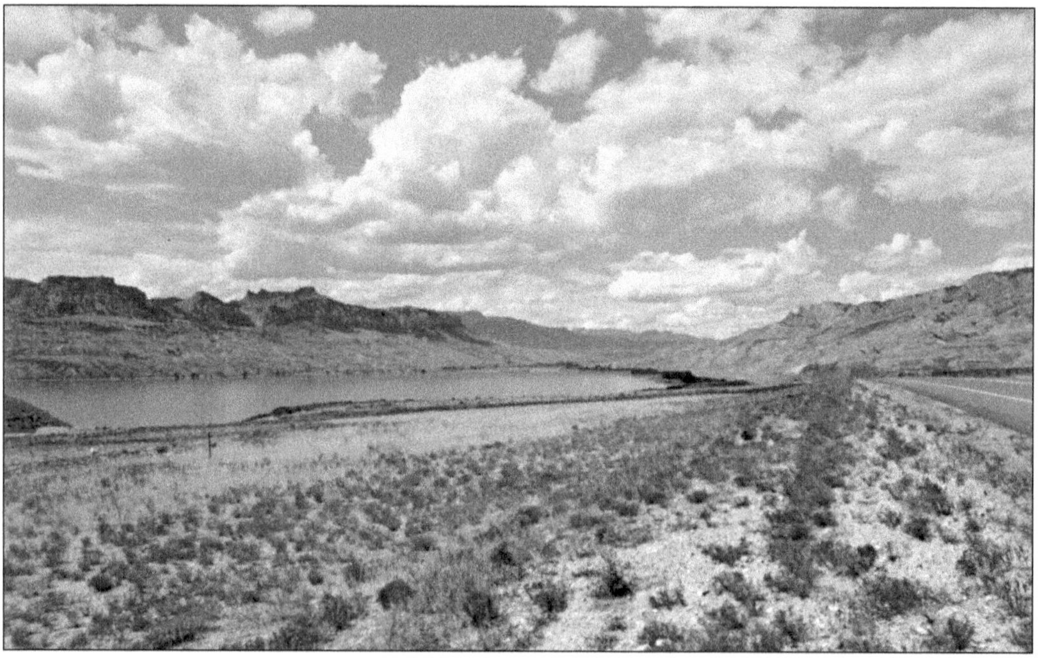

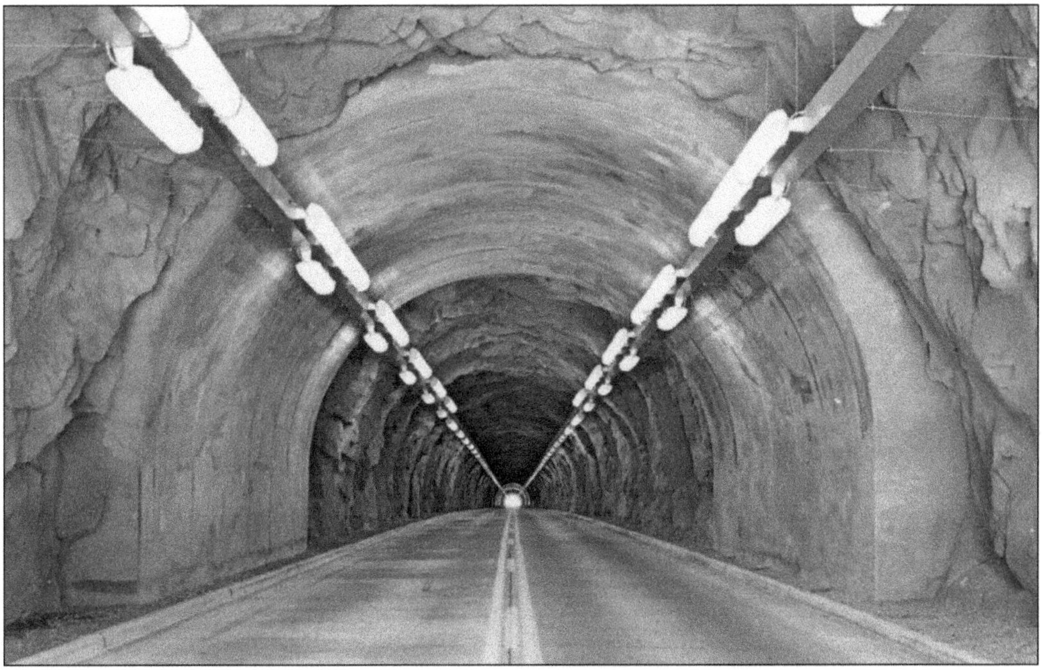

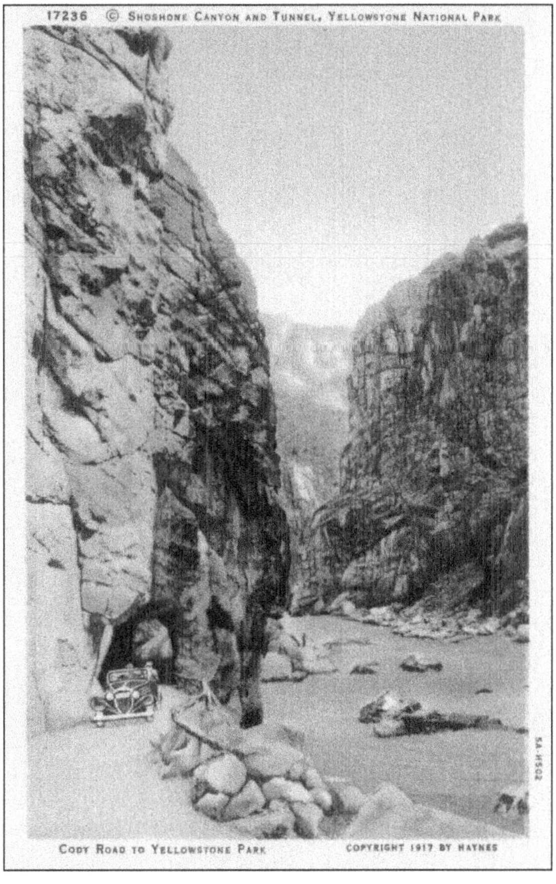

World's Longest Lighted Tunnel, Cody Road. The marvel of Cody Road's engineering is exemplified by the tunnel shown on this card. The granite wall through which the tunnel passed was a major obstacle in opening the highway that enabled visitors coming from the east to have easier access to Yellowstone National Park. The tunnel was three quarters of a mile in length and lighted by electricity. It is still in use.

Cody Road to Yellowstone Park. Early engineers confronted several places along Cody Road where the alternatives were to drill a tunnel or remove the entire face of a cliff to the level of the roadbed. At that time, a tunnel frequently was the most effective solution, both economically and as a means to allow the passage of traffic while not defacing the beauty of the mountain.

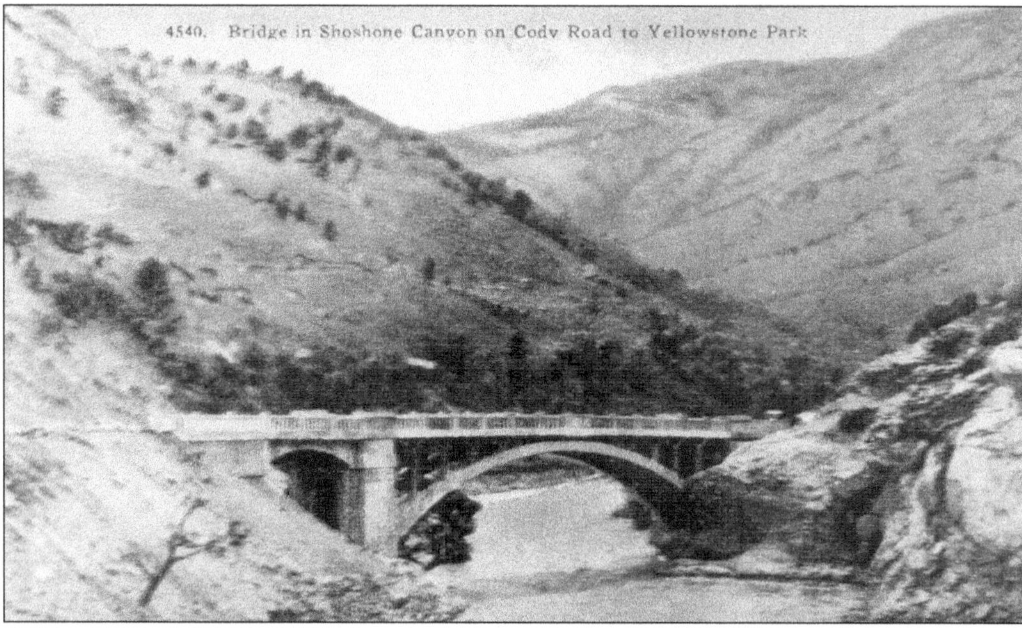

Hayden Arch Bridge in Shoshone Canyon, Cody Road. This bridge was completed in 1925 and is still standing. Special attention was given to safeguard travelers on their way to Yellowstone National Park. Several crossings of the Shoshone River and lesser streams were required during construction of Cody Road. The philosophy of the engineers was straightforward: "Where bridges are necessary they must be the finest that can be constructed."

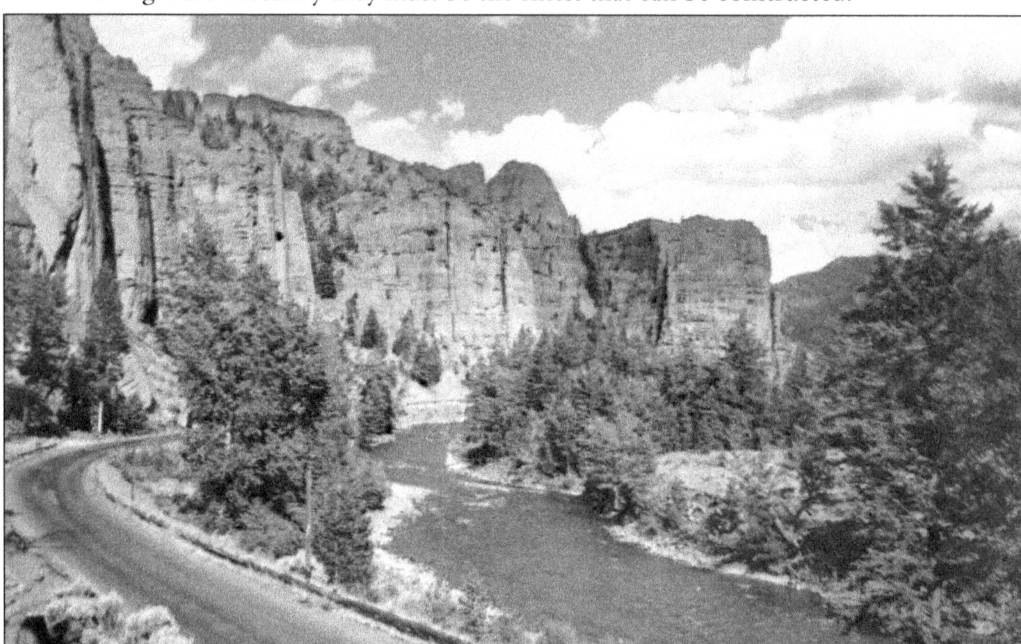

North Fork, Shoshone River, Cody Road. Scenes such as this were frequent as motorists drove along historic Highway 20 between Cody and Yellowstone National Park. The combination of towering mountain cliffs, a pristine mountain stream, and lush vegetation gave ample evidence of the claim that Cody Road traversed the 50 most scenic miles in the country.

Box Canyon, Cody Road. This linen postcard is from the 1940s and shows how another challenge met by the engineers was surmounted. The caption on the back states that construction of the road at this point required the base of the cut to be blasted through solid granite to establish the roadbed between the cliffs. It is estimated that the construction cost was $100,000 per mile.

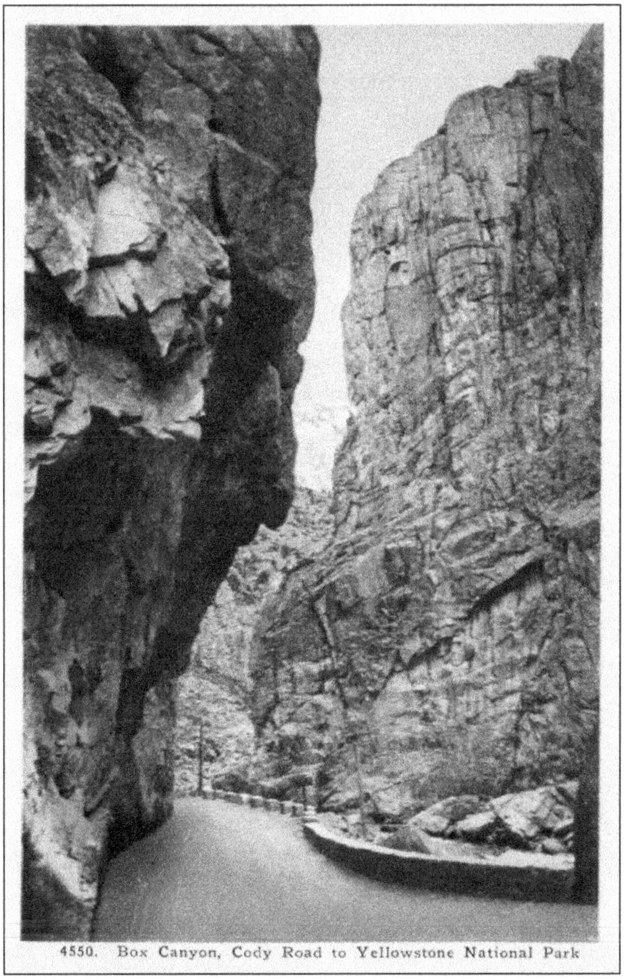

Mountain View Lodge, Cody Road. This lodge is located at the halfway point along Cody Road, at the eastern portal to the Shoshone National Forest. For years, it has been a popular location for hunting, fishing, and hiking enthusiasts, as well as those who stopped for gas or a meal. The service station featured Texaco products, and the lodge provided cabins and home-cooked meals.

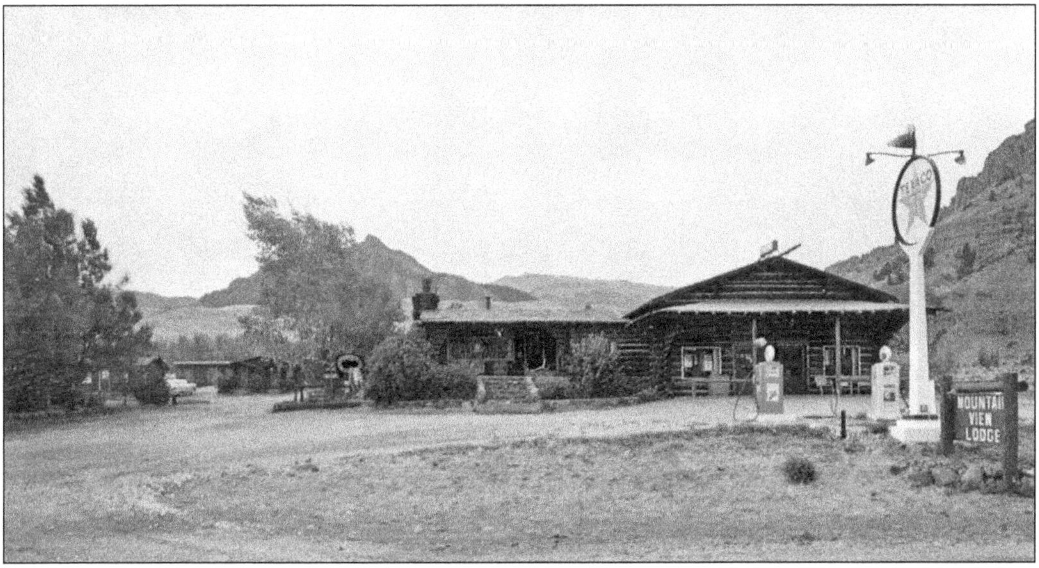

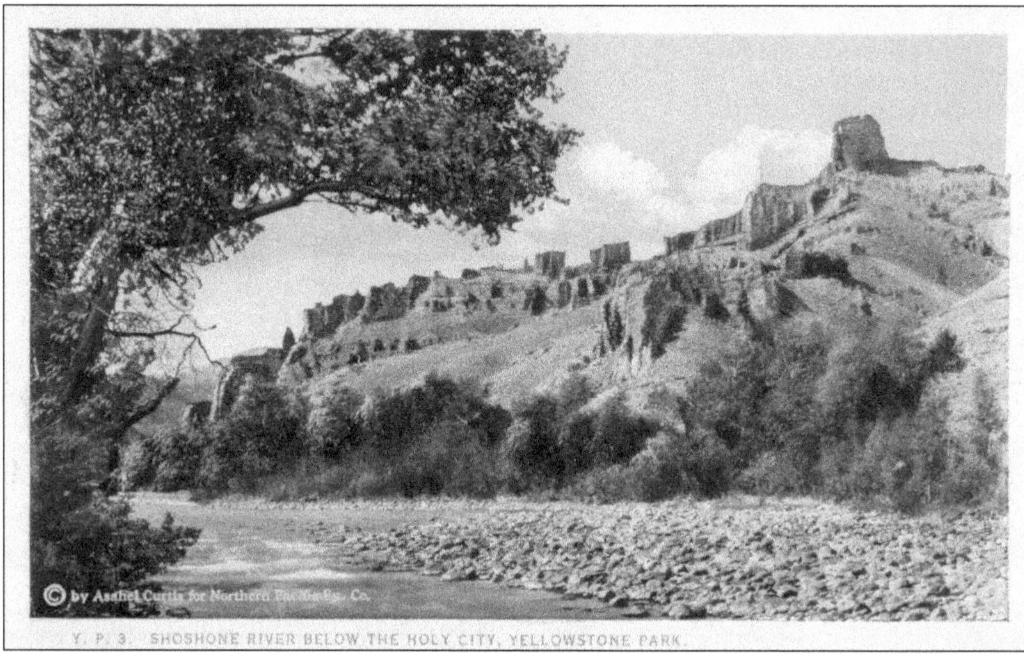

HOLY CITY, CODY ROAD. The high cliffs on either side of Cody Road contain interesting rock formations that have been carved by centuries of erosion by wind, rain, and volcanic activity. Colorful names have been applied to describe these figures, some of which test the viewer's imagination, whereas others are quite straightforward in appearance. For more than 100 years, these rocks have provided additional interest for travelers among the highway's already spectacular scenery. The Holy City rock formation shown in both images is located north of the highway just after entering Shoshone National Forest. Some early observers felt the rocky pinnacles resemble the skyline of Jerusalem. Interestingly, Holy City is adjacent to another similar formation of tall spires called Devil's Elbow.

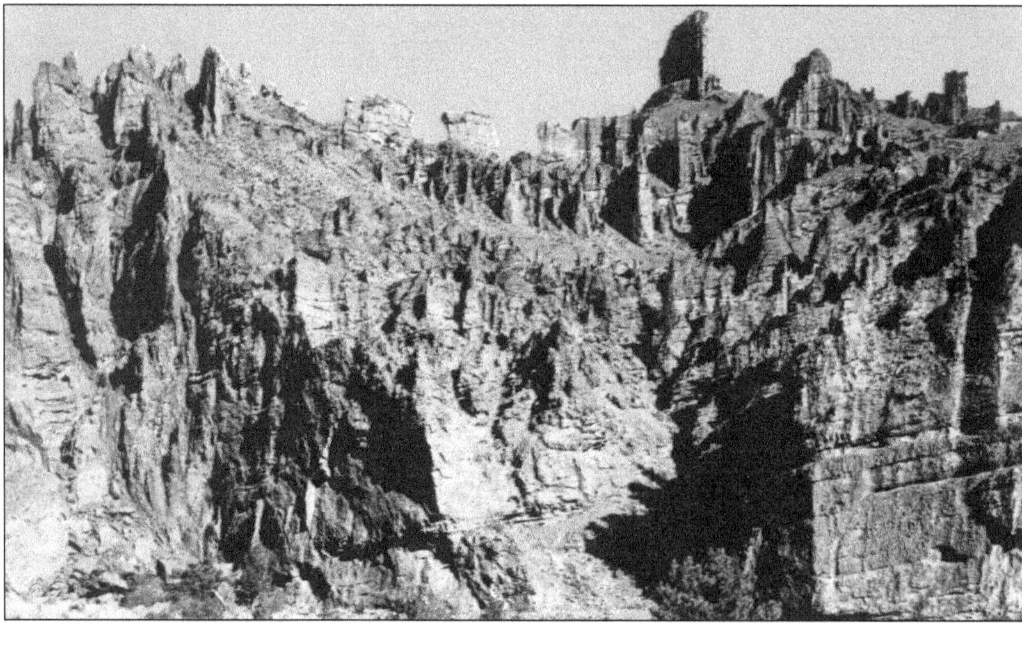

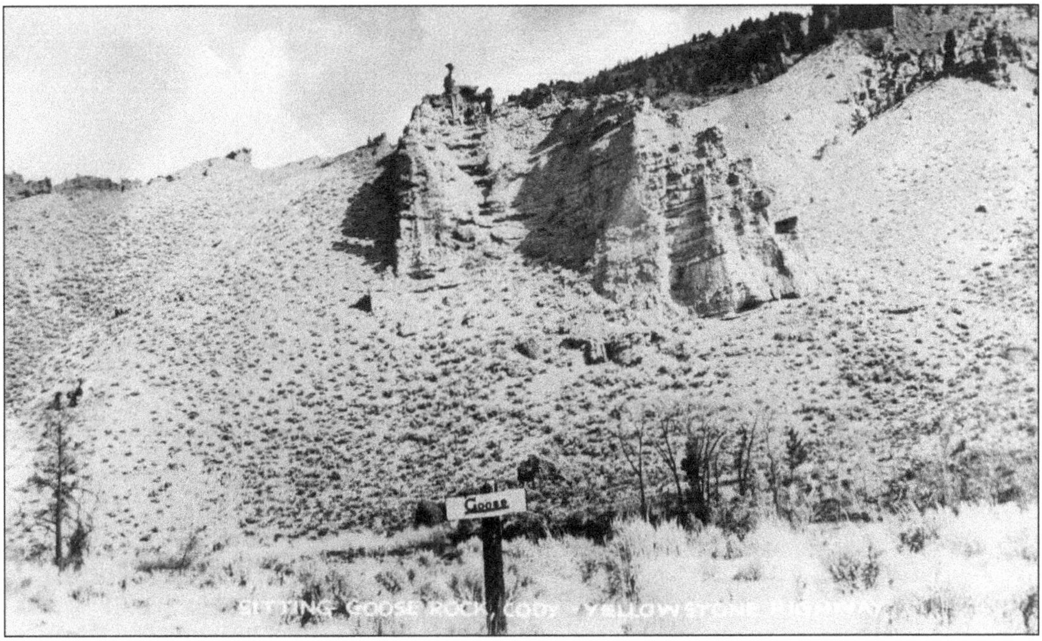

SITTING GOOSE ROCK, CODY ROAD. Sitting Goose is located high on the mountain peak near the Holy City rock formation. The unique rock projects clearly above the larger rock upon which it sits. When this postcard was produced in the 1930s, a sign at the side of the road saying simply "Goose" let visitors know that this was the best place to view the Sitting Goose.

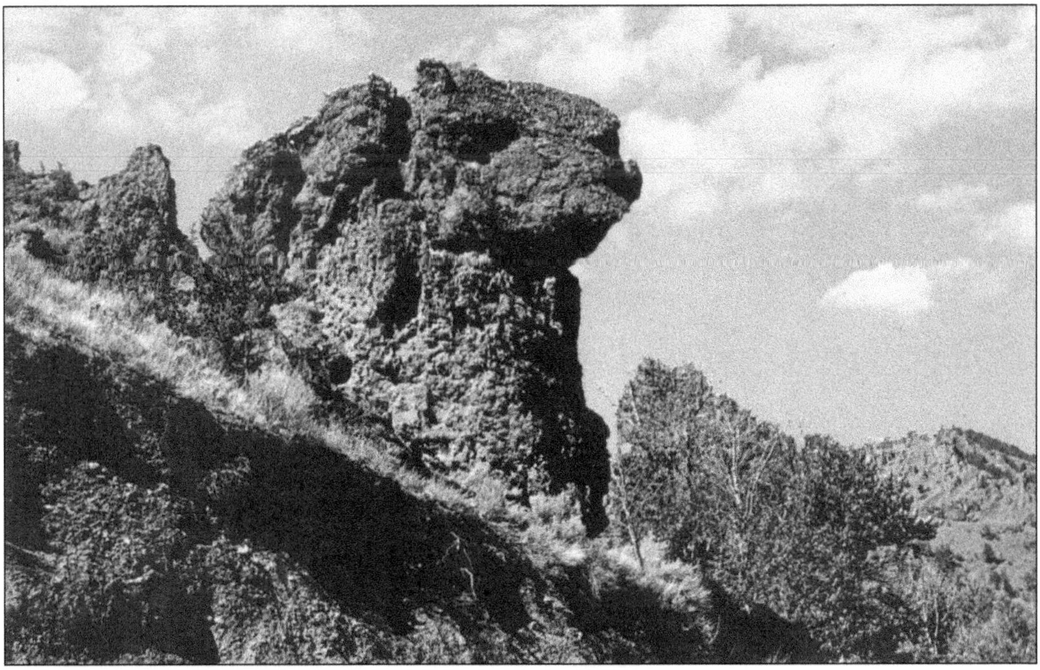

LAUGHING PIG ROCK, CODY ROAD. The Laughing Pig rock formation requires a more creative imagination to conceptualize the object being described. Going west, Laughing Pig is on the left side of Cody Road opposite Holy City. Bighorn sheep, elk, and other wildlife have been known to roam the area surrounding Laughing Pig.

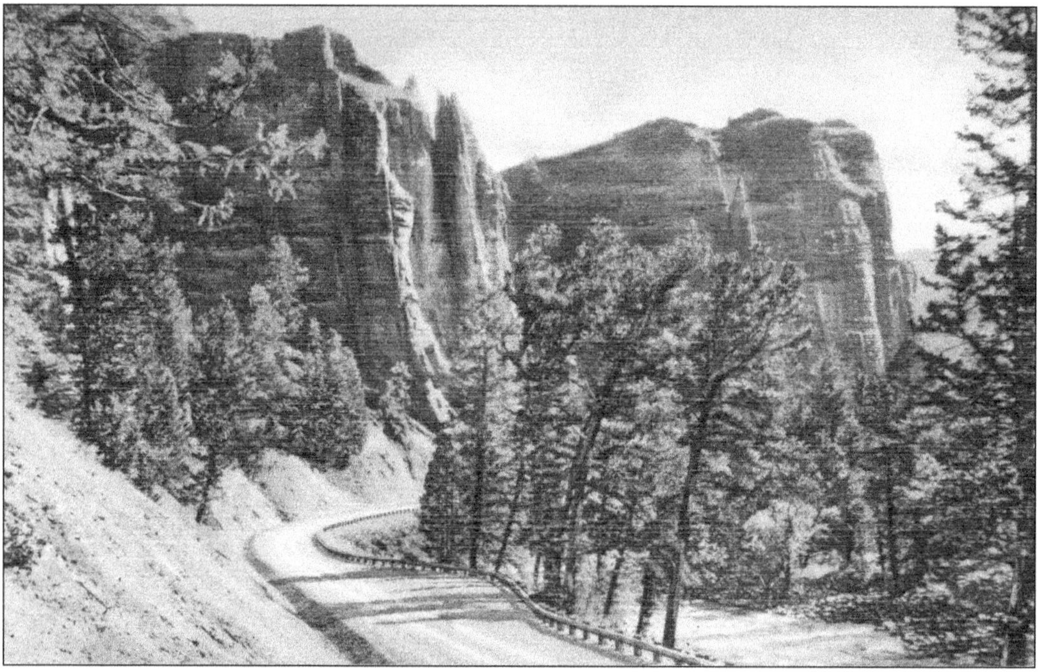

The Palisades and Shoshone River, Cody Road. This scenic section of Cody Road is located between the Wapiti Ranger Station and Absaroka Lodge, approximately 14 miles from the east gate of Yellowstone Park. The combination of precipitous cliffs on the south side of the road and the river on the north made this a favorite place to take photographs. A convenient parking area encouraged tourists to enjoy the view.

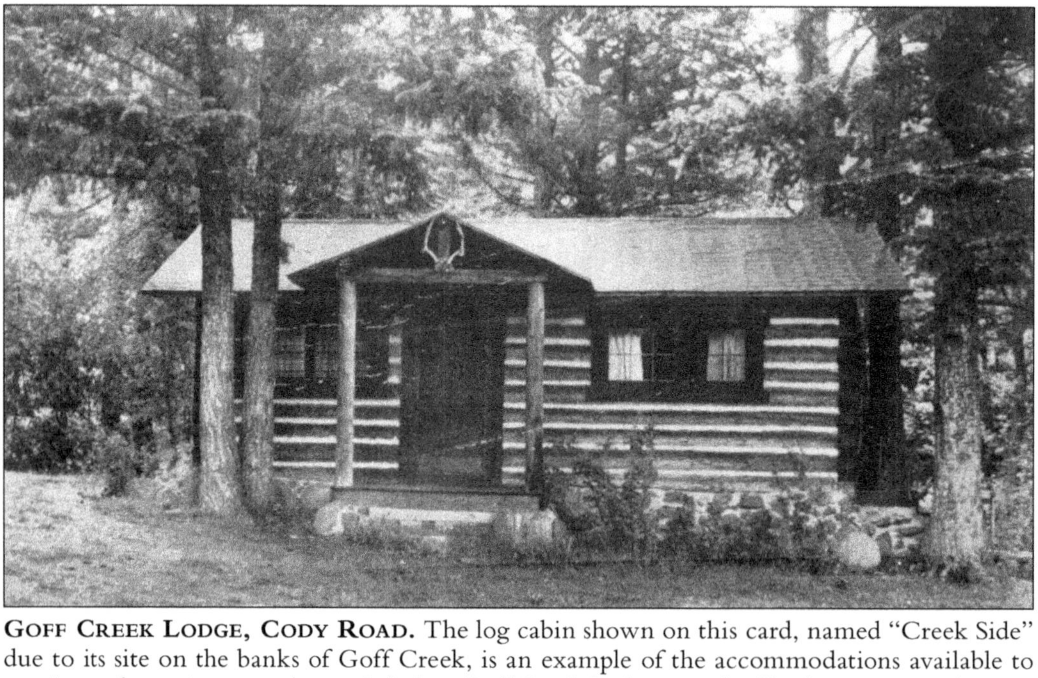

Goff Creek Lodge, Cody Road. The log cabin shown on this card, named "Creek Side" due to its site on the banks of Goff Creek, is an example of the accommodations available to tourists and vacationers at the rustic lodge. Goff Creek Lodge is in the Shoshone National Forest near the Palisades rock formation.

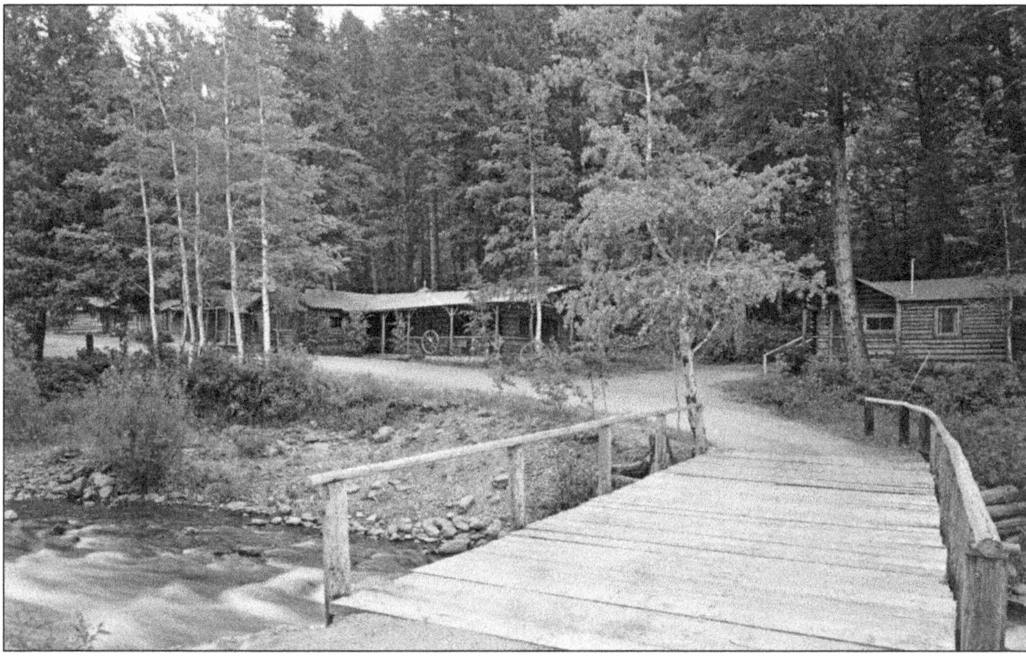

ABSAROKA LODGE, CODY ROAD. The rustic bridge over Gunbarrel Creek shown in the photograph above leads to the century-old Absaroka Lodge, nestled among the pines adjacent to Cody Road. It was begun in 1910 and called Gunbarrel Lodge in honor of its namesake creek. The lodge is located approximately 13 miles east of Yellowstone National Park and at one time was owned by the grandson of Buffalo Bill Cody. In 1925, the name was changed to Absaroka Lodge. It was a favorite of Pres. Theodore Roosevelt, who stayed at the lodge in a cabin similar to those in the image below during some of his western trips. The elevation of 6,000 feet assured cool nights, and nearby Gunbarrel Creek provided exciting trout fishing. Absaroka Lodge is listed in the National Register of Historic Places.

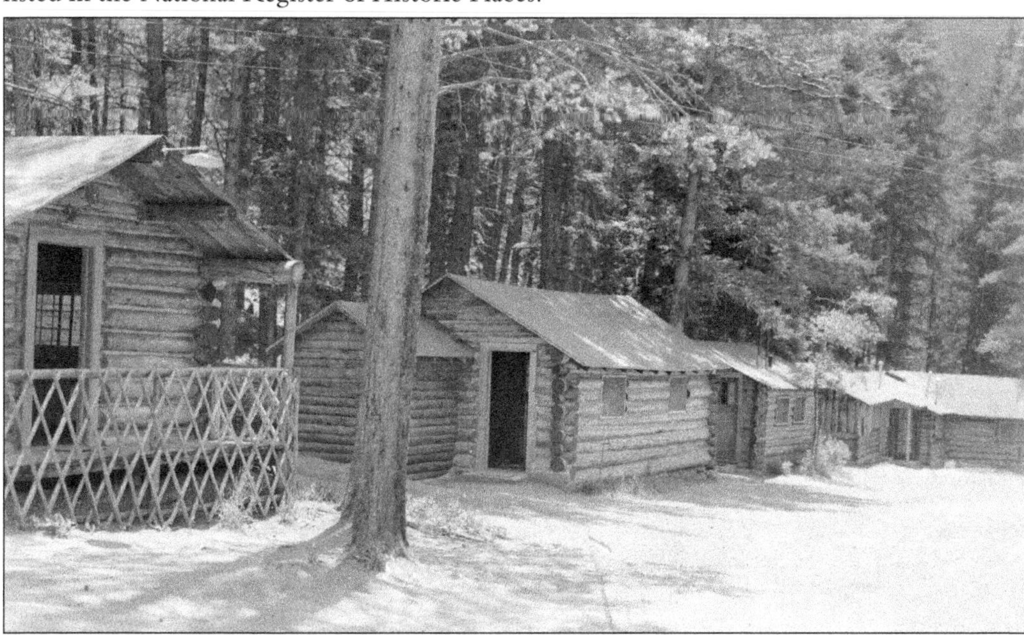

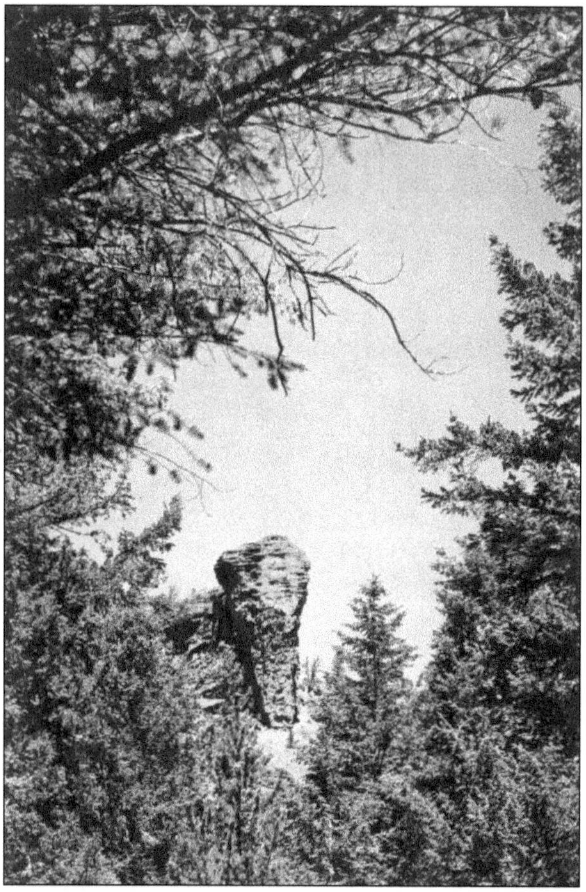

ELEPHANT HEAD ROCK AND ELEPHANT HEAD LODGE, CODY ROAD. This is one of the easier rock formations to identify. Going west, it is on the right side of the road, approximately 12 miles from the east entrance to Yellowstone National Park. It is a spectacular sight for all viewers, but it is a special attraction for children, who have no difficulty understanding why the name has been applied. The Elephant Head Lodge near the road beneath the rock opened in 1910. It offered modern cabins, home-cooked meals, saddle horses, and pack trips for hunting and fishing.

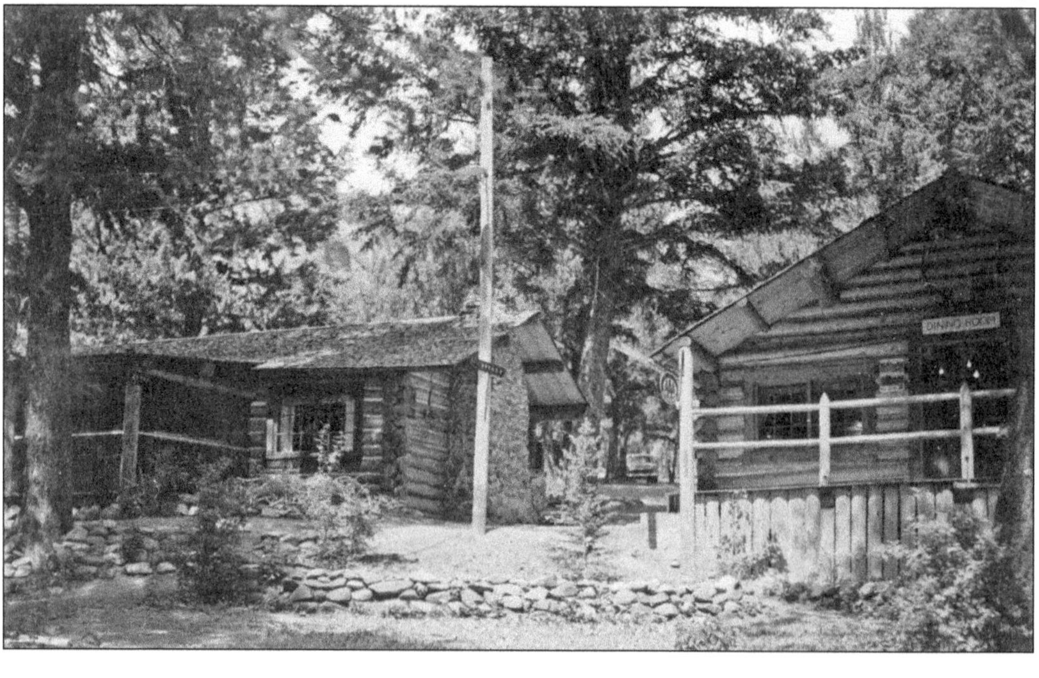

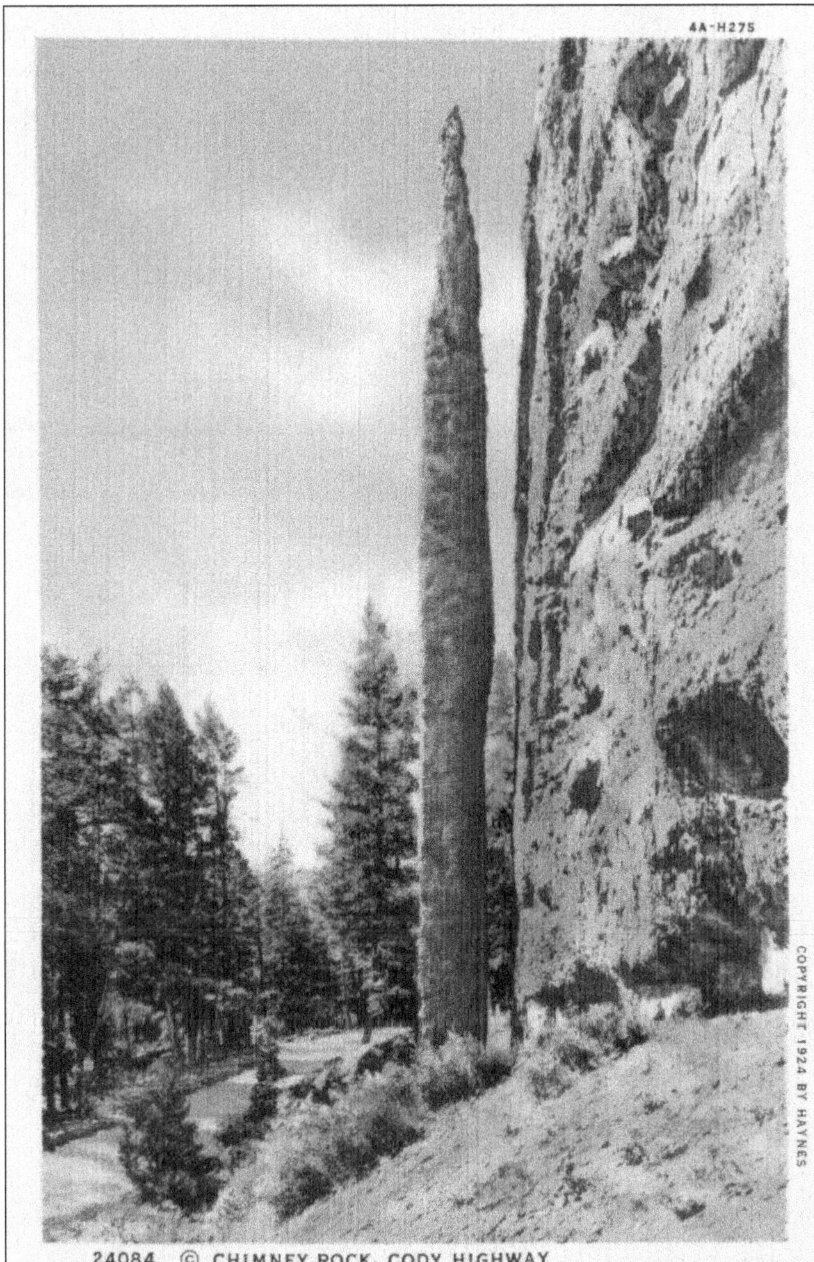

CHIMNEY ROCK, CODY ROAD. Although there are several Chimney Rocks throughout the West, this unique formation on Cody Road is among the most popular. Its position close to the highway makes it particularly easy to view. Unlike most similar formations, the base of this Chimney Rock does not appear to be part of another stone; rather, it seems to come from the earth totally separate from it neighbors. The thin rock formation, similar in form to a church spire, rises to a height of 125 feet. All such rocks were formed by the forces of nature, especially rain and wind acting on the indigenous rock over many millennia. Its prominent roadside position is 11 miles from the east entrance of Yellowstone National Park. Throughout the entire life of the highway, Chimney Rock has been one of the most photographed structures.

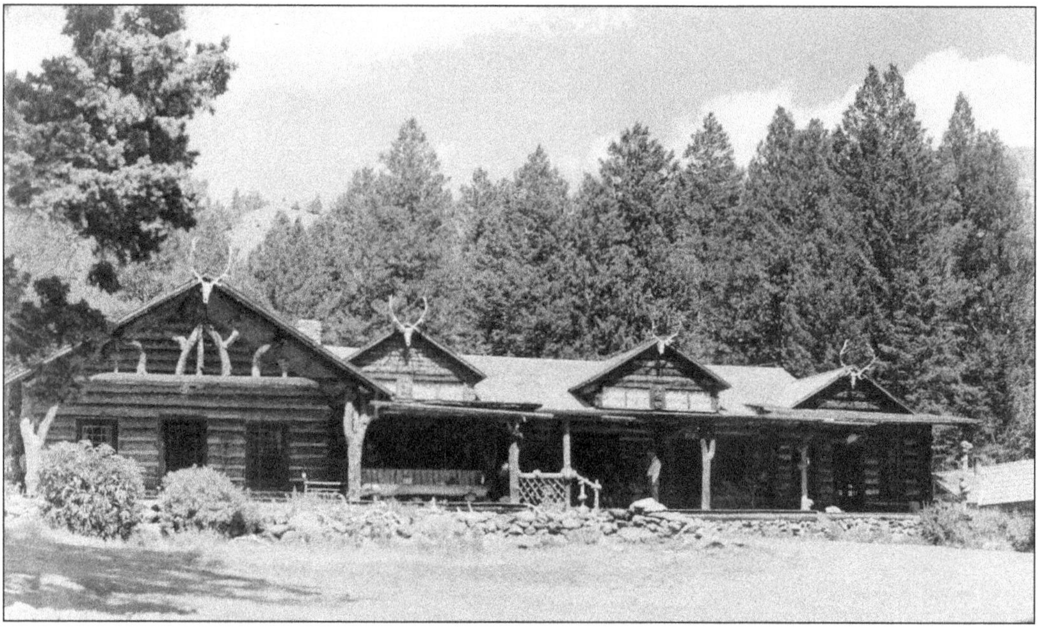

Holm Lodge, Cody Road. Holm Lodge is located seven miles east of Yellowstone National Park. It opened in 1898 as a stagecoach stop. The original 1903 lodge was destroyed by fire, and in 1906 a new, larger lodge was built. Most guests were accommodated in tents with wooden floors, but rooms for "unescorted ladies" were provided in the main lodge. The latter building also contained the dining room and lounge. After the opening of the Sylvan Pass Road enabled easier travel to the interior of the park, Holm Lodge became the primary midpoint stagecoach stop between Cody and the Lake Hotel at Yellowstone Lake. In addition, Holm Lodge was a tourist destination in its own right. Guide services were available for camping and hunting both within the park and in the rugged countryside outside the park limits.

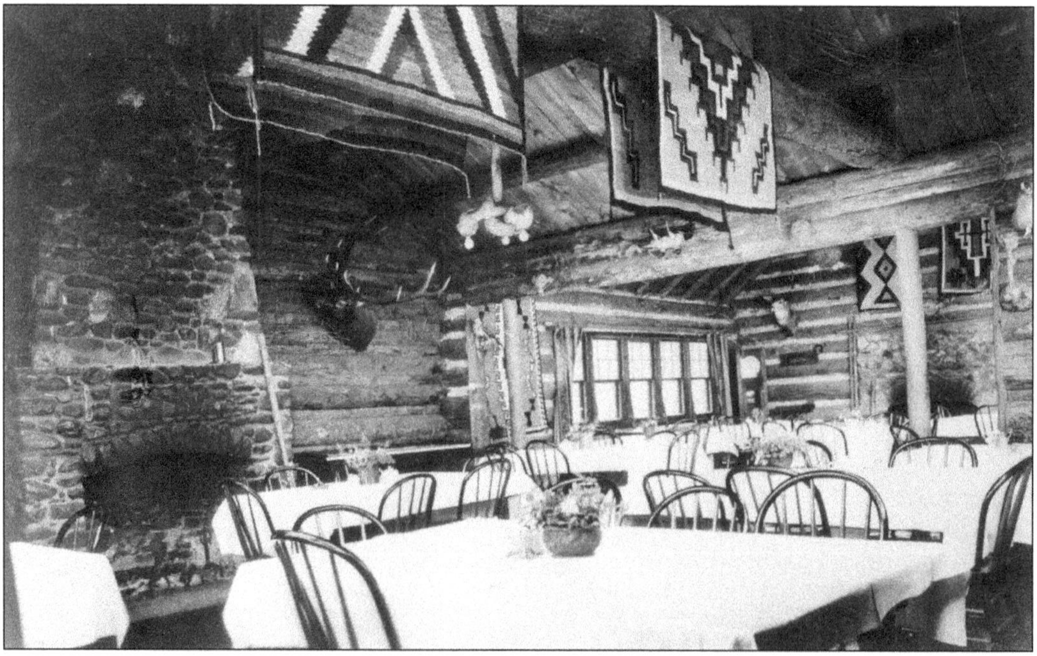

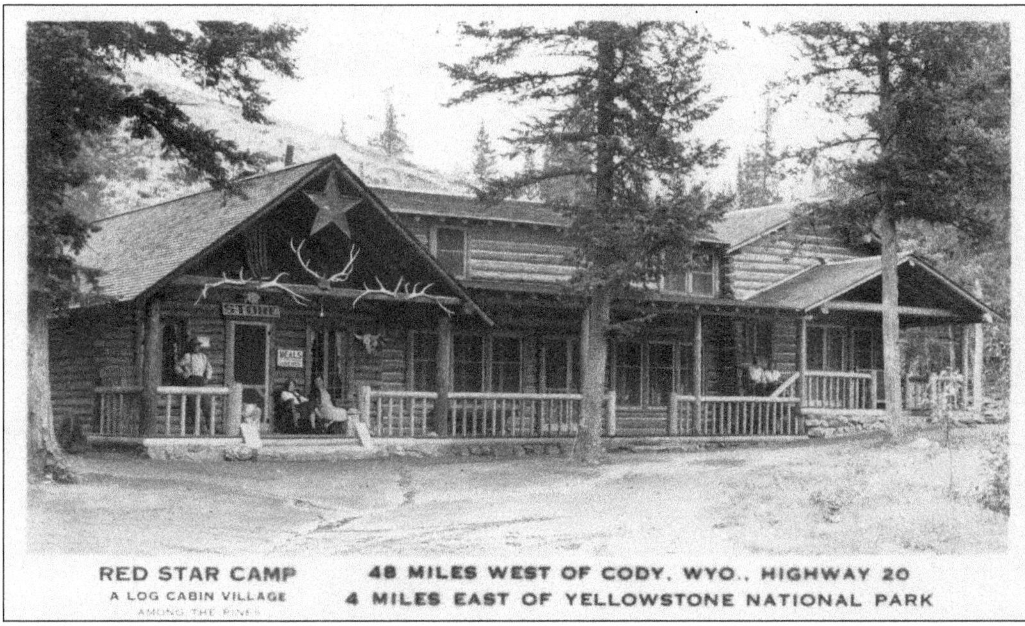

RED STAR CAMP, CODY ROAD. This camp, located four miles from the east gate of the park, called itself a "log cabin village among the pines." It is another example of the early tourist lodgings along Cody Road. Accommodations included housekeeping cabins and furnished rooms, all with electric lights, showers, and pure spring water. Light lunches and full meals were available, and a gas station was also on the premises.

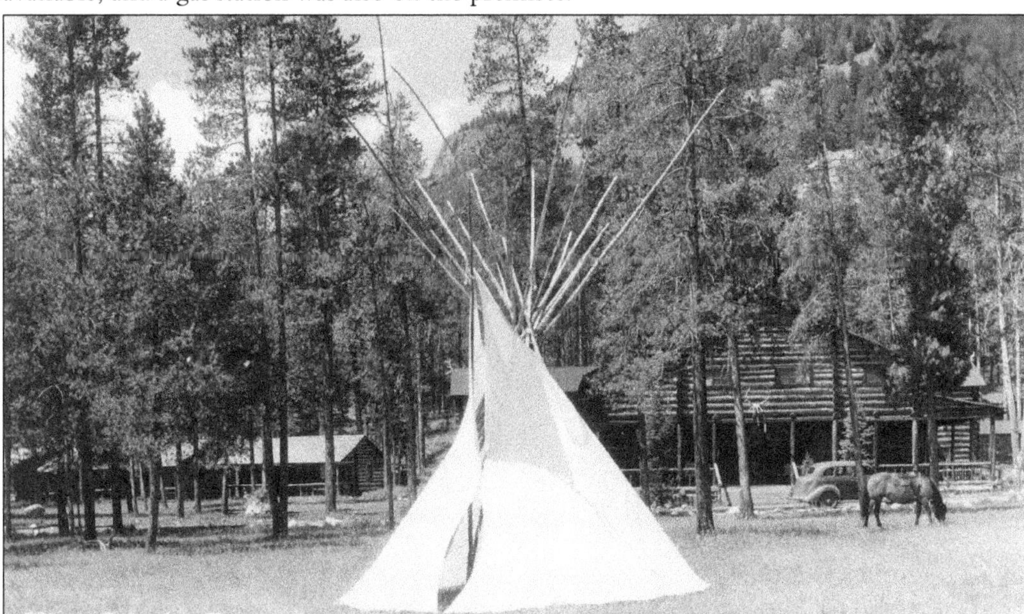

PAHASKA TEPEE LODGE, CODY ROAD. An authentic Lakota Tepee greeted guests at Pahaska Tepee Lodge. Among the lodge's many outdoor activities were horseback excursions into the rugged forest in the surrounding area. The horse grazing by the tepee was one of many that were available to lodge guests. The model of the car indicates that this card was produced in the mid-1930s.

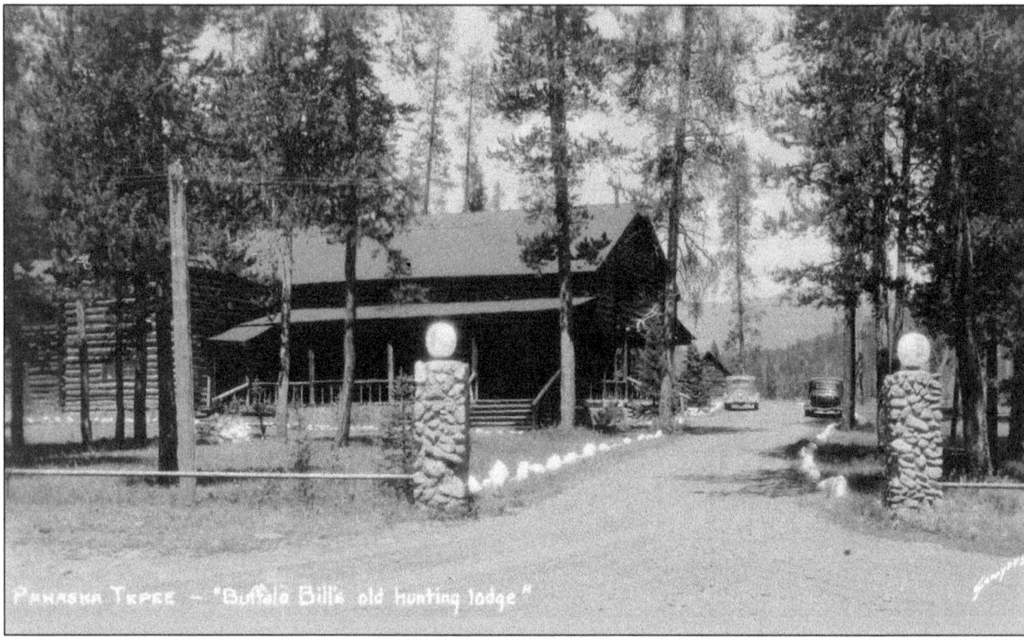

Pahaska Tepee Lodge, Cody Road. Built in 1904 and now listed in the National Register of Historic Places, this lodge is well into its second century of serving hunters, fishermen, trappers, and visitors to the park. The lodge was said to be Buffalo Bill Cody's favorite retreat, and its log construction amid tall pine trees and sparkling streams in the Shoshone National Forest befitted his outdoor personality.

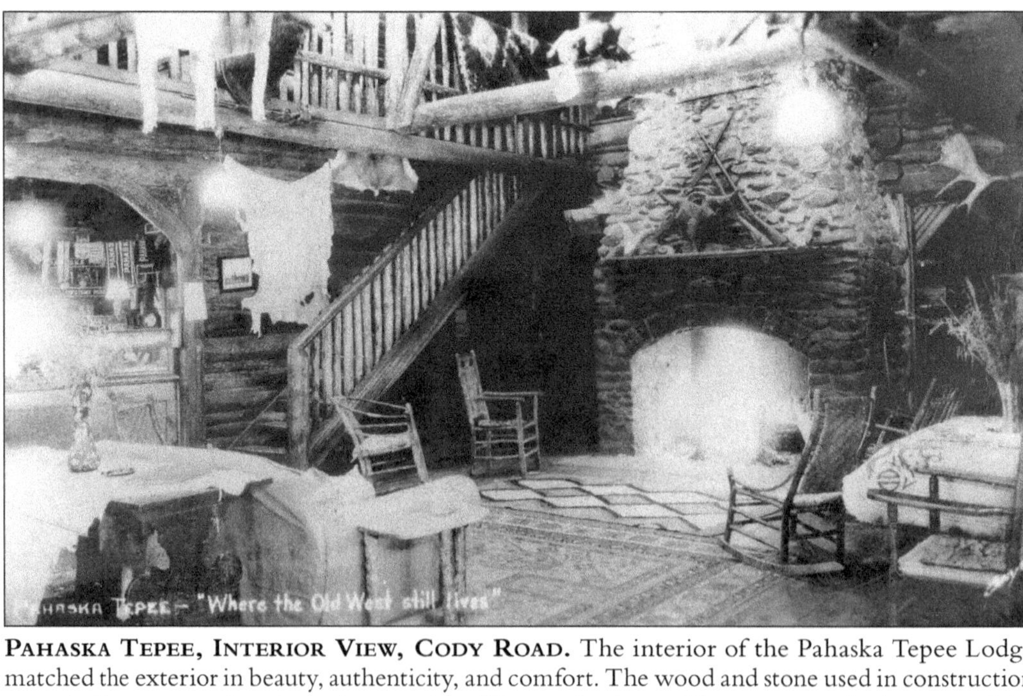

Pahaska Tepee, Interior View, Cody Road. The interior of the Pahaska Tepee Lodge matched the exterior in beauty, authenticity, and comfort. The wood and stone used in construction were indigenous to the site and stressed its Western heritage. The motto at the bottom of the card sums up the lodge's philosophy: "Where the old west still lives."

Six

Yellowstone National Park

Highway 20 is unique among the original cross-country highways. It has two distinct sections with Yellowstone National Park as the connecting link. From 1926 to 1940, the eastern section extended from Boston, Massachusetts, to the east gate of the park. In 1940, the western section of the highway was extended from the park's west gate to Newport, Oregon, on the Pacific Coast. For over 90 years, cross-county travelers on historic Highway 20 have looked forward to driving directly through Yellowstone National Park. For most, it has been the highlight of their journey.

The Grand Loop Road, Yellowstone Park's main thoroughfare, is designed in a roughly figure-eight pattern encircling the park with spurs extending to each of the park's five entrances. Highway 20 travelers from the east began their drive on the East Entrance Road crossing Sylvan Pass (elevation 8,524 feet) and passing beautiful Sylvan Lake. The road continued along the north shore of Yellowstone Lake to the famous Fishing Bridge over the Yellowstone River, where it connected with the Grand Loop Road. Historic Highway 20 typically is shown continuing along the west shore of the lake until reaching the Lake Hotel, the oldest of the original Yellowstone hotels. There, the road turned west passing Old Faithful Inn, thought to be the world's largest log building, and Old Faithful Geyser, the park's premier attraction. The Grand Loop Road continued to Madison Junction, and from there the West Entrance Road went 15 miles to the western gate at West Yellowstone, Montana. From the east entrance to the Fishing Bridge, the road geographically lies within Park County. From the Fishing Bridge until entering Montana, the 70-mile stretch is located in Wyoming's Teton County, although county designations are superseded by the federal identification of Yellowstone National Park.

In addition to spectacular scenery, attractions include animals that are native to the area. Motorists, dating to even the automobile's earliest time, have confronted traffic jams caused by buffalo, bears, and other animals crossing the roads. Visitors are encouraged not to interfere with the animals, and feeding them is prohibited.

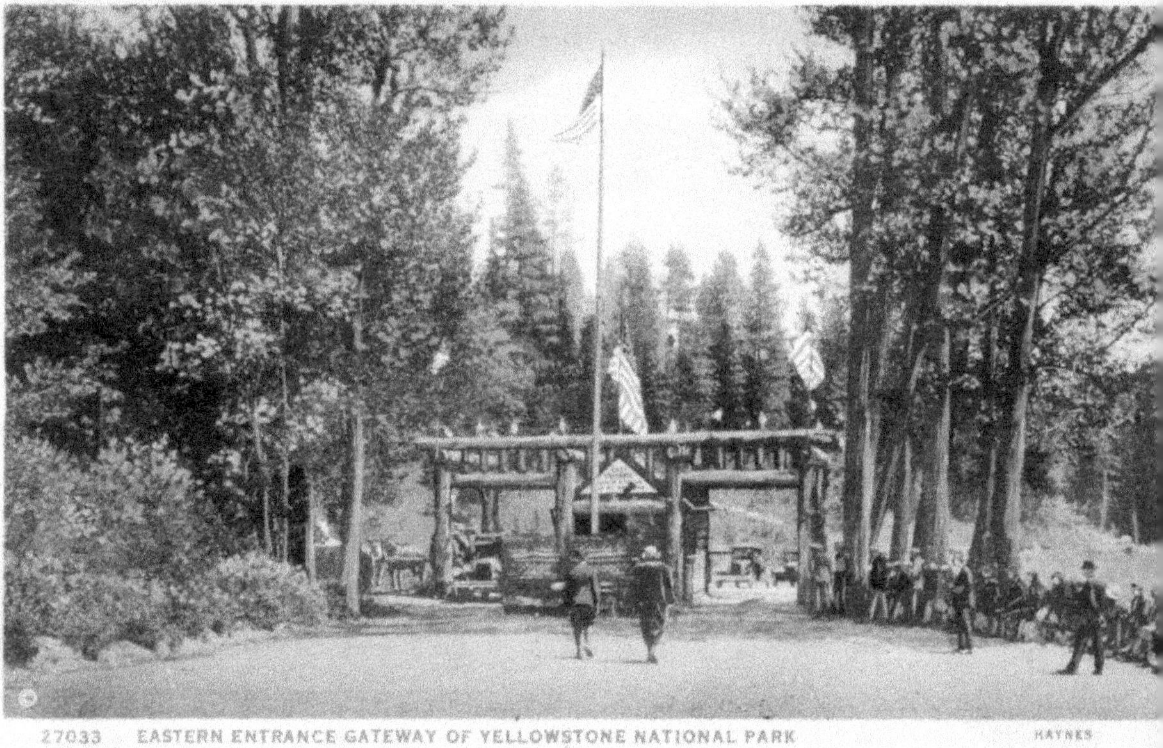

EASTERN ENTRANCE GATEWAY OF YELLOWSTONE NATIONAL PARK. This rustic gateway marked the western terminus of the eastern section of historic Highway 20. It is considered by many to be the most scenic of Yellowstone Park's five entrances. The character of the gate was an introduction to the scenery travelers would encounter on the road ahead. The wilderness setting among tall pine trees and mountainous terrain was especially attractive to persons who were looking forward to a rugged outdoor experience. Unlike its counterpart at the western extremity of the park, there is no town at the eastern border; rather, travelers were accommodated at lodges and cabin courts along the Cody Highway. Motorists entering Yellowstone Park from the east proceeded along the East Entrance Road, which became known as the Sylvan Pass Road as it approached the pass and Sylvan Lake in the Absaroka Mountain Range. After several miles, it joined the Grand Loop Road. That road and the east and west access roads are the connecting links between the eastern and western sections of original Highway 20.

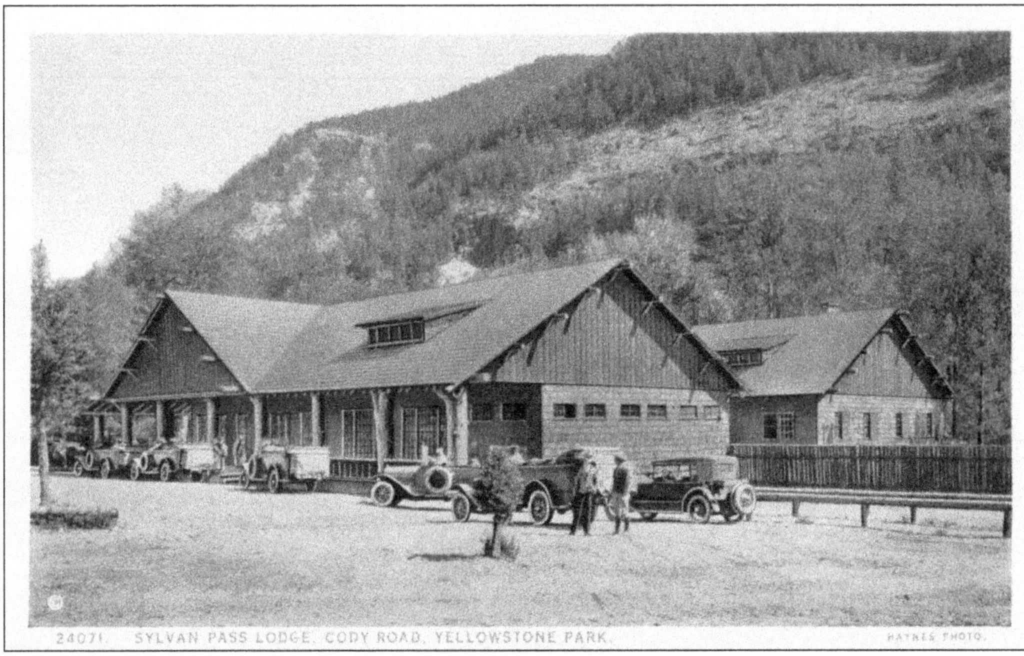

Sylvan Pass Lodge. This rustic lodge was located at the base of Sylvan Pass Road near the east entrance to Yellowstone Park. It was the last lodge built in the park and was intended to be a rest stop for tourists who were making the journey from Cody to the park's famous Lake Hotel. The lodge operated for only 10 years and was finally torn down in 1940.

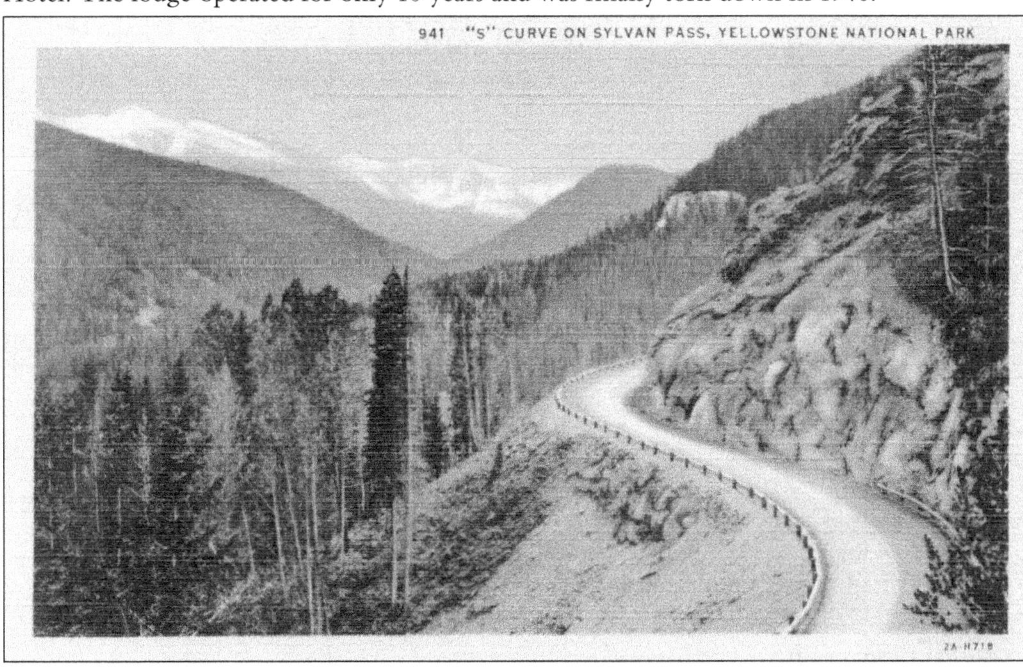

Sylvan Pass Road, Yellowstone National Park. The East Entrance Road leads directly to Sylvan Pass in the Absaroka Mountain Range, approximately seven miles from the east entrance. The road passes through high mountains featuring dazzling curves, shear rocky cliffs, and volcanic beauty. The pass was named after the tree-lined Sylvan Lake that the highway overlooks.

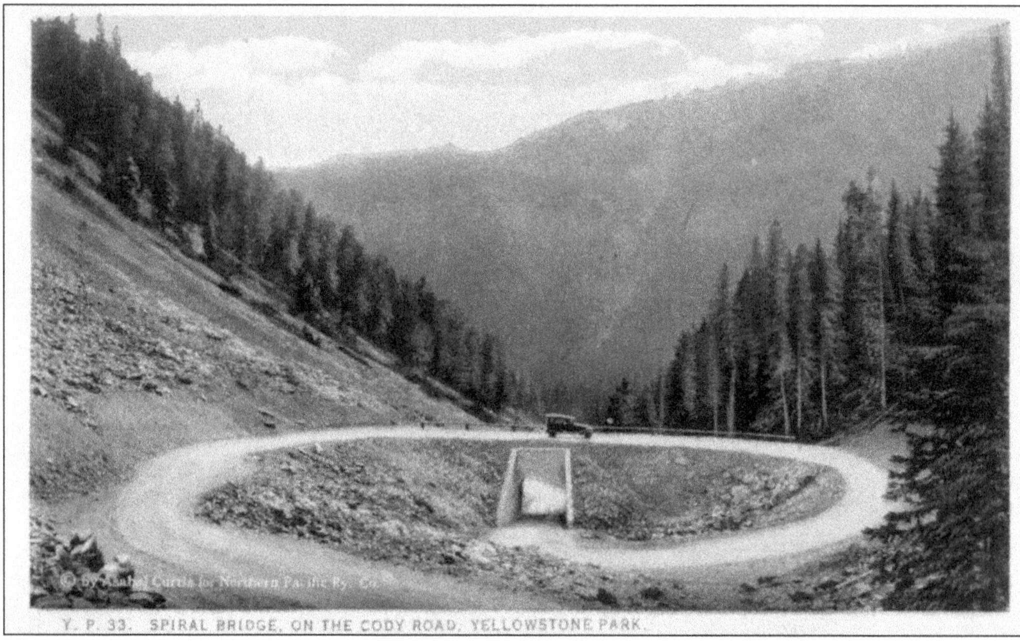

SPIRAL BRIDGE, SYLVAN PASS ROAD, YELLOWSTONE NATIONAL PARK. This engineering marvel opened in 1921. It was located near Sylvan Pass and is identified on some old postcards as Sylvan Pass Loop. The unique design actually followed principles established by railroads in the West when difficult mountain grades were encountered. A loop extended the length of the road and thereby enabled a more gradual change in grade.

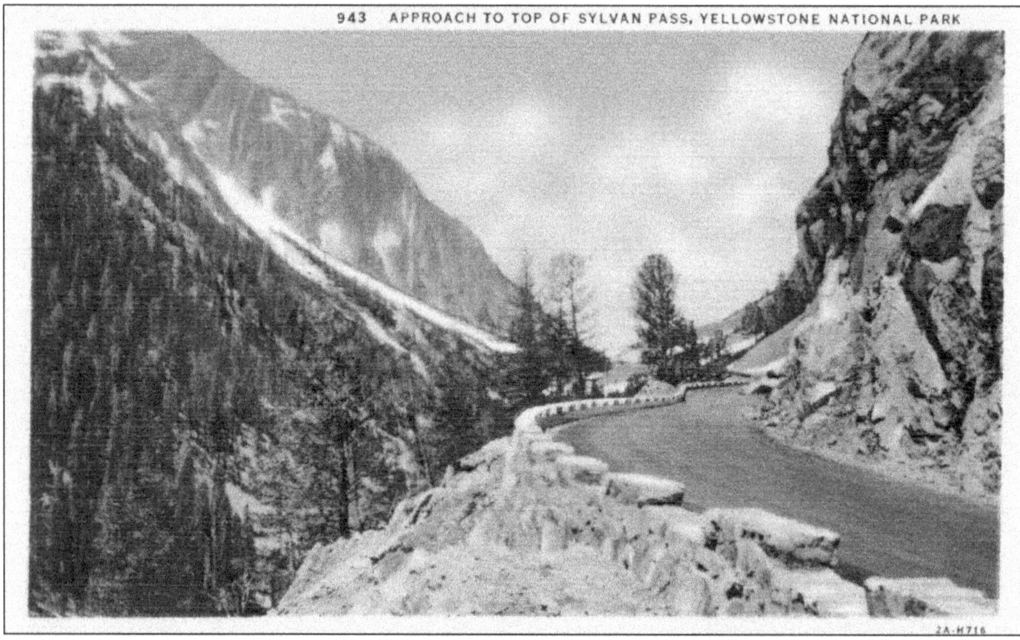

APPROACH TO TOP OF SYLVAN PASS, YELLOWSTONE NATIONAL PARK. The road over Sylvan Pass is one of the premier scenic features of Yellowstone National Park. At its crest, the pass reaches an elevation of 8,524 feet. Drivers had to maintain careful control of their cars as the low rock walls provided little protection from a fall over the precipitous cliffs.

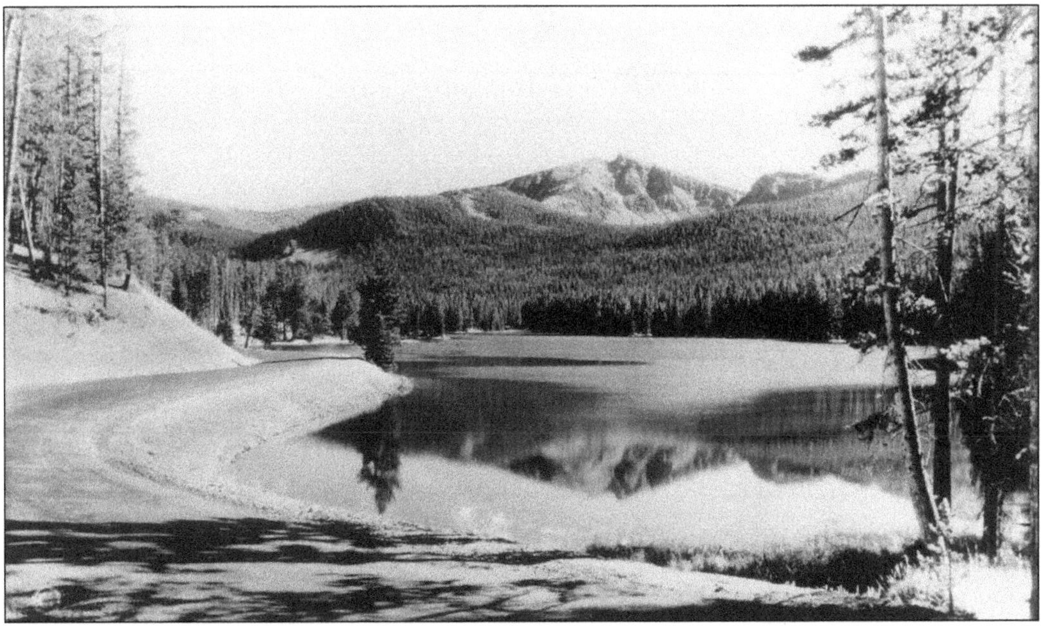

SYLVAN LAKE, YELLOWSTONE NATIONAL PARK. Shortly after cresting Sylvan Pass, the road passes beautiful Sylvan Lake. The Sylvan Lake surface was smooth as glass the day this photograph was taken, resulting in a mirror image reflection of the mountains, including Top Notch Peak (10,238 feet high) in the distance.

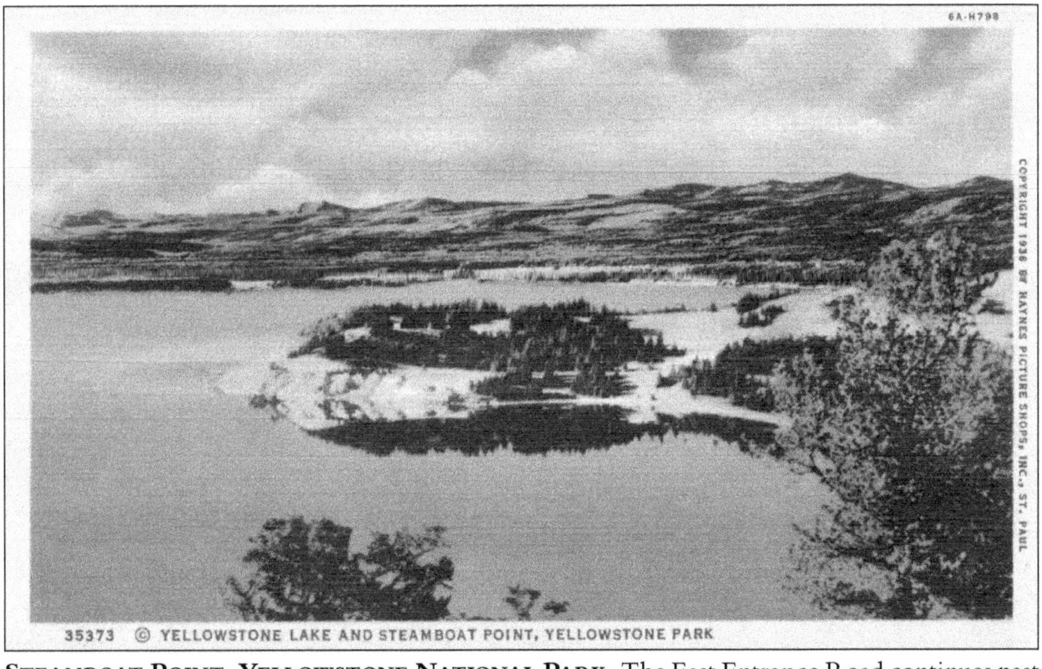

STEAMBOAT POINT, YELLOWSTONE NATIONAL PARK. The East Entrance Road continues past this scenic spot on the northeastern shore of Yellowstone Lake, only a few miles from the road's junction with the Grand Loop Road. The name was applied by the Heyden Survey Expedition in 1871 due to regular puffs of steam that emanated from nearby Steamboat Springs. The thermal emissions in this area are among the hottest in the lake.

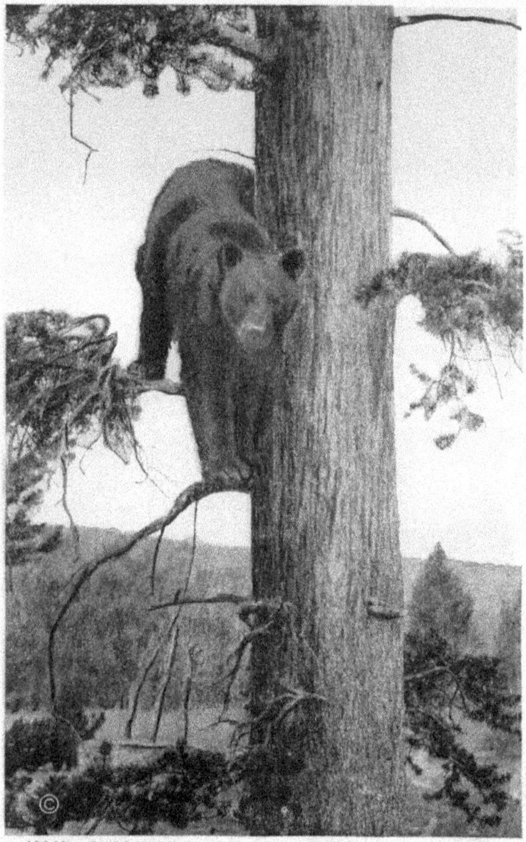

16348. A BLACK BEAR IN TREE, YELLOWSTONE NATIONAL PARK.

Wildlife, Yellowstone National Park. Animals native to the area are a frequent sight within the park. The caption on the back of the card at left reads, "Long renowned as a refuge, Yellowstone contains a wide variety of animals. Among the most popular are bears and buffalo which are frequently seen along the highways throughout the park." Spotting wild animals has long been a highlight when visiting Yellowstone National Park, and seeing them in their natural habitat is especially thrilling. Feeding animals was allowed during earlier times, but fortunately attempting to interact with the wildlife is now strictly prohibited. Visitors to the park are encouraged to view the animals and take photographs, but not interfere in any way with their normal activities.

© 21202—BUFFALO (AMERICAN BISON, BULL) YELLOWSTONE NATIONAL PARK

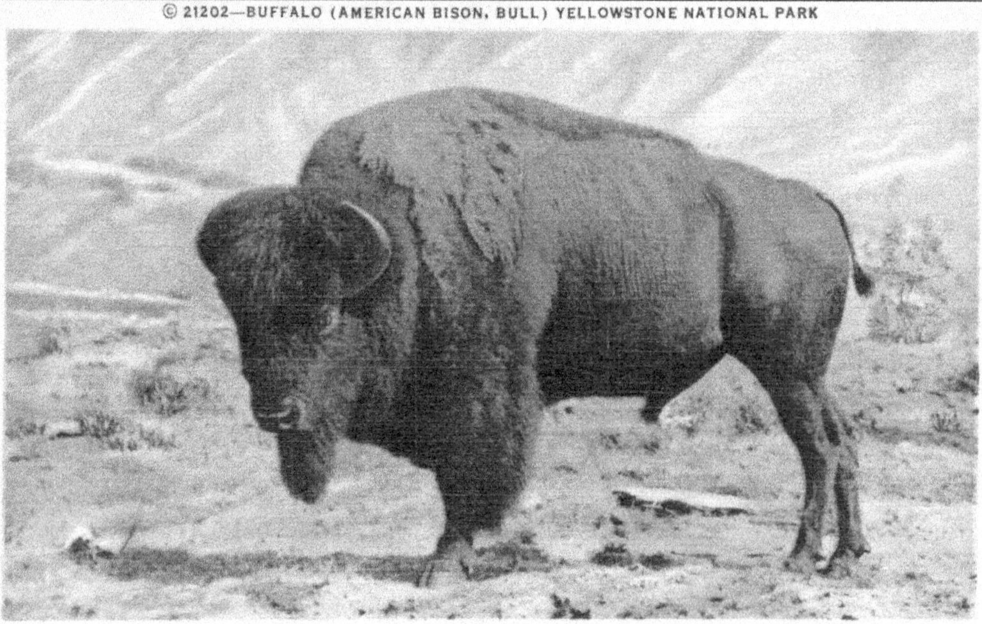

COPYRIGHT BY HAYNES INC., YELLOWSTONE PARK, WYOMING

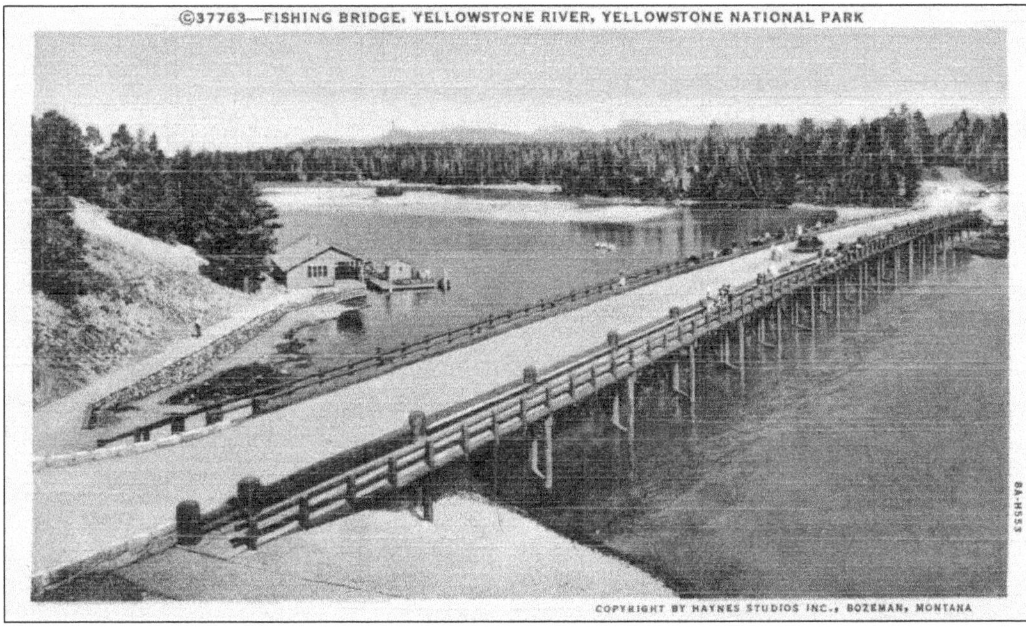

FISHING BRIDGE, YELLOWSTONE NATIONAL PARK. Fishing Bridge is located on the Grand Loop Road at the point where the Yellowstone River emerges from Yellowstone Lake. Formerly, it was a popular spot to fish for cutthroat trout, but fishing has been prohibited from the bridge since 1973. An original log bridge was built in 1902 and remained in use for 35 years. The bridge pictured here opened in 1937.

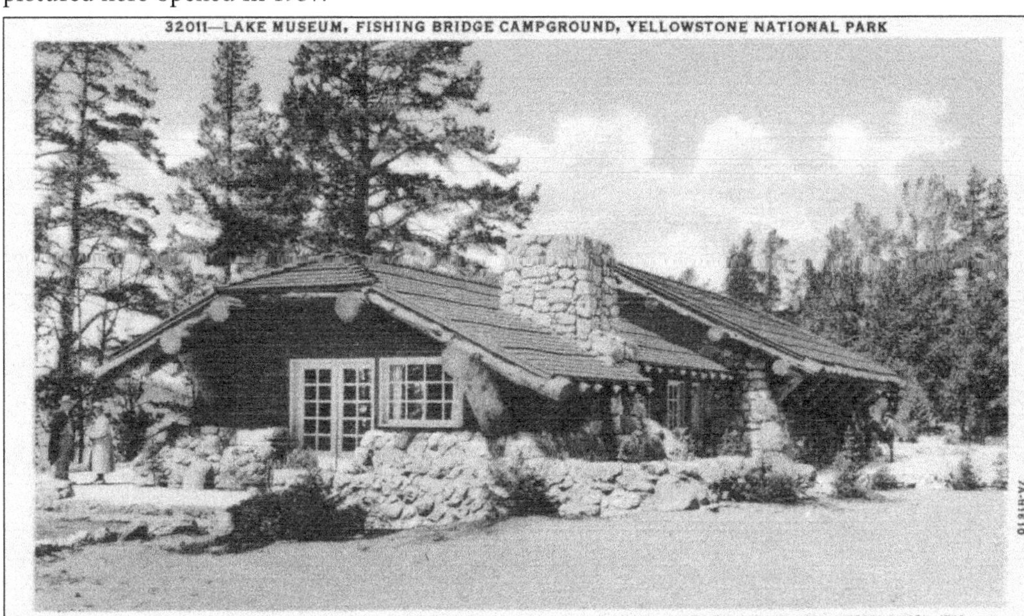

LAKE MUSEUM, FISHING BRIDGE CAMPGROUND, YELLOWSTONE NATIONAL PARK. The attractive Lake Museum is centrally located near Fishing Bridge. It was built in 1931 and is listed in the National Register of Historic Places. Exhibits of fish and local wildlife are featured inside the building, and on the roofed patio outside visitors could relax and enjoy a meal or beverage. An amphitheater where lectures were given was located nearby.

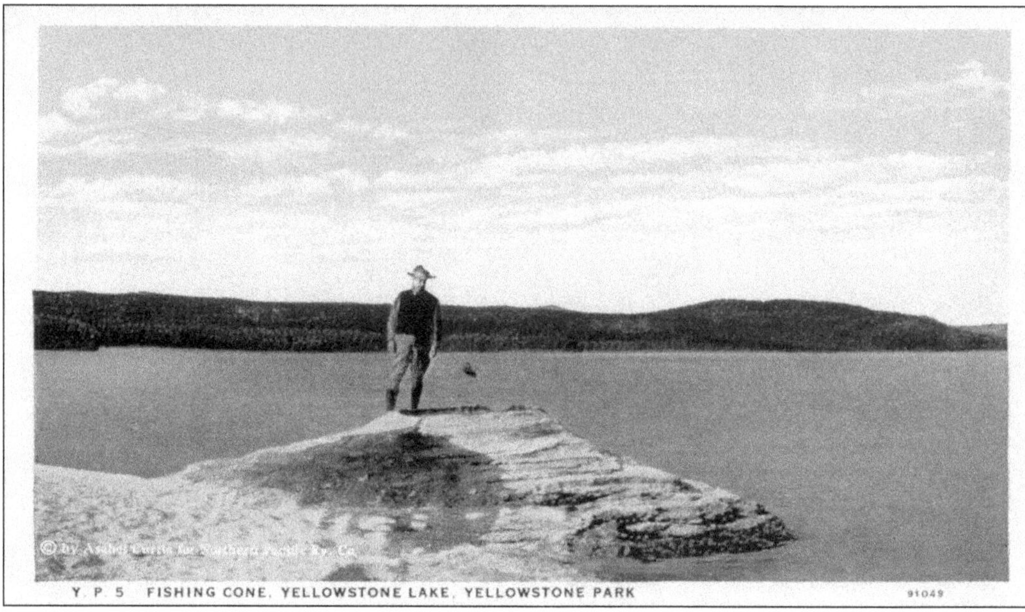

FISHING CONE, YELLOWSTONE LAKE, YELLOWSTONE NATIONAL PARK. Fishing Cone is a unique geological structure in the West Thumb of Yellowstone Lake near the Grand Loop Road. Originally a geyser, it was said that a fish could be cooked while it was still on the hook! The water has now cooled near the cone, although it is still considered a hot spring. Fishing from the cone has been prohibited since 1912.

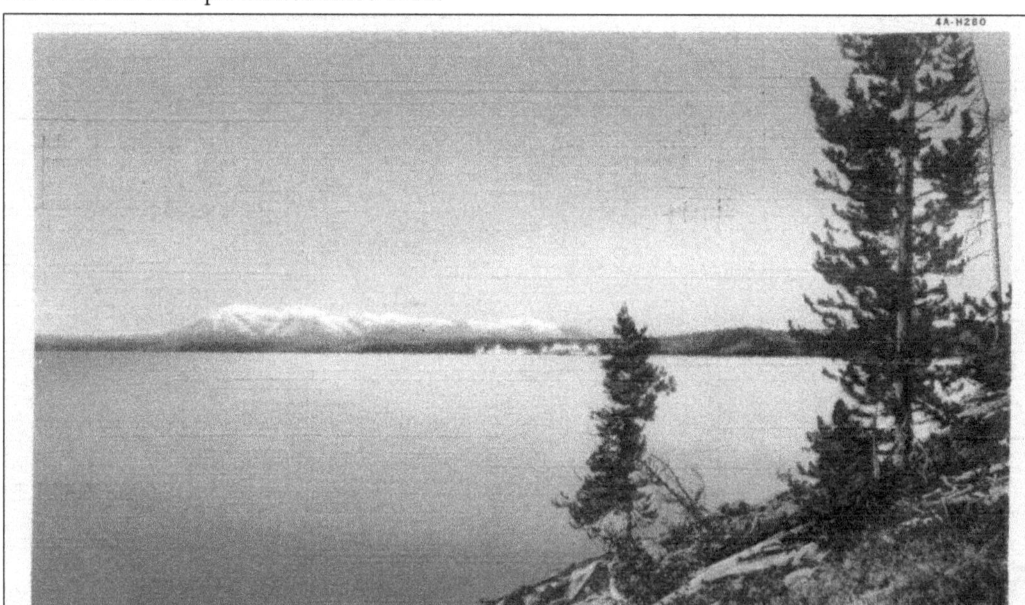

YELLOWSTONE LAKE AND MOUNT SHERIDAN. At 7,732 feet above sea level, Yellowstone Lake is the largest body of water in North America at such an altitude. Snow-covered Mount Sheridan (elevation 10,250 feet) lies only a few miles to the south. For decades, the mountain has been a favorite of hiking enthusiasts where deer, elk, grizzly bears, and a large variety of birds, including bald eagles, can be spotted.

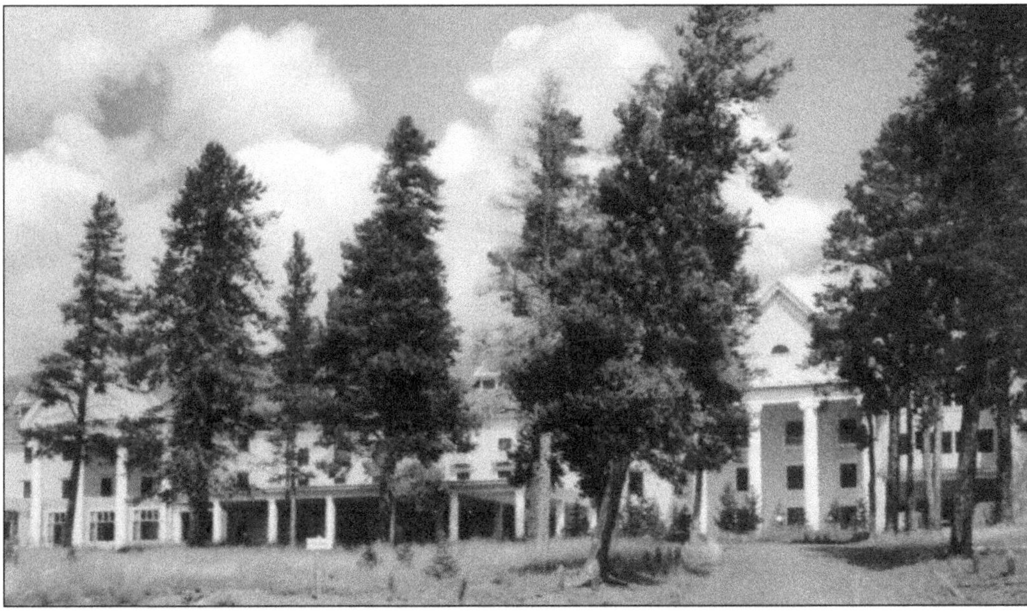

LAKE HOTEL, GRAND LOOP ROAD, YELLOWSTONE NATIONAL PARK. This hotel on the west shore of Yellowstone Lake opened in 1891. It is the oldest of the standing Yellowstone hotels and is listed in the National Register of Historic Places. Lake hotel has 296 rooms, and ever since opening it has remained true to its original objective of offering elegant accommodations and first-class service.

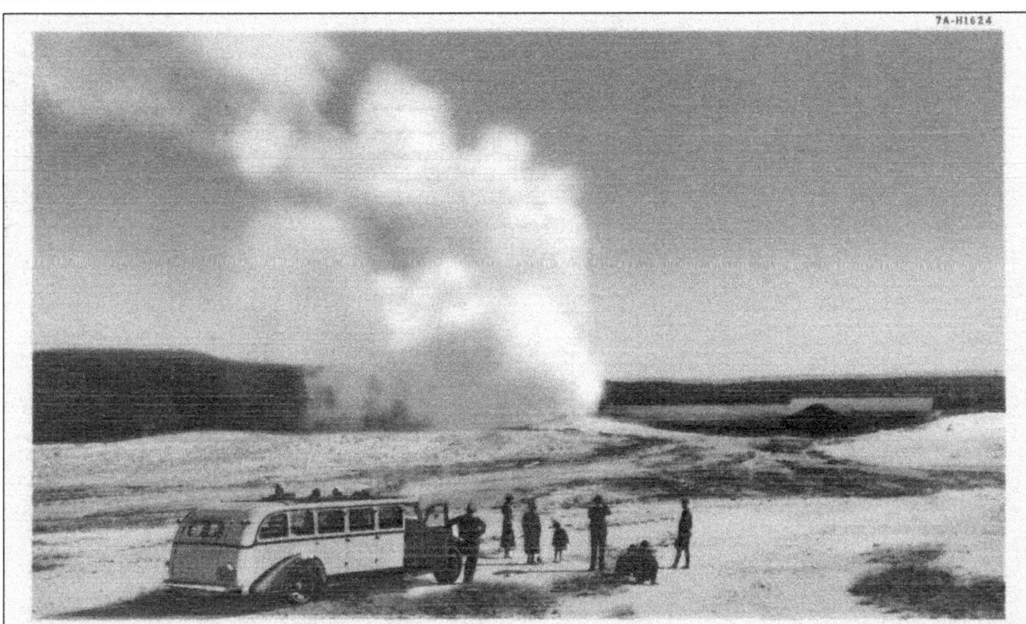

OLD FAITHFUL GEYSER, GRAND LOOP ROAD, YELLOWSTONE NATIONAL PARK. As the most famous geyser in the United States and possibly the world, Old Faithful has been the centerpiece of Yellowstone National Park since its designation in 1872. This 1930s photograph shows Old Faithful Geyser as it is erupting. The yellow bus was a common conveyance used to transport tourists to the geyser from various locations in the park.

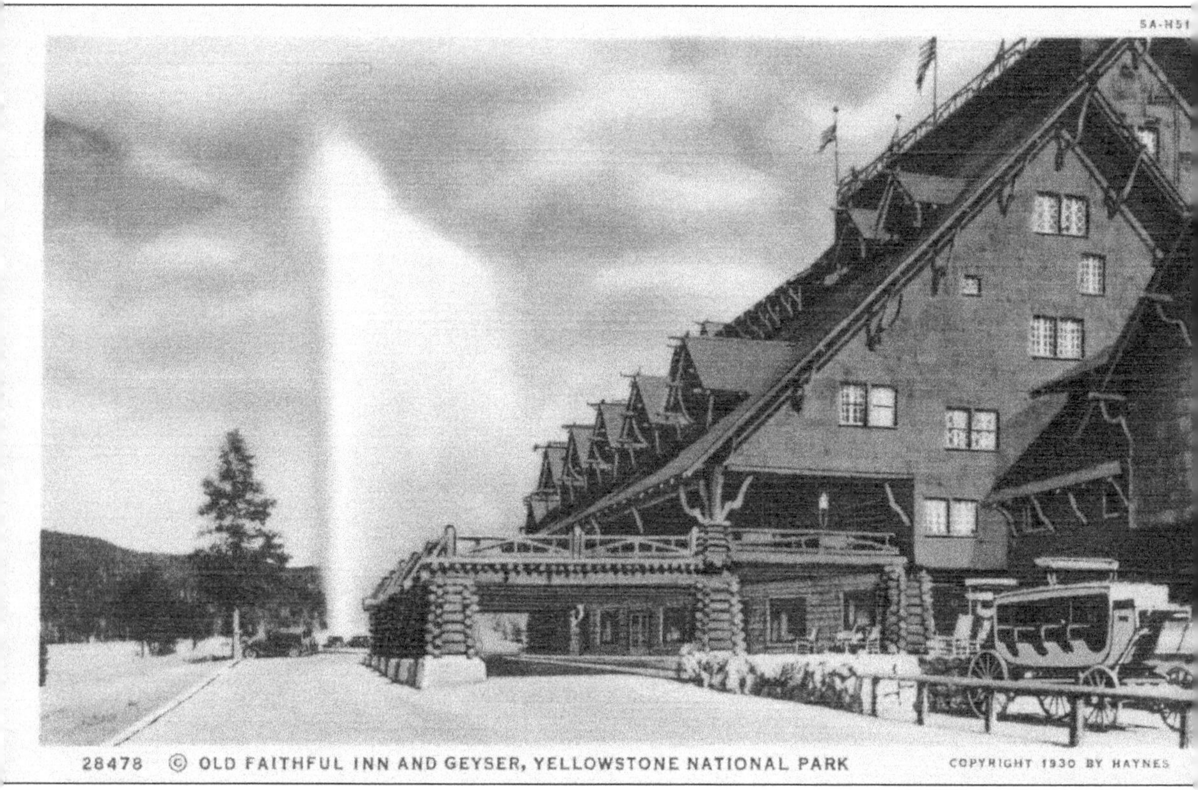

OLD FAITHFUL INN, YELLOWSTONE NATIONAL PARK. Located adjacent to Old Faithful Geyser, the Old Faithful Inn is a rustic, exposed log and wood-frame structure that is seven stories high. It is one of the few remaining log hotels in the United States. The building was designed by architect Robert Reamer and was constructed in three major phases. The first phase, in 1903, included the main section known as the Old House. In 1913–1914, the east wing was added, followed by the west wing in 1927. Many modifications have been made over its 100-year history, but all have been true to the original design. Old Faithful Inn has been termed the queen of rustic hotels in the national parks. It is listed in the National Register of Historic Places.

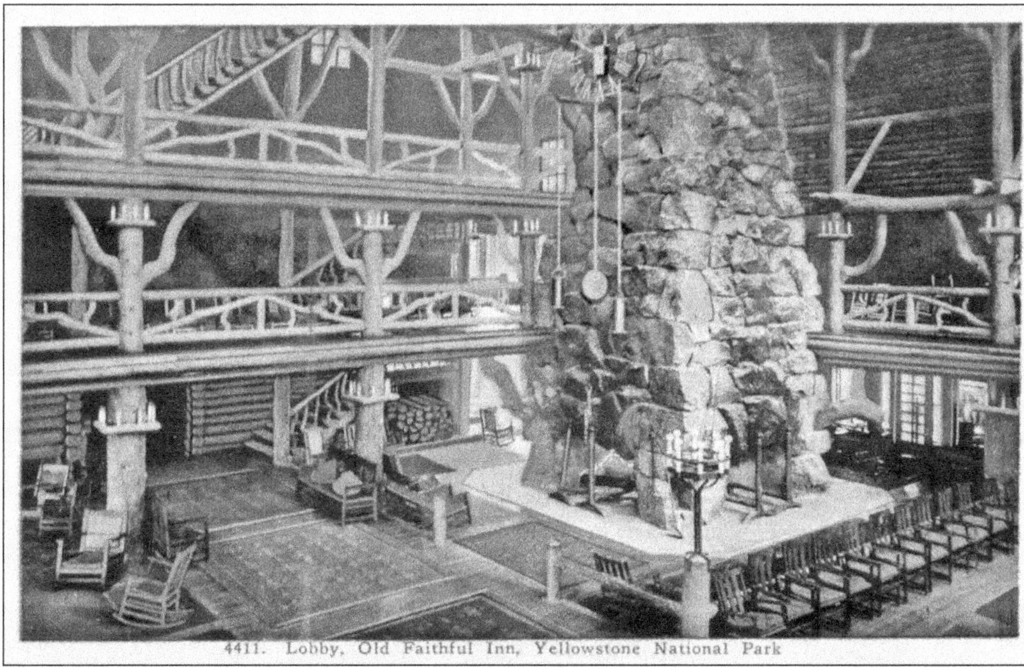

OLD FAITHFUL INN, LOBBY AND DINING ROOM, YELLOWSTONE NATIONAL PARK. The elaborate lobby of the Old Faithful Inn is remarkable for its size and construction. When possible, all materials used in the building were indigenous to the area. The huge logs that support the building, together with those forming the walls and decorative railings, were harvested locally. The 500 tons of rock used to build the massive fireplace were quarried from a hillside nearby. The giant clock adorning the fireplace was made from the design of architect Mr. Reamer and hammered out on the grounds before being suspended from the fireplace chimney. The image below shows the inn's popular dining room decorated with a tasteful wildlife theme.

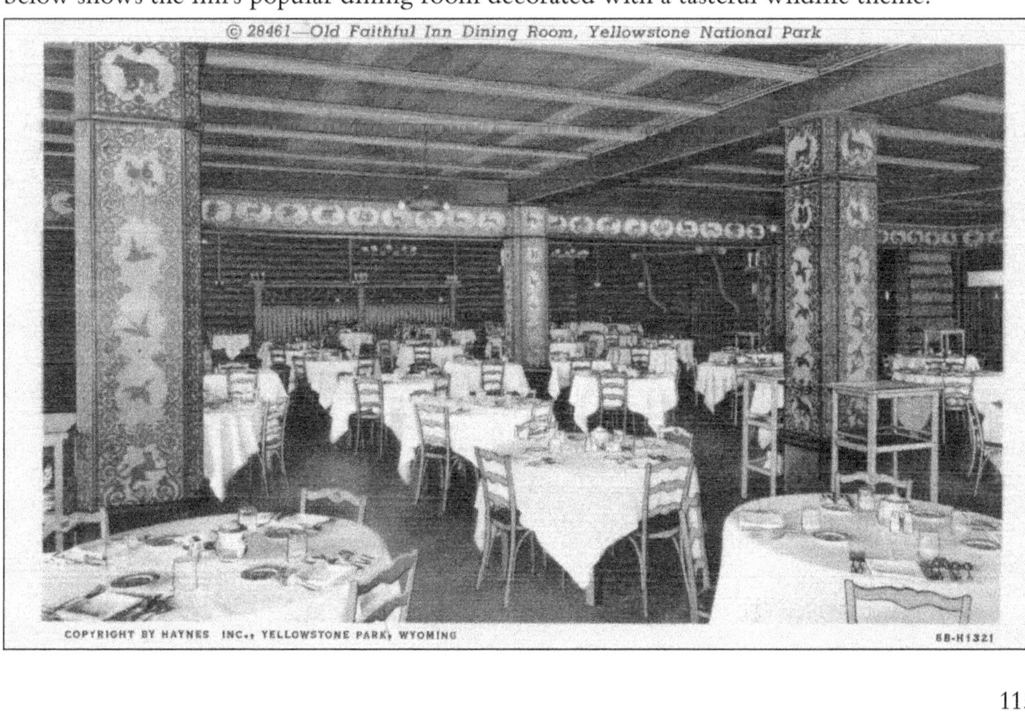

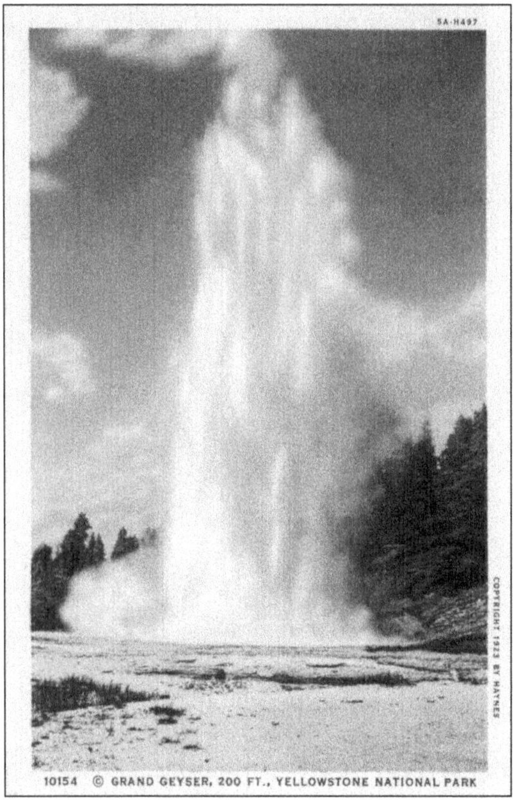

GRAND GEYSER, YELLOWSTONE NATIONAL PARK. Located only 15 minutes from Old Faithful, this geyser exceeds Old Faithful in eruptive force, sometimes reaching a height of 200 feet. The Grand Geyser erupts more irregularly, with the usual span being between 6 and 15 hours. This variance is the reason it has received less notoriety than its famous neighbor; nonetheless, its eruption has been a spectacular sight enjoyed by lucky tourists who visit at the right time.

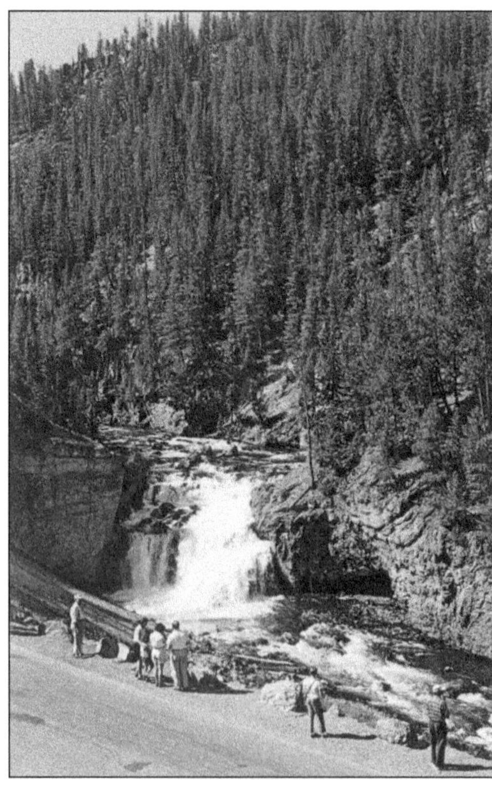

FIREHOLE FALLS, YELLOWSTONE NATIONAL PARK. The short but interesting Firehole River extends from slightly south of Old Faithful to the Gibbon River near Madison Junction. It has long been recognized as a first-class trout stream abounding in brown, brook, and rainbow trout. Firehole Falls is a 40-foot drop in the river approximately one mile south Madison Junction. Access to the falls is from the Grand Loop Road.

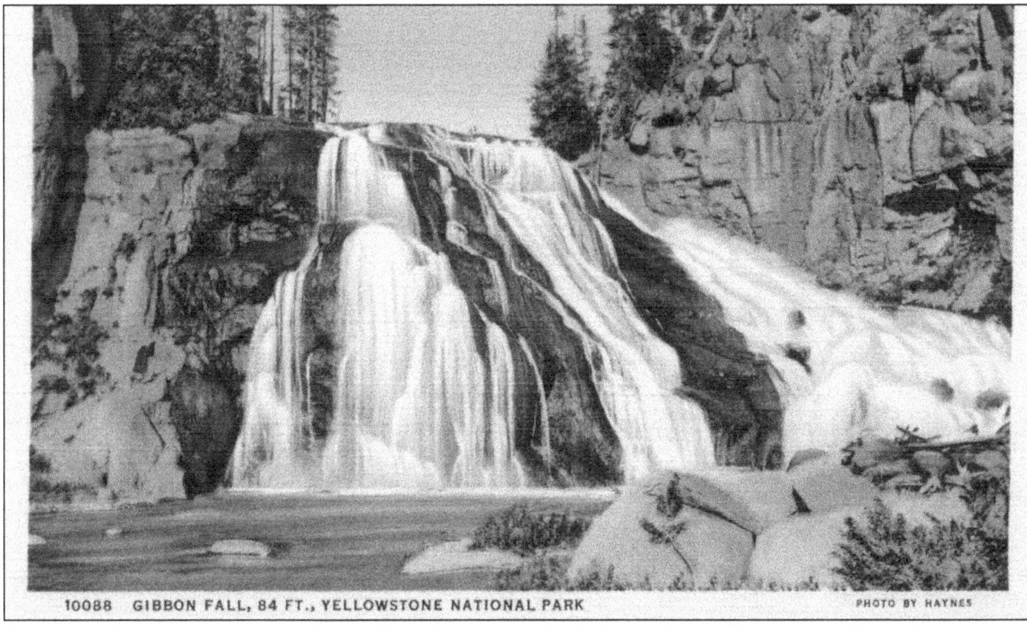

GIBBON FALLS, NEAR MADISON JUNCTION, YELLOWSTONE NATIONAL PARK. This waterfall is located on the Gibbon River only a short distance from that river's confluence with the Firehole River. The falls, which drops approximately 84 feet, emerges from the forest only four miles east of Madison Junction, and many tourists on the Grand Loop Road make the short side trip to take in its beauty.

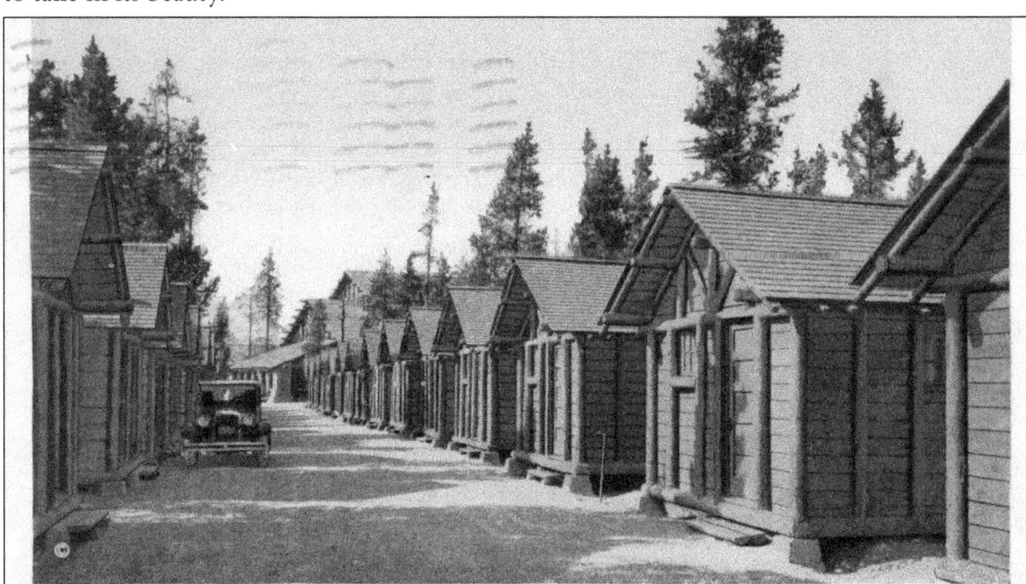

PARK LODGE COMPANY SLEEPING CABINS, YELLOWSTONE NATIONAL PARK. These were among the earliest cabins in Yellowstone Park, built specifically for visiting tourists and vacationers. The Lodge Company featured an orderly arrangement of substantial facilities that included well-furnished sleeping accommodations. The sender of this card reported that this was where she had stayed and that it was very comfortable. She may have been driving the late-1920s car in the image.

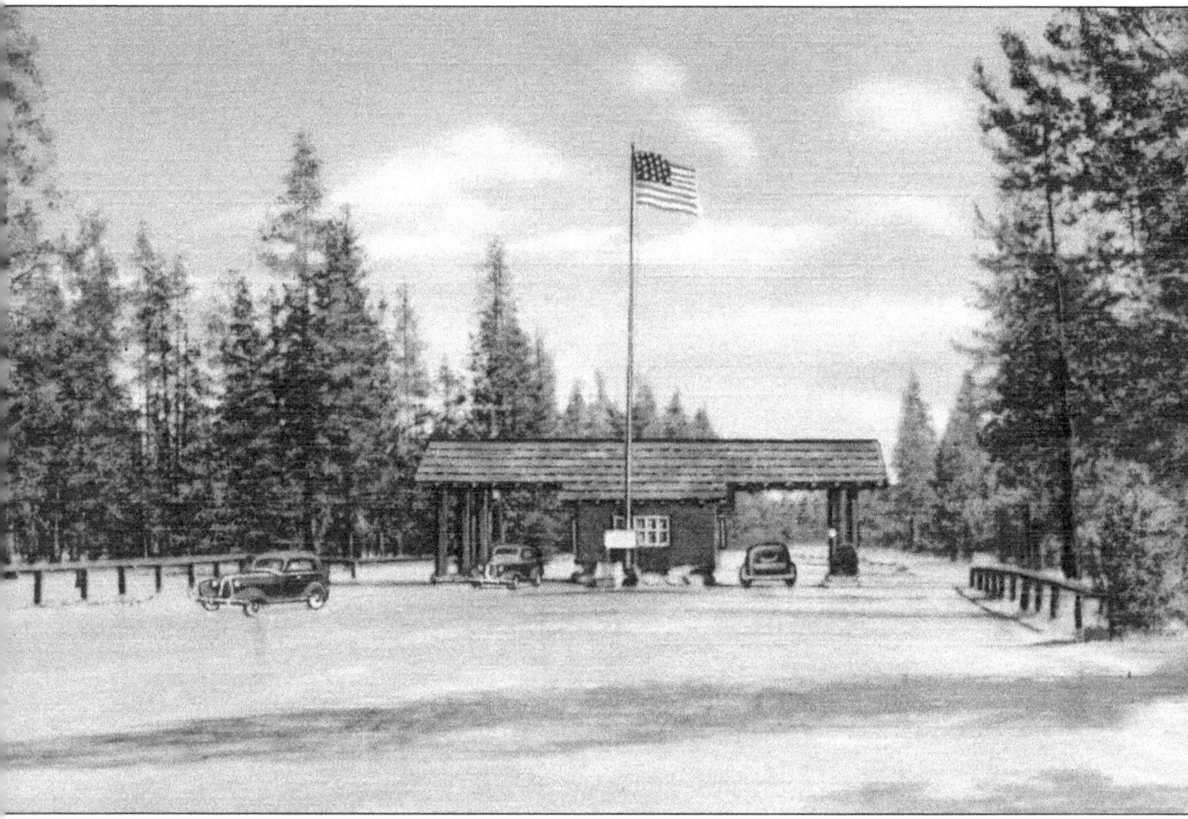

WEST GATE TO YELLOWSTONE NATIONAL PARK, WEST YELLOWSTONE, MONTANA. The Wyoming-Montana state border passes through Yellowstone Park approximately two miles east of the gate shown on this card, and thus this entrance/exit gate is in Montana. It holds the dual distinction of being the western limit of Yellowstone National Park and the beginning of the western section of historic Highway 20. The western section of the road opened in 1940 and extended from this point to Newport, Oregon. When this postcard was produced in the early 1930s, the area surrounding the gate was a wilderness, but over the ensuing years urbanization inevitably occurred. The population of West Yellowstone, Montana, grew in accordance with the increasing popularity of the park, and the country road became a city street. Tourists were greeted by an expanding community that anxiously awaited their arrival.

Seven

West Yellowstone, Montana

The majority of Yellowstone National Park is in Wyoming, with the exception of the extreme northern and western sections, which extend into Montana and Idaho. The town of West Yellowstone, Montana, has been the western gateway to the park since the late 1800s. In contrast to the eastern entrance where the nearest town, Cody, Wyoming, is 53 miles away, the park's western gate is actually the demarcation between the town and the park. Historic Highway 20 begins its journey to the Pacific Ocean in West Yellowstone. Despite the park's attraction, the population of West Yellowstone has remained small. It was under 200 in the early 1900s and remained under 400 during the 1920s and 1930s, reaching only slightly more than 1,200 by 2010. The town was incorporated in 1966.

The arrival of the railroad in West Yellowstone in the early 1900s made getting to the park easier and more comfortable than via stagecoach. Both the Union Pacific and Northern Pacific Railroads promoted the park, and in 1905 a rail extension from Ashton, Idaho, to the west entrance of Yellowstone National Park was planned. That spur, called the Oregon Short Line Branch, delivered the first trainload of passengers to West Yellowstone on June 11, 1908. The steady influx of visitors prompted further development in West Yellowstone. Restaurants, hotels, bars, and other businesses soon followed. Those arriving from the east welcomed the west gate, as it led directly to the town's many amenities. Tobacco and alcohol were prohibited in the park, and many visitors found the opportunity to enjoy a smoke and a favorite beverage at one of the town's establishments highly appealing.

West Yellowstone conveys the appearance of a typical Western frontier town. The majority of the buildings are constructed using materials native to the area, thus there are many log and stone structures. The town's economy is almost completely dependent on tourists. West Yellowstone hosts millions of visitors during the summer months. Throughout the cold-weather months, some West Yellowstone businesses close, whereas others turn their attention to winter-related activities.

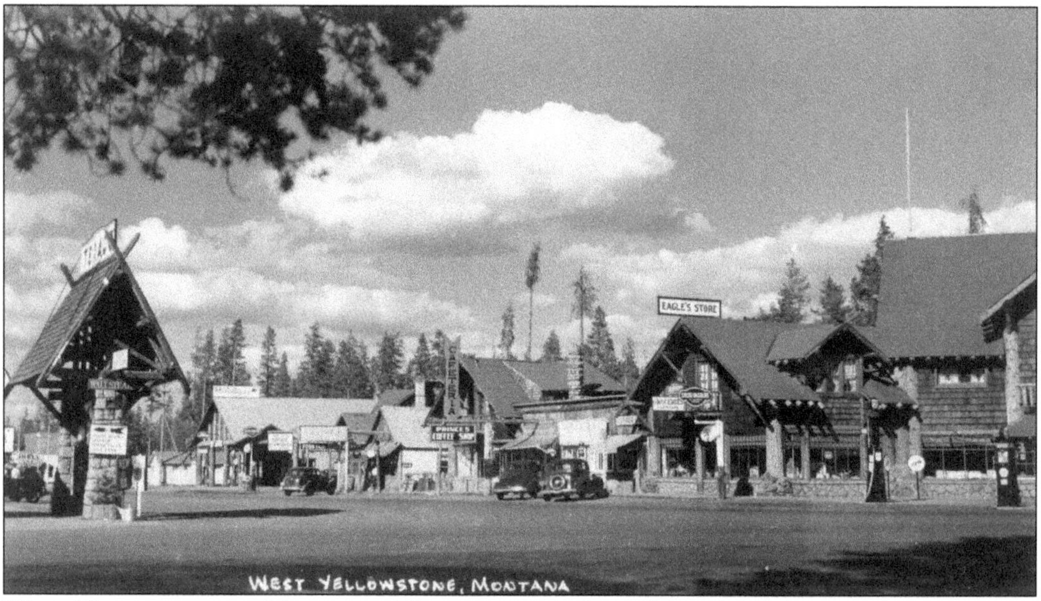

WEST YELLOWSTONE, MONTANA. The western section of historic Highway 20 began in West Yellowstone, which by the 1930s and 1940s had evolved into a complete tourist destination. Tourist-related retail stores dominated the business district, including the famous Eagle store shown on this card. The business was founded in 1908, and the present store and service station only a short distance from the gate were built between 1927 and 1930.

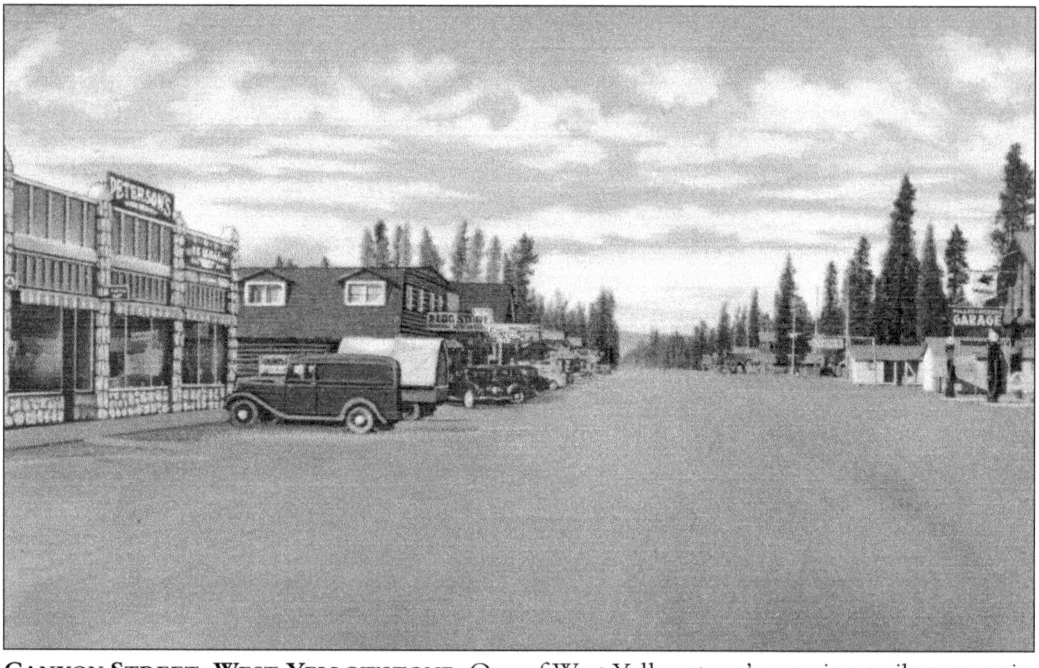

CANYON STREET, WEST YELLOWSTONE. One of West Yellowstone's premier attributes was its beautiful setting among pine trees and snowcapped mountain peaks. The town's natural beauty, complemented by a vibrant business district and proximity to Yellowstone Park, assured a steady influx of visitors to the community. They were rewarded with this broad street and rustic storefronts constructed of indigenous materials, projecting an image of a rugged frontier village.

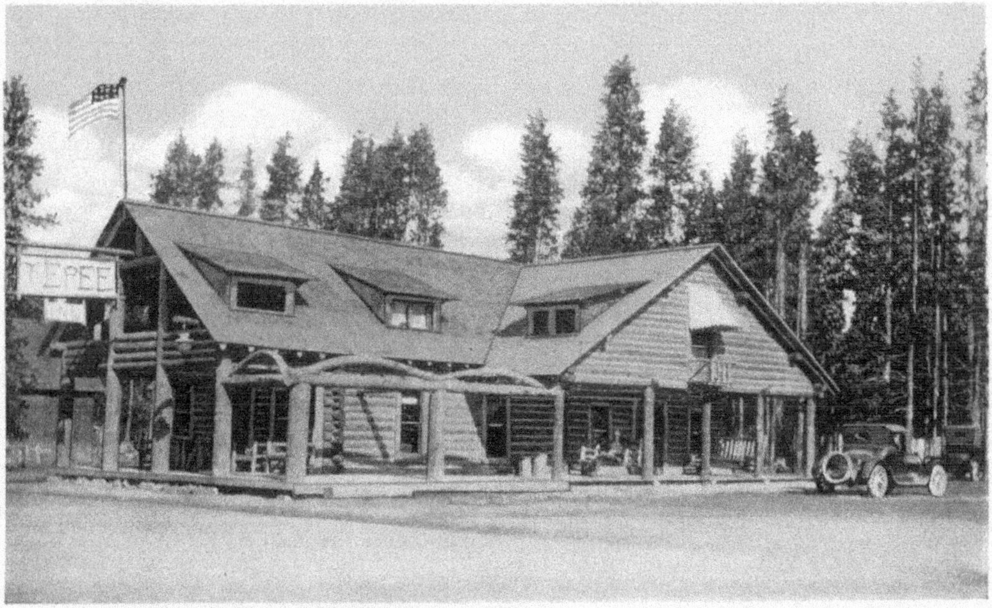

TEPEE INN, WEST YELLOWSTONE, MONTANA 98411

TEPEE INN, 217 YELLOWSTONE AVENUE, WEST YELLOWSTONE. The Tepee Inn was a popular stop for early visitors to West Yellowstone. It dates to 1926, and in spite of suffering through three serious fires and several ownership changes, it has continued to survive and contribute to West Yellowstone's business district. The car indicates that this card was produced soon after the Tepee Inn opened.

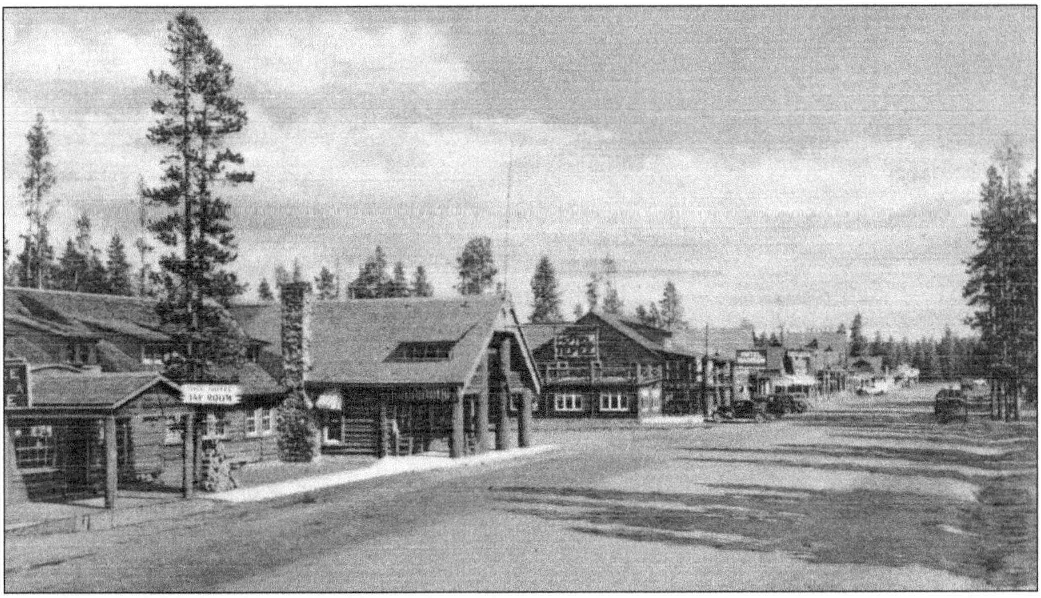

STREET SCENE, WEST YELLOWSTONE. This card describes West Yellowstone as "one of the most picturesque towns in the west." The historic Tepee Inn and Tap Room are in the left foreground, and the historic Madison Hotel is the building across the street on the left. The sender of this card in 1942 had just been married in Salt Lake City and was spending her honeymoon in Yellowstone Park.

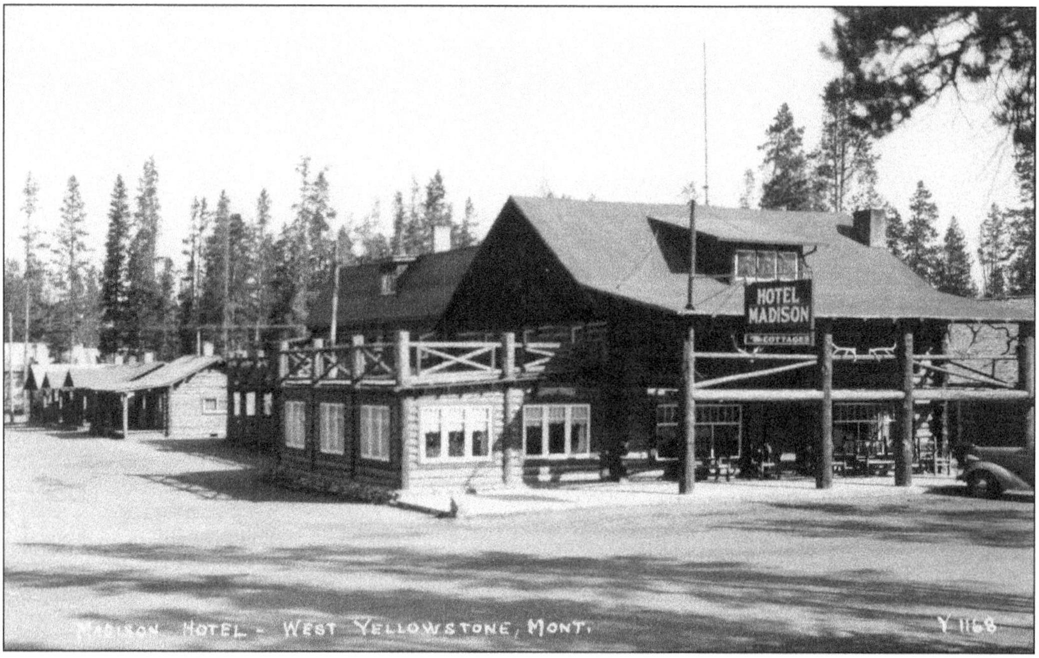

MADISON HOTEL, 137 YELLOWSTONE AVENUE, WEST YELLOWSTONE. The Madison Hotel shown in the photograph above has been a fixture on Yellowstone Avenue for more than a century. The original building opened in 1912 and was enlarged in 1922. Running water was added in 1930. It is the only remaining hotel from the early days of tourism in the park. The hotel is listed in the National Register of Historic Places. Typical of most vacation communities, stores in West Yellowstone were full of souvenirs. Among the most popular were Western attire, boots, rugs, baskets, and Native American artifacts. The image below of the Madison Hotel Gift Shop gives ample testimony to this practice. Visitors were invited to browse the aisles and see for themselves the thousands of items at all price ranges on display.

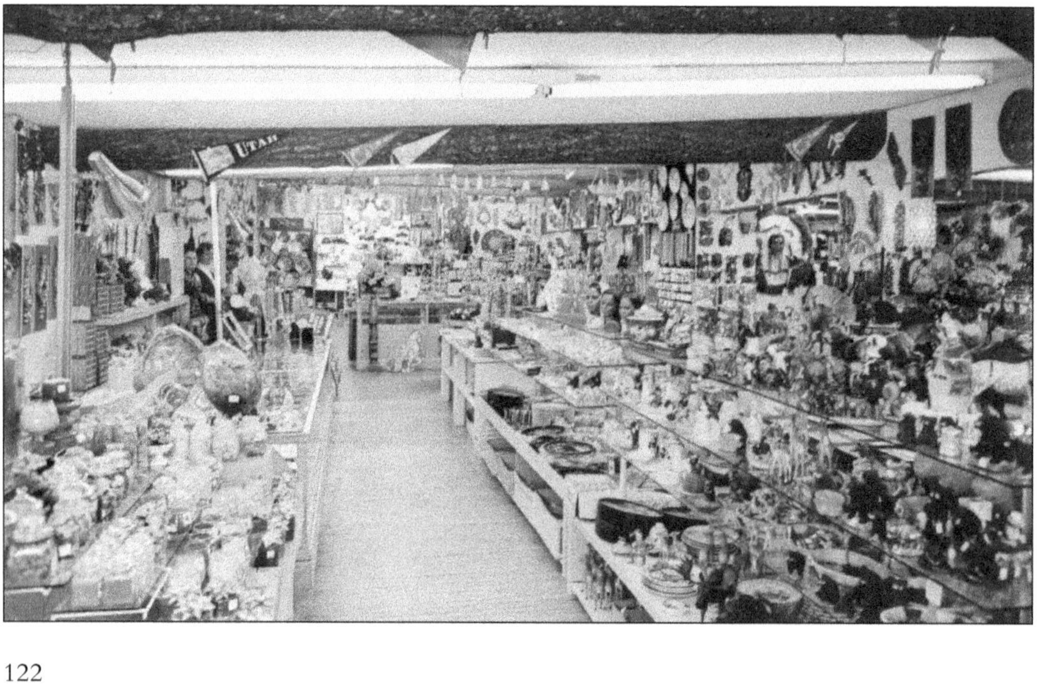

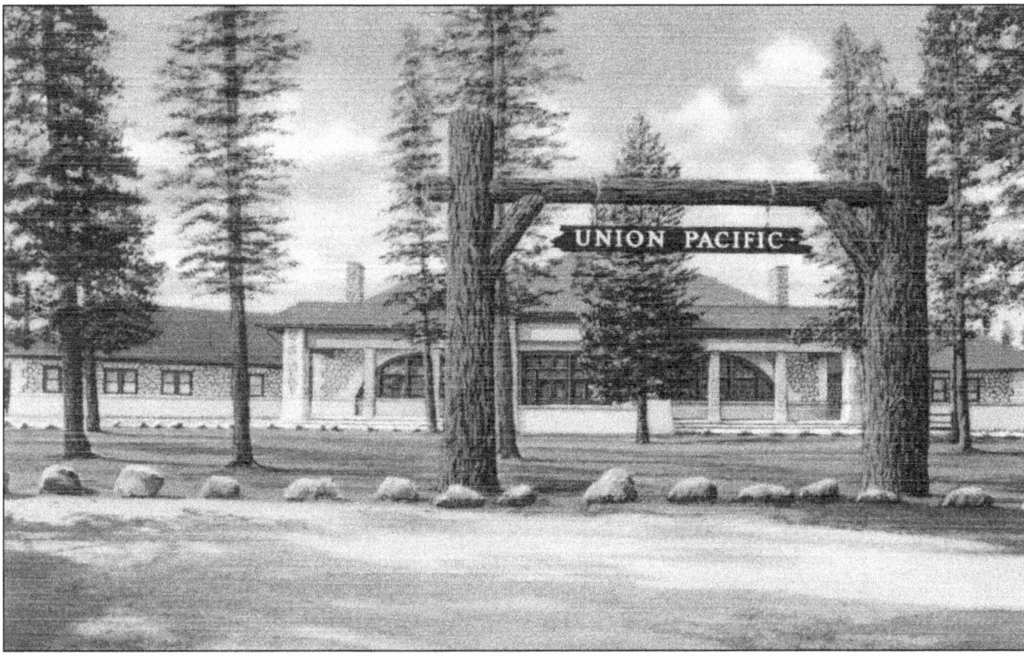

UNION PACIFIC DEPOT AND DINING LODGE, 104 YELLOWSTONE AVENUE, WEST YELLOWSTONE. The Union Pacific Depot in the image above is one of the oldest buildings in West Yellowstone. It was built in 1908 and included a dining hall, but after only a few years it was found to be too small. By 1920, the increasing popularity of the park and convenient rail transportation demanded expansion. The Dining Lodge seen below was completed in 1925 and had the capacity to serve up to 1,000 meals per day. After many years of service to the community, the facility was converted into the Yellowstone Historic Center Museum. There have been few modifications since the lodge opened. The Oregon Short Line Historic District, with the depot as its centerpiece, was added to the National Register of Historic Places in 1983.

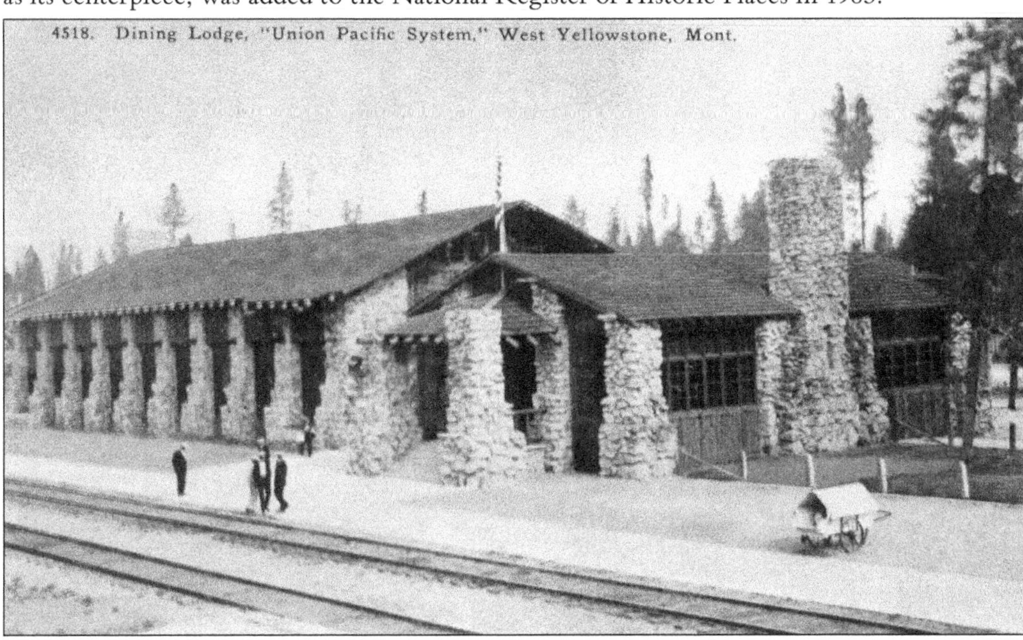

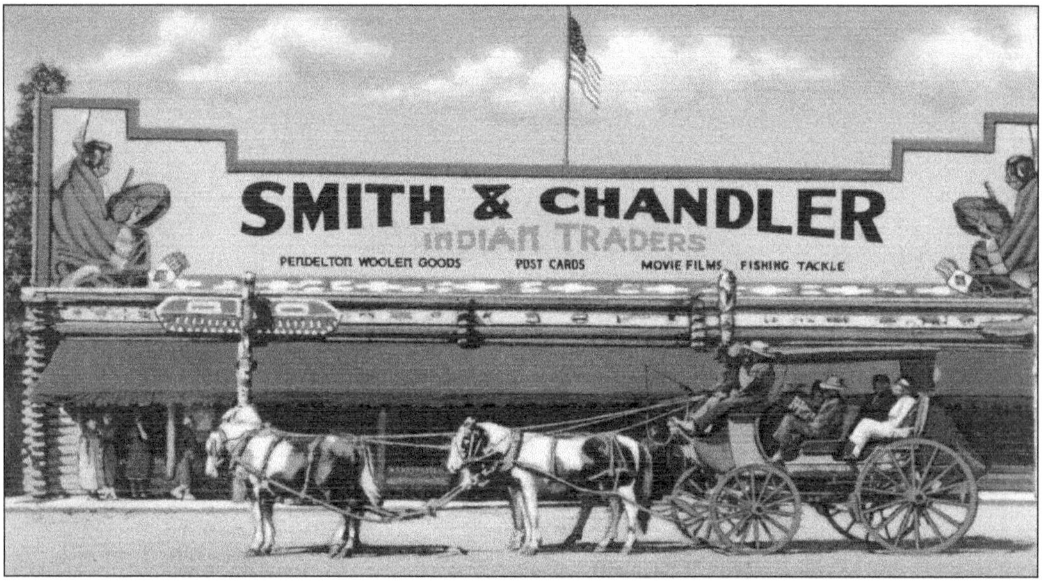

SMITH & CHANDLER, 121 YELLOWSTONE AVENUE, WEST YELLOWSTONE. This large mercantile opened in 1926 and has been a dominant retail outlet throughout its entire existence. The colorful storefront introduces the many Western artifacts within, and very few persons leave West Yellowstone without visiting the store. The open stagecoach illustrates the mode of transportation between the Union Pacific Depot and Yellowstone Park during the early years of the community.

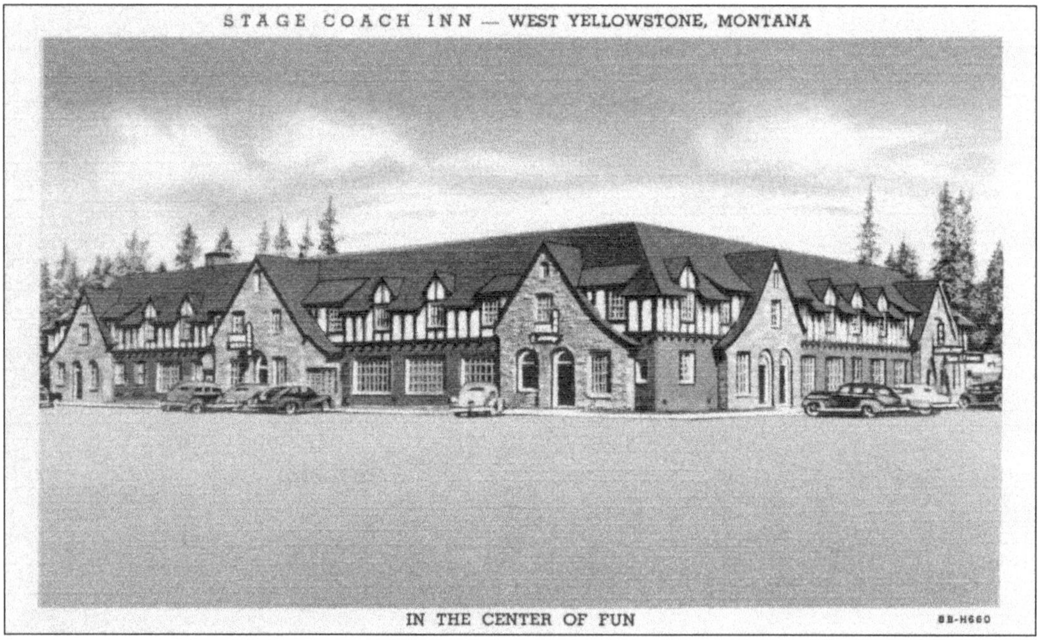

THE STAGECOACH INN, 209 MADISON AVENUE, WEST YELLOWSTONE. This hotel, built in 1946, was uniquely designed to project both a Western and Alpine appearance. Over the years, it has become a landmark in West Yellowstone and a favorite location for residents and tourists. The lobby features a huge flagstone fireplace and a large collection of taxidermy. The back of the card states that this is "the trout fisherman's paradise."

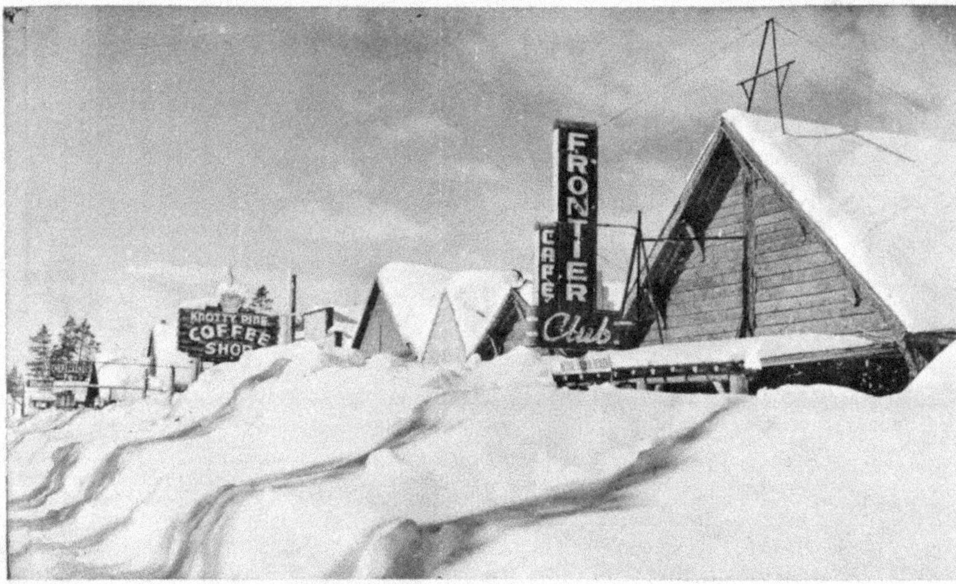

Frontier Club — West Yellowstone, Montana

FRONTIER CLUB, WEST YELLOWSTONE. Many roads to Yellowstone Park were closed in winter, as evidenced by the photograph above. Adorned in its winter coat, the Frontier Club was centrally located in the business district just minutes from the west entrance to Yellowstone National Park and across the street from the Union Pacific Depot. When weather permitted, the club capitalized on West Yellowstone's reputation that it offered the best trout fishing in the world and was a haven for fishermen and hunters. The menu, emphasizing charcoal-broiled steaks, prime rib, and fresh fish, plus nightly dinner music, ensured a pleasant evening for guests. Below is the Frontier Club's large bar decorated with a wildlife theme. The bar was unoccupied when this photograph was taken, possibly on the same day of the snowstorm seen above.

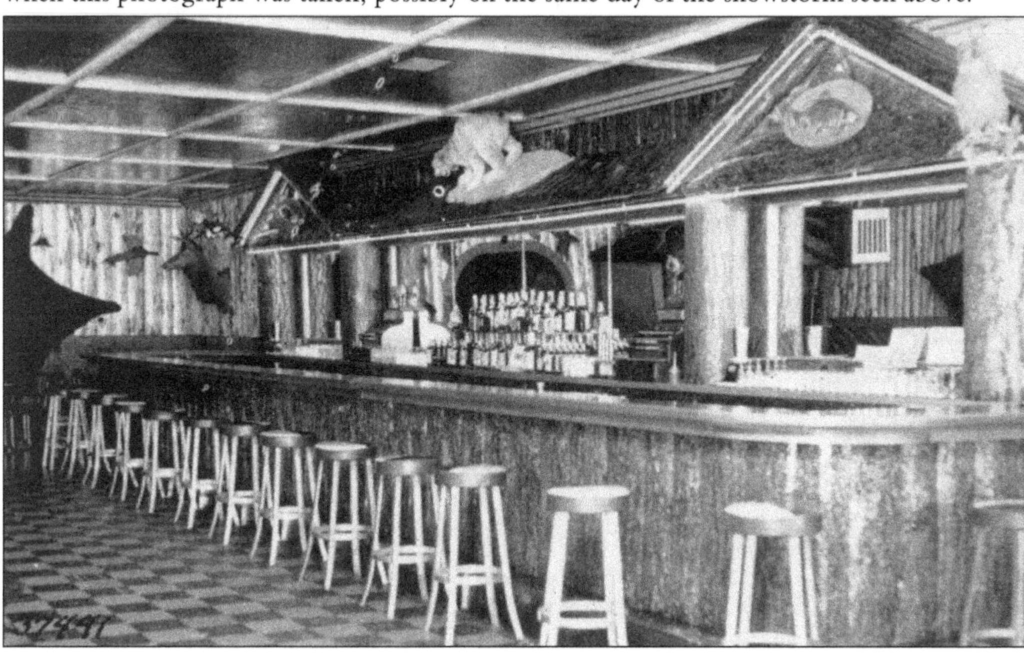

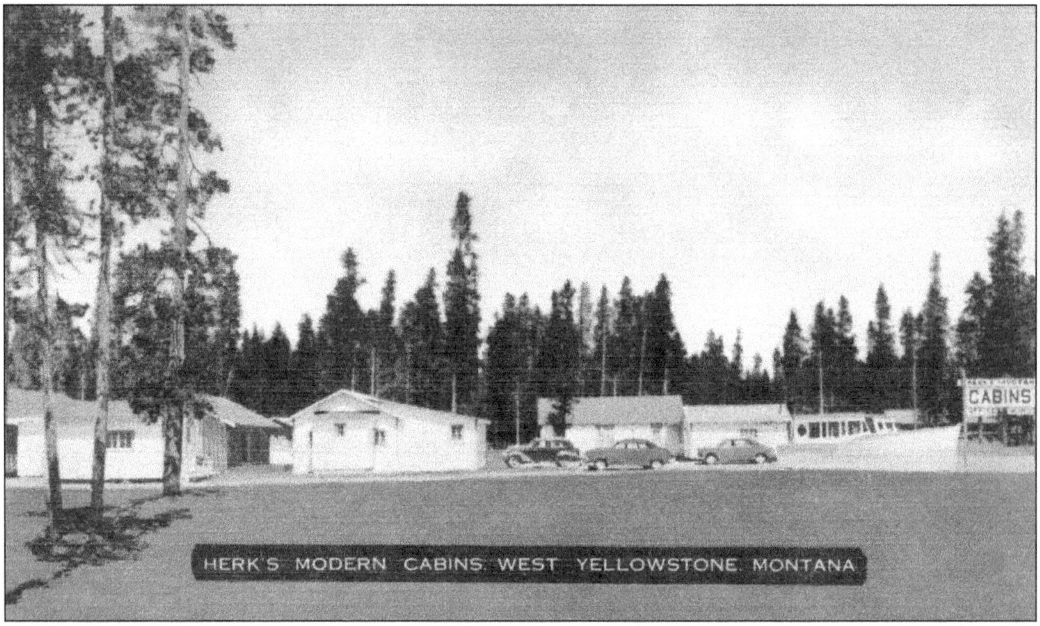

HERK'S MODERN CABINS, NEAR CENTER OF TOWN, WEST YELLOWSTONE. This card was published before the western section of Highway 20 opened, but Herk's continued to be popular long after the US 20 designation was added to Highway 191. Tourists could relax after a day of sightseeing in Yellowstone National Park or before embarking on a visit to the park the following day. The cabins featured modern kitchens, deluxe beds, and private showers.

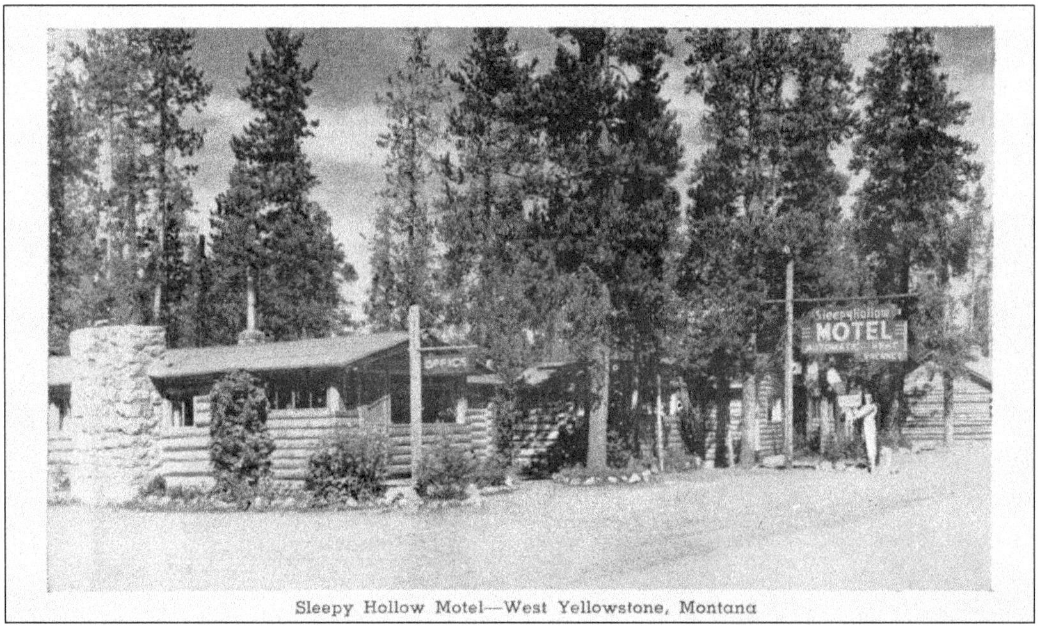

SLEEPY HOLLOW MOTEL, 124 ELECTRIC STREET, WEST YELLOWSTONE. Located near the west entrance to Yellowstone National Park, this rustic motel appealed both to park visitors and sportsmen who looked to the surrounding mountains and streams to pursue their favorite outdoor passion. The motel offered 11 completely modern units, including individual cottages to accommodate two to eight people.

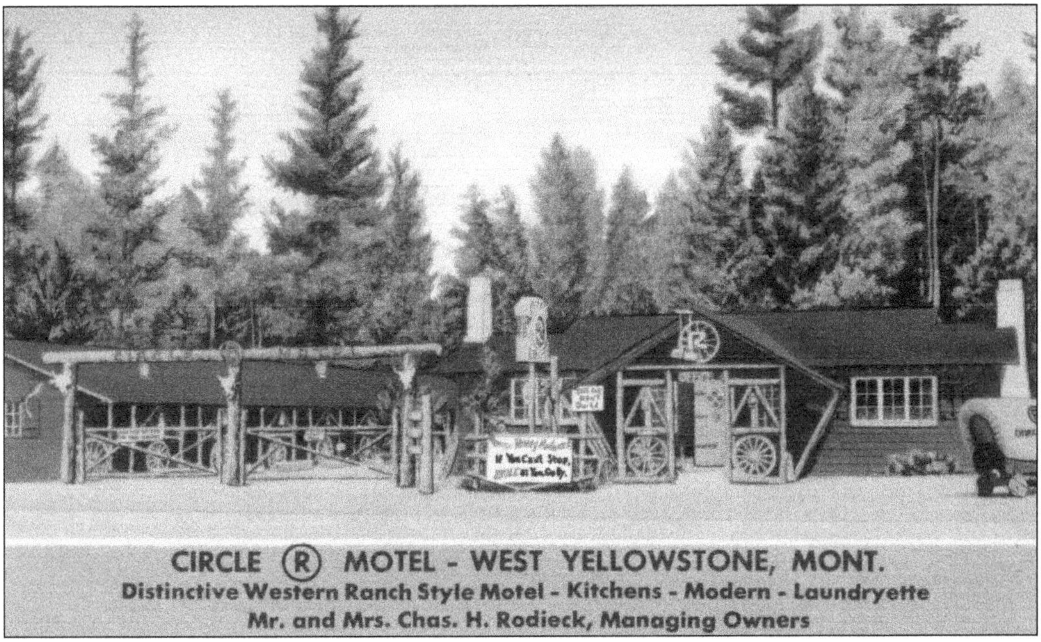

CIRCLE R MOTEL, 321 MADISON LANE, WEST YELLOWSTONE. The sign in front of this Western-themed, 1950s motel offered a friendly greeting to all travelers: "Howdy Pardner! If you can't stop, smile as you go by." The motel touted itself as being the headquarters for seeing Yellowstone National Park, but nearby fishing, hunting, horseback riding, and hiking were also available in this scenic area.

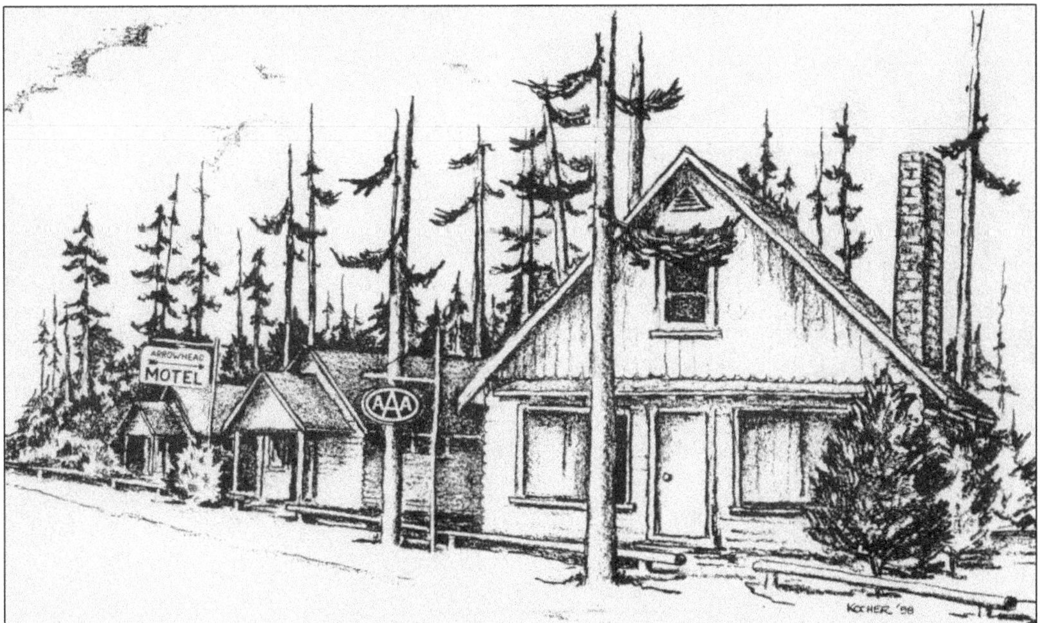

ARROWHEAD MOTEL, 301 HAYDEN STREET, WEST YELLOWSTONE. The artistic rendering on this card illustrates the rustic setting of the Arrowhead Motel. In contrast to other accommodations in the area, this motel was strictly seasonal, open only from May 30 through Labor Day. Vacationers who chose this motel were guaranteed deluxe log cottages and Western hospitality.

www.ingramcontent.com/pod-product-compliance
Lightning Source LLC
LaVergne TN
LVHW072040150926
847810LV00055B/439
* 9 7 8 1 4 6 7 1 1 5 9 8 8 *